AF574360

Painterly Enlightenment

Bettie Allison Rand Lectures in Art History

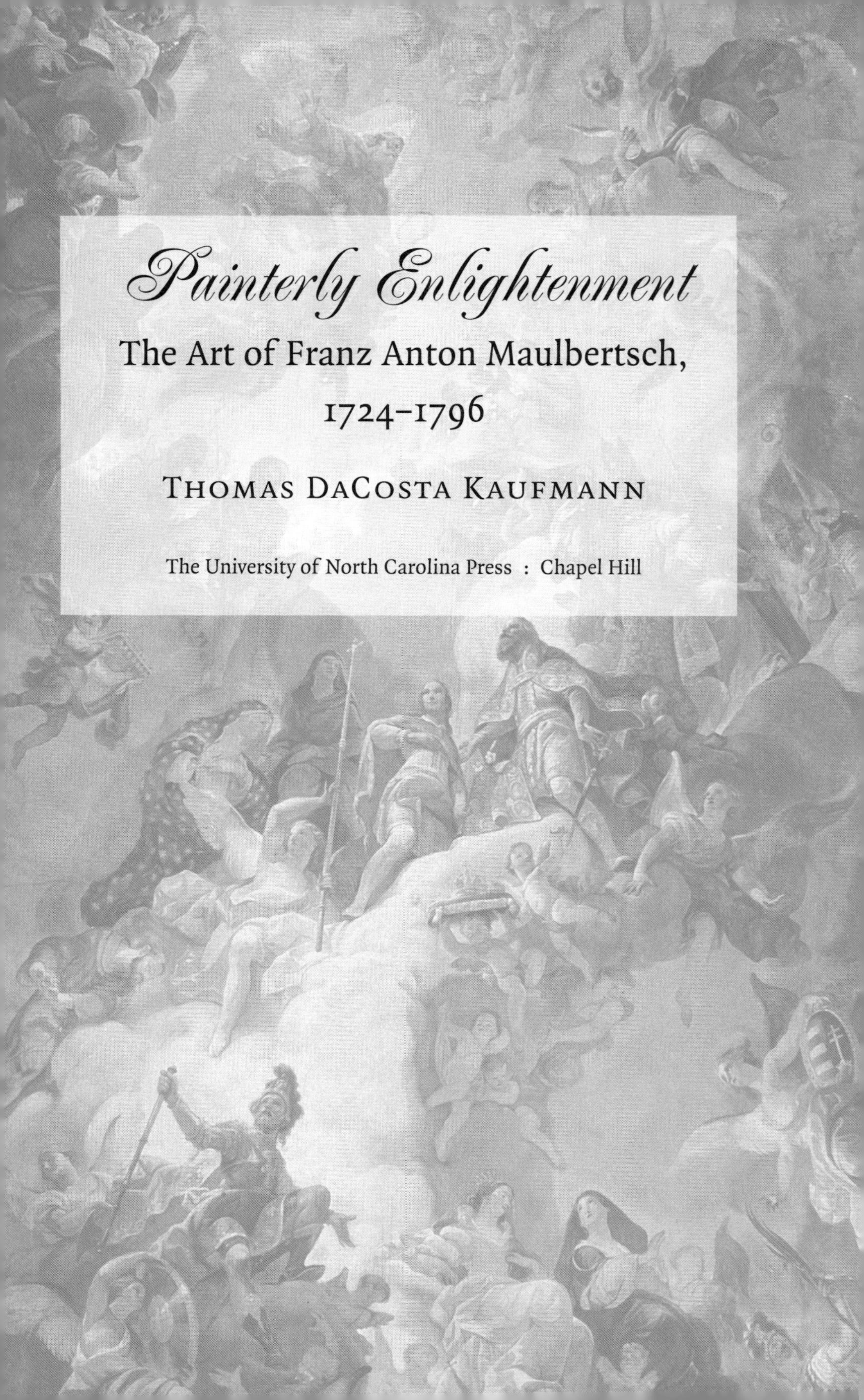

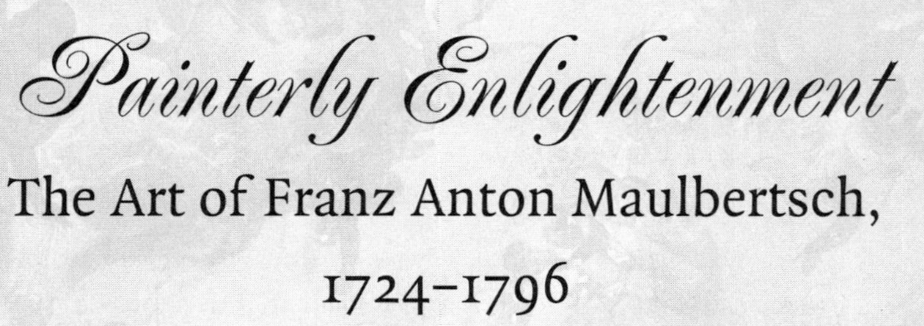

Painterly Enlightenment

The Art of Franz Anton Maulbertsch, 1724–1796

Thomas DaCosta Kaufmann

The University of North Carolina Press : Chapel Hill

© 2005
THE UNIVERSITY OF NORTH CAROLINA PRESS
All rights reserved

The publication of books in this series is made possible through the generous support of William G. Rand in memory of Bettie Allison Rand.

The publication of this book was also supported by a subvention from the Publications Committee, Department of Art and Archaeology, Princeton University.

Designed by Heidi Perov
Set in Quadraat & Poppl Residenz by Tseng Information Systems, Inc.
Manufactured in the United States of America

The paper in this book meets the guidelines for permanence and durability of the Committee on Production Guidelines for Book Longevity of the Council on Library Resources.

Library of Congress Cataloging-in-Publication Data

Kaufmann, Thomas DaCosta.
Painterly enlightenment :
The art of Franz Anton Maulbertsch, 1724–1796 /
Thomas DaCosta Kaufmann.
p. cm. — (Bettie Allison Rand lectures in art history)
Includes bibliographical references and index.
ISBN 0-8078-2956-0 (alk. paper)
1. Maulbertsch, Franz Anton, 1724–1796—Criticism and interpretation.
2. Mural painting and decoration, Austrian—18th century.
I. Maulbertsch, Franz Anton, 1724–1796. II. Title. III. Series.
ND511.5.M34K38 2005
759.36—dc22 2004027169

09 08 07 06 05 5 4 3 2 1

Freunden und Kollegen
in Mitteleuropa
in Dankbarkeit
gewidmet

Contents

Preface

On September 29, 1974, during the final afternoon of a major exhibition held to commemorate the 250th anniversary of the birth of Franz Anton Maulbertsch, who was born 1724 and died in 1796, I visited the Piarist Church of Maria Treu in Vienna's Seventh District. Many drawings, oil sketches, and some altarpieces by the artist were displayed in the church and adjacent spaces. Most impressive of all were the paintings on the ceilings of the church, a building most likely designed by the noted Austrian architect Johann Lucas Hildebrandt, which also possesses an organ on which Anton Bruckner had played as church organist. (See plate 1.) My reaction particularly to the astounding frescoes by Maulbertsch above me—of the Virgin who seemed to explode upward into heaven, for instance—was so compelling that I then traveled around in Austria and in neighboring countries to see more works by an artist about whom I had never previously heard—even though I was working on my dissertation in Central Europe—but whom I found to be increasingly intriguing.

The impact made on me by Maulbertsch's work was a dim echo of the intense response that Oskar Kokoschka had experienced, although I did not know about it at the time. Kokoschka spoke of "the inner fire of the colors of the painter of luminosity" in the Church of Maria Treu, where he had sung as a choir boy. Once when he was singing as a soloist in a Mozart mass, Kokoschka's voice broke. Overpowered by the majestic cupola fresco by Maulbertsch before his eyes, he fainted. Later, he says, Maulbertsch helped determine his course as a painter.

Although obviously not as powerful or important as Kokoschka's, the impression made by paintings in the Piarist church in Vienna and in places like Heiligenkreuz-Gutenbrunn in Austria, Kroměříž in Moravia, Trenčianské Bohuslavice in Slovakia, and Sümeg in Hungary confirmed my first reaction that Maulbertsch was a great, if to me hitherto unknown, master, one who was responsible for the production of many luminously beautiful paintings. That experience led ultimately to the writing of the present book.

I am grateful to have received an invitation from the Department of Art of the University of North Carolina to deliver the Rand Lectures, because I still would not have taken on this subject as a major project if such an opportunity had not presented itself. Some reasons for my initial reluctance to deal more comprehensively with Maulbertsch may be suggested by the circumstances discussed in the first chapter. Previously I have only had the opportunity to write briefly on Maulbertsch in *Central European Drawings, 1680–1800* (Princeton, 1989) and in *Court, Cloister, and City: The Art and Culture of Central Europe, 1450–1800* (Chicago and London, 1995). But this chance enabled me to work more intensively on Maulbertsch, to rethink many of my ideas about him, and to treat an extraordinary artistic phenomenon in what will be the first book on the artist in English.

When I was first invited to give the lectures, I proposed speaking about a topic in the theory or historiography of art, but I was informed that William Rand wished to have beautiful works of art discussed. I immediately suggested Maulbertsch, and I hope that on this score the lectures and the resulting book will not have disappointed him. However, I also hope that other readers will not be disappointed, either, since I have indeed discussed issues of art theory, historiography, and intellectual and cultural history in relation to Maulbertsch. Maulbertsch created very beautiful works that engage many important issues of interpretation, some of which I have considered here.

Above all I wish to thank Mr. Rand for making these lectures and the ensuing publication resulting from them possible. I also gratefully acknowledge grants from the Spears Fund of the Department of Art and Archaeology at Princeton University, which supported travel and the initial purchase of photographic materials, and from the department's Publications Fund, which allowed for the publication of additional color images and helped defray related costs of gaining permissions for illustrations.

My hosts in North Carolina provided a congenial and stimulating environment in which to deliver these lectures. I wish to thank Mary Sturgeon, Michael Cole, Mary Pardo, Madeleine Viljoen, Frances Huemer, and the graduate students who attended the lectures and posed many stimulating questions. Lindsay Fulenwider adeptly arranged all details.

I wish to thank Peter Miller for inviting me to present an earlier version of this project in a lecture at the Colloquium Graduate Program at Bard College. Similarly, I am grateful to Felice Aarons, Kevin Hatch, Noriko Kotani, and Kris Neville, members of a seminar on art, historiography, and art theory in the eighteenth century for listening to and commenting on the lectures. I wish also to thank the audience at a conference on Rubensism at which I gave a lecture derived from chapter 4 on April 2, 2004; that lecture will be published in a version in French, in a volume to be edited by M.-C. Heck.

Paul Betz was a great help in preparing the manuscript for publication, and I thank him. I also wish to thank the following individuals who in one or many ways have helped in supplying me with photographs or in enabling me to acquire them, facilitating access to monuments, sending me publications, accompanying me to visit monuments, or giving me advice or suggestions: Angelika Arnoldi, Eduard Beranek, Kalliopi Chamanikolasová, A. Czere, L. Daniel, Monika Dachs, Péter Farbaky, Geza Galavics, Ivan Gerát, Terez Gerszi, Annemarie Jordan-Gschwendt, Shari Kenfield, Manfred Koller, Jiří Kroupa, Bruce Livie, Miklos Mojzer, Friedrich Polleroß, Jens Rosigkeit, Martina Sošková, Károly Szelényi, Vilmos Szentai, Claudia Wöhrer, Zora Wörgötter, and Monika Zsámbeky. I am also grateful to all those owners and institutions who allowed me access to their collections. Finally I wish to express my appreciation to Elizabeth Pilliod for her participation in this Central European adventure.

Painterly Enlightenment

There's no lack of excellent draftsmen;
great colorists are few.
DENIS DIDEROT, *Salon of 1765*

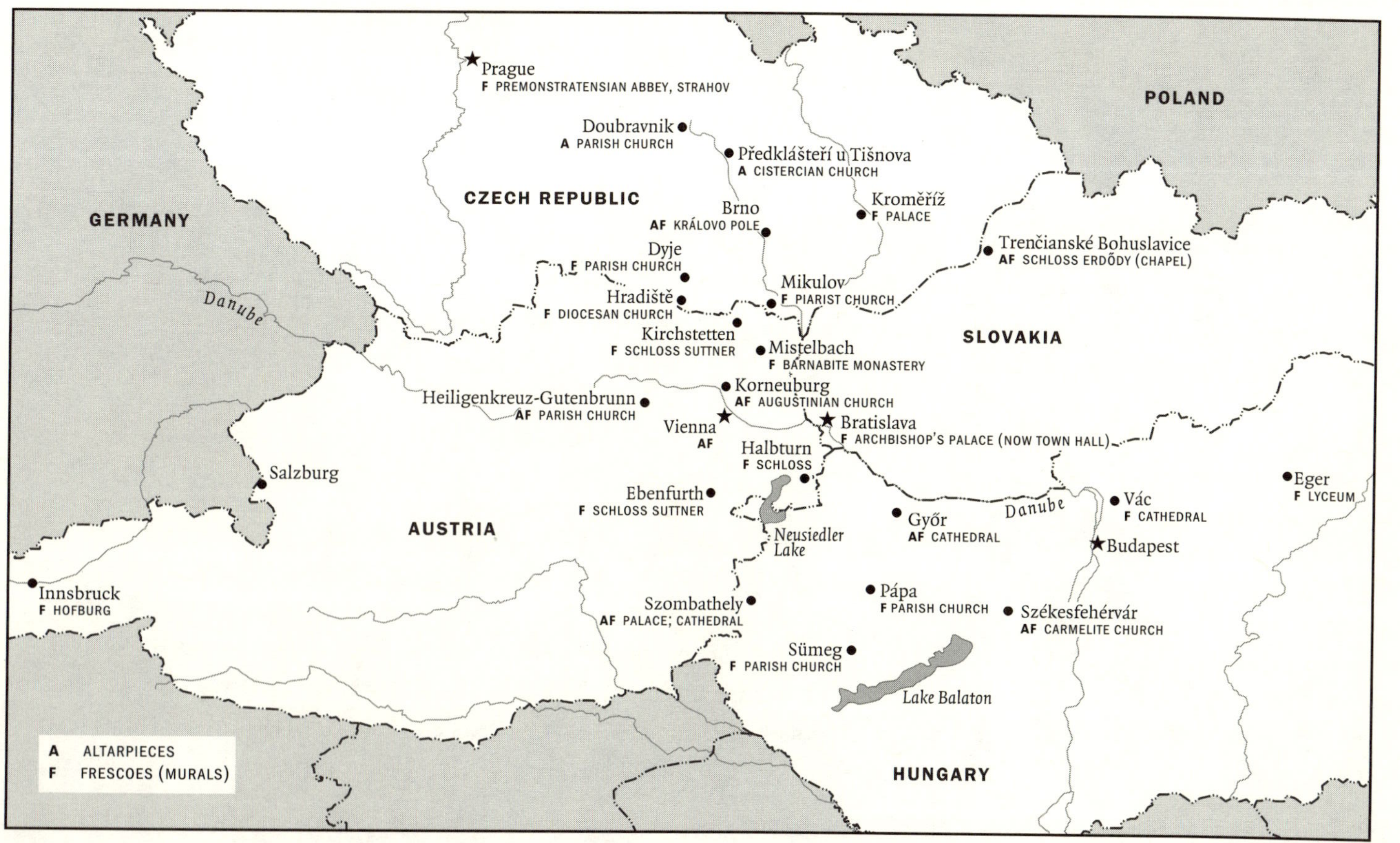

Location of works by Maulbertsch discussed in the text

ONE

Introducing an Original Strangeling

In the region where his works are located, Franz Anton Maulbertsch (1724–96) is recognized as one of the greatest masters of fresco and oil painting of the eighteenth century, yet he may also be considered one of the "odd men out" in the history of art.[1] Maulbertsch painted frescoes in churches and palaces in almost sixty places, and over thirty such works survive (Figure 1; Plate 1). These paintings are spread throughout the present states of Austria, Hungary, Slovakia, the Czech Republic, Romania, and Germany, while his oil sketches and drawings are found in collections in many other countries as well. Maulbertsch's astonishing use of color, luminous compositions, and bold inventions have in Central Europe gained for him a reputation of genius. Several noted Germanophone art historians and the well-known painter Oskar Kokoschka have compared him to his contemporary Mozart.[2] However, Maulbertsch has also long been treated as strange, odd, and eccentric. Outside Central Europe he has still not obtained the broader attention that he would seem to deserve.

This story starts with some of the first writings in the history of art (*Kunstgeschichte*) as such, where Maulbertsch's originality is emphasized. In a manuscript that was probably compiled during the years 1785–92,[3] Andreas Schweigel, the leading sculptor of the later eighteenth century in Moravia, and often a collaborator of Maulbertsch, calls him a "Viennese Academic Painter," yet includes him in a survey of the fine arts in Moravia ("Anmerkung der bildenden Künste in Betreff der schönen Gebäuden, Malereien und Statuen in Mähren") because of the mass of work he executed in that margravate. Schweigel praises Maulbertsch, saying that he was to be considered a true original (*ein wahres eigenes Originel zu*

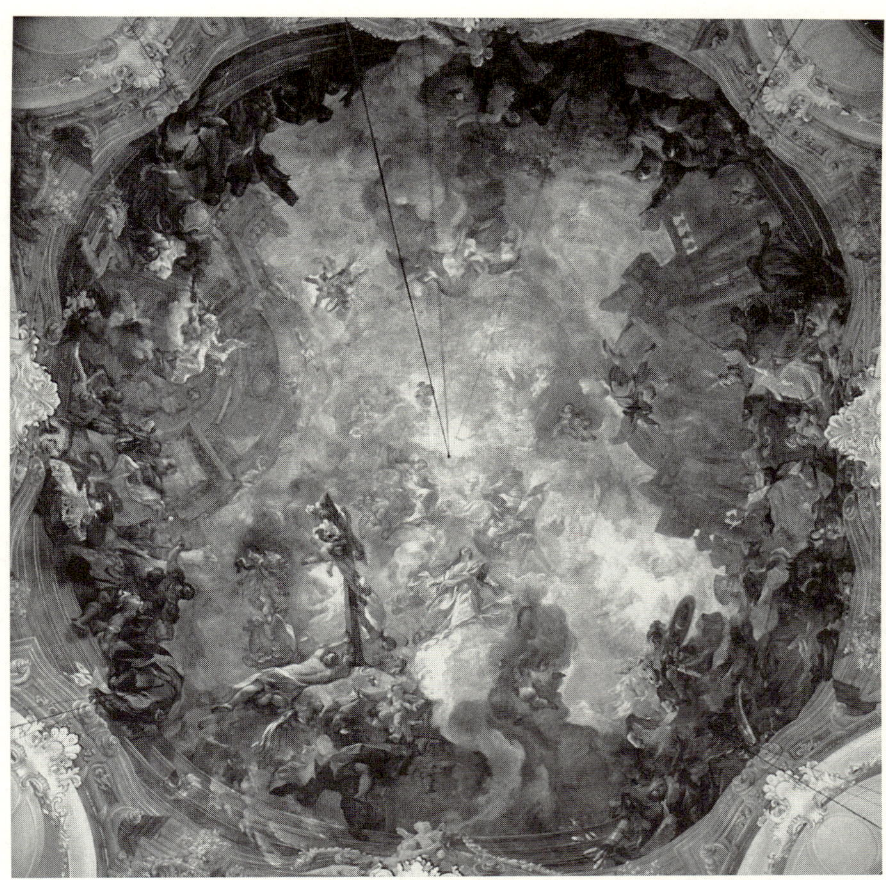

FIGURE 1. F. A. Maulbertsch, *Assumption of the Virgin*, cupola painting, 1752, Piarist Church of Maria Treu, Vienna (Photograph: Eduard Beranek)

betrachten).[4] In the context of Schweigel's discussion, and in light of the language of eighteenth-century criticism, originality is here to be regarded as a virtue.[5]

Yet within a decade Maulbertsch's originality was being treated quite differently in one of the earliest accounts to call itself a history (*Geschichte*) of art. In a history of the fine arts in Vienna (*Geschichte der bildenden Künste in Wien*) published in 1801, Hans Rudolf Füßli, a member of the famous Swiss family of artists and writers, criticized Maulbertsch and his contemporaries. He attributes what he believes to have been a decline of history painting (the painting of significant human action, including religious subjects) in Vienna to the fault of instruction in the academy of art, and thus says that it was good that Maulbertsch had never become director there. Füßli writes: "But Maulbertsch, an original strangeling, who at the time began to set the tone in the great field of historical painting, regardless of his valuable qualities as an artist, would have been more damaging than useful to young academicians, if he had assumed direction over them; because it is far more risky to allow beginning artists to stray completely from the circle of fundamental rules than to burden them with too great an amount of rules."[6]

Taste had changed since Maulbertsch had set the tone at the academy, which Füßli also had attended and where he had worked as librarian. Instead of writing more fully about Maulbertsch, Füßli published favorable biographies of Hubert Maurer, Heinrich Friedrich Fuger, and Franz Caucig, all of whom are now regarded as exemplars of classicism in Vienna.[7] According to the lights of classicist precepts, which established a canon based on ancient Greek and Roman art and thus advanced aesthetic doctrine based on emulation of the antique, the antecedent period of eighteenth-century art could not be appreciated. Consequently Maulbertsch could at best be considered a talented eccentric who had strayed from the rules of art.

Füßli's opinions are, to be sure, an expression of a distinctive taste of his time, but the norms that he and other like-minded writers promoted helped to determine the shaping of the canon of the history of art as it was subsequently written. Füßli's description of Maulbertsch as a strangeling has had many echoes in the last two centuries. Furthermore, in spite of Maulbertsch's supposed originality, he was not celebrated during the early nineteenth century, when it might have been thought that this quality would have appealed to tendencies that are identified with "romanticism." Even though some nineteenth-century lexica repeated earlier commentary on the painter, and he is occasionally mentioned in local literature,[8] Maulbertsch and other artists of his milieu were not incorporated into the canon of art history as it evolved during the nineteenth century. The development of art historical literature and institutions during an era of growing nationalism, in which many European nation-states were born, may also have played a role in this process of exclusion, because Maulbertsch is hard to claim for any nationalist cause: he was born in Germany, and later painted works for churches there, but lived in Vienna, and provided paintings for places throughout the multinational realms of the Habsburgs.[9]

In any case, Maulbertsch and his contemporaries remained of little interest to scholarship until the end of the nineteenth century. They were then briefly mentioned, for example by Albert Ilg, who has been called the "father of Austrian baroque research."[10] Ilg said that Maulbertsch was especially skillful (*tüchtig*) in history painting, and most inventive in his (oil) sketches, but too sweet and delicate in his coloring.[11]

It was not until Austrian scholars and critics had their eyes opened by impressionist painting and, significantly, became associated with early twentieth-century expressionism that there was a greater appreciation of Austrian baroque painting, the stylistic phenomenon with which Maulbertsch came to be identified. Later, Maulbertsch himself was deemed to be a forerunner of expressionism.[12] Tellingly, one of the first major essays on Austrian ceiling painting was published by Hans Tietze:[13] Tietze was portrayed together with Erika Tietze-Conrat in a work painted by Oskar Kokoschka in his expressionist mode (New York, Museum of Modern Art). The famed Viennese professor Max Dvořák, who had also written about El Greco, and evidently also was responding to painting of his own time, penned the first major modern art historical essay to make strong positive comments about Maulbertsch.[14]

Dvořák treated Maulbertsch as the culminating artist in a survey of ceiling painting in Vienna. Paintings like Maulbertsch's early ceiling fresco in the Piarist church in Vienna are deemed products of his inexhaustible power of imagination, which make him a high point of the great idealistic art of fantasy. While his expressive means are gained from his contemporaries, in Maulbertsch these take on "an individual stamp of unprecedented power and originality. Movements in his paintings increase into a hurricane, colors and light effects into real orgies, and forms are united into unimagined possibilities; his earthly-heavenly compositions are bound by the power of individual invention into new unities."[15]

This view of Maulbertsch helped shape opinions formed between the two world wars; Kokoschka's own statements about Maulbertsch were informed by circles around Dvořák. Kokoschka says that while El Greco never appealed to him, Maulbertsch, who was original and bound to popular culture, showed him the true way to art. In his youth Kokoschka came to admire the "extremist," "revolutionary fresco painter of the Baroque, Maulbertsch." Kokoschka spoke further of this "illusionist's magic color, born in the master's unbound imagination" and remarked that he "soon became aware of and was caught by the Austrian Baroque artist's indocility to the classicist Italian conventions of harmony." However, Kokoschka realized that these qualities lacked appeal to his own twentieth-century contemporaries.[16]

Kokoschka may have been correct in this last observation. Maulbertsch was mentioned in some studies and surveys of the interwar period, such as that by Adolf Feulner, where he is called the greatest fresco painter of Austria,[17] and he was the subject of an important essay by Otto Benesch.[18] F. M. Haberditzl prepared a comprehensive monograph on him, but for a variety of reasons Haberditzl's book did not appear until 1977.[19] Hence not until 1960 was the first monograph on Maulbertsch published, a fundamental work by Klára Garas.[20] Significantly, the slightly revised and shortened monograph on Maulbertsch by Garas that appeared in 1974 bears a preface by Kokoschka.[21]

Garas's books represent a turn in studies of Maulbertsch, and more generally of the art of his time in Central Europe. As Garas noted in a 1979 review, more had been published in the field of Austrian, or, as she corrects herself, Central European baroque art (meaning that of the later seventeenth and earlier and mid-eighteenth century) in the preceding decade than in the preceding 150 years altogether.[22] The 250th anniversary of Maulbertsch's birth in 1974 was commemorated by a series of major exhibitions in Austria and Hungary that brought more attention to the painter.[23] Since 1974 three exhibitions in his birthplace of Langenargen on Lake Constance have been devoted to Maulbertsch and the art of his time in Swabia, Vienna, and Hungary, all with extensive catalogs containing numerous scholarly essays;[24] a show of drawings was to be seen in Salzburg;[25] another summary exhibition has been held in Vienna, with a catalog containing a compilation of documents;[26] and his works have been included in many other exhibitions. Over a hundred essays, books, and reviews have been written on the artist in the past three decades alone. Maulbertsch has thus become a familiar phenomenon in the artistic terrain of Central Europe, where he is often regarded as the outstanding painter of his time.

In contrast, Maulbertsch has not obtained a comparable place in the larger canon of European art. It is probably safe to say that he remains largely unknown even to many professional art historians outside Central Europe. Although paintings by him are scattered throughout the world, they are unstudied in France, unknown in Italy, and not given attention elsewhere in Western Europe.[27] Some paintings and drawings are owned by American museums, where they have occasionally been included in exhibitions, yet only a handful of scholarly articles on Maulbertsch, none of them concentrating on his wall paintings, have appeared in English.[28] Although Maulbertsch has been handled positively in a few English-language works on art of his period in Central Europe,[29] he is treated in a very cursory fashion in more general surveys.

Moreover, not only the same images, but many of the same ideas regularly reappear in publications: if he is mentioned at all, Maulbertsch is often characterized as a personal example of baroque hyperbole or as an emotional artist.[30] For instance, a recent book on the baroque describes Maulbertsch's ceilings in the Piarist church as less intellectual in comparison with the famous ceiling by

Andrea Pozzo in Sant'Ignazio, Rome; Maulbertsch's paintings are said to "focus on extreme emotions." The image of Maulbertsch the strangeling also remains current: further discussion of his work in the same book is limited to a frequently reproduced image of a painting of an unidentified saint (Vienna, Österreichische Galerie). This is called a "strange painting," "an extreme instance of the eccentricity of baroque vision, which delights in strange angles of approach, as if to suggest that oddity is a kind of norm."[31]

The present book aims to make the apparently strange seem familiar. It argues that while Maulbertsch's art reveals outstanding, even personal, qualities, he may be regarded as more than an eccentric. Maulbertsch's work is rooted in the historical situation and artistic practices of his time in Central Europe, but he is also of greater interest than as a local phenomenon. His work evinces many tendencies that are far from being strange, regressive, or retardataire: it engages with many intellectual and aesthetic issues of his day. Thus this book attempts not only to recover Maulbertsch for the European art historical canon, but also to call for reconsideration of the visual aspects of culture in Central Europe in the age of the Enlightenment.

Furthermore, although Maulbertsch's art was forged in the contexts and crises of the eighteenth century, it also illuminates problems that have continued to be posed to painters since then. While Maulbertsch has been seen as a painter of what art historians used to call the baroque or rococo, and considered to be one of the last great mural painters of the ancien régime, several aspects of his art anticipate issues that attend modernist painting, as it is usually understood. Kokoschka once asked if Maulbertsch had anything to say to the twentieth century.[32] This book answers that Maulbertsch is not only of historical interest: some of the concerns engaged by his art may also still have something to say to the twentieth-first century as well.

Why, then, if it can be claimed that Maulbertsch is such a significant art historical figure, who also still has something to say to the present time, has he not gained broader attention? In the first place, some reasons for his exclusion from the art historical canon result from aesthetic prejudices and historical preconceptions. Outside of art history as it is written in Central Europe Maulbertsch may seem an uncanonical eccentric because his paintings cannot easily be accommodated to normal art historical criteria or historical paradigms; he does not fit easily into many of the usual categories.

Maulbertsch was a mural painter at a time of transition to easel painting. Color is a key element in his art during a period in which color was not appreciated by some major writers on art. He worked in a time of transition for artistic styles; even his latest works do not fit the norm of neoclassicism, as represented in painting by his younger contemporary Jacques-Louis David. In contrast with intellectual and social developments associated with the Enlightenment and revolution in France, in the Habsburg realms humanism was suppressed, Enlightenment delayed, revolution opposed, and Jacobinism (sympathy with the French Revolution) crushed.[33] Maulbertsch painted many works with religious themes during a time in which secular subjects were becoming more popular. He continued to work for monarchs and for religious orders at a time when they were being overthrown or eliminated. While in revolutionary France images of the Virgin were being destroyed, and churches converted into temples of reason, he painted a Marian cycle in a cathedral in Hungary, and showed critics of religion, probably *philosophes*, being fought and driven down in a fresco painted on the ceiling of a monastic library in Prague.

Neglect of Maulbertsch also has much to do with the peculiar perimeters of the geography of art. In general, art in Central Europe between the time of Albrecht Dürer and that of romanticism is not much studied outside the region.[34] The course of art history is cast in a trajectory that leads from French art of the eighteenth and nineteenth centuries to modernism in Europe and America. Only a few examples of artistic production in other countries, for instance in eighteenth- or early-nineteenth-century England, in eighteenth-century Rome or Venice, and in twentieth-century Russia or Germany, get much recognition. Most accounts allow little place for supposedly peripheral phenomena like Maulbertsch.

With Maulbertsch the problem of location is even more acute than it is with many other painters, such as Giovanni Battista Tiepolo (Tiepolo's frescoes are also strewn about the Veneto), to whose art his own has often been compared.[35] Many of Maulbertsch's important works are located in sites that are far from major centers. They can be reached only with difficulty, and some even now only by private transport. Major paintings by Maulbertsch are found in small churches in provincial Hungary, rural Slovakia, and the Austrian countryside. Other frescoes are found in small towns or minor cities in Moravia that also lie off the beaten track. Moreover, many of these places were not accessible except to the most intrepid or determined traveler for half a century, until the fall of the Berlin Wall and the collapse of the Soviet bloc in 1989.

In contrast with painting in these parts of Central Europe, German palaces and pilgrimage churches of what is called the rococo (the ornamental style of the eighteenth century) have received some sporadic attention, and the frescoes of Tiepolo in Würzburg are well known. However, these eighteenth-century works do not provide the best comparisons for Maulbertsch.[36] His paintings are usually not subordinated to a decorative ensemble that includes stucco and other media, as they define the German rococo (including paintings by the Tiepolos at Würzburg). In several cases Maulbertsch's frescoes cover an entire church, creating ensembles made purely out of paint. In the parish church in Sümeg, Hungary (Figure 2 and Plate 2), even the altarpieces, including their fictive frames, are painted in fresco. There is also a problem of chronology here: Tiepolo's frescoes in Würzburg were painted during the 1750s, when Maulbertsch was just beginning to work in the medium; most of Maulbertsch's major paintings were executed later than the well-known German paintings of the rococo with which he is supposedly comparable. Among German painters Januarius Zick—sometimes called the last important fresco painter of southern German rococo—is the only artist who is fairly comparable for the time and place in which he worked.

Maulbertsch's paintings possess qualities of execution, including freedom of handling, broad brushwork, bright contrasting color, and extraordinary light effects that despite the superficial similarities they reveal with the works of these artists, not only differ from those of Tiepolo, as will be further discussed in Chapter 4, but also from those of his German contemporaries. In these regards he can be better compared to several other Austrian painters of his time, as has often been remarked.[37] Such features are, however, more pronounced in Maulbertsch's painting than they are in those of other Austrian artists of the period. While standing for the tradition of Austrian—better said, of Central European painting—Maulbertsch has thus rightly been regarded as its paramount personality.[38]

Yet the very celebration of Maulbertsch's color suggests another reason why there have been problems for the reception of his art. Color has often been regarded as a secondary quality in perception. It has been disparaged as arbitrary, unreal, and superficial, and as incapable of contributing to beauty. A very recent critique has even labeled this misapprehension of color chromophobia.[39]

Whether or not this is so, it is true that drawing is associated in the literature of art with thought, while color, and the emotions it provokes, often leaves words impotent to explain.[40] Art historians are used to talking about texts, narratives, signs, symbols, and subjects, but do not have an easy time describing color, or qualities of execution, that are essential to considerations of an artist like Maulbertsch. In comparison with other topics, a limited literature and a relatively poor vocabulary exist for discussions of color. Hence, though color theory, colorism, and color effects have increasingly been studied, the discussion of such topics remains comparatively limited.[41]

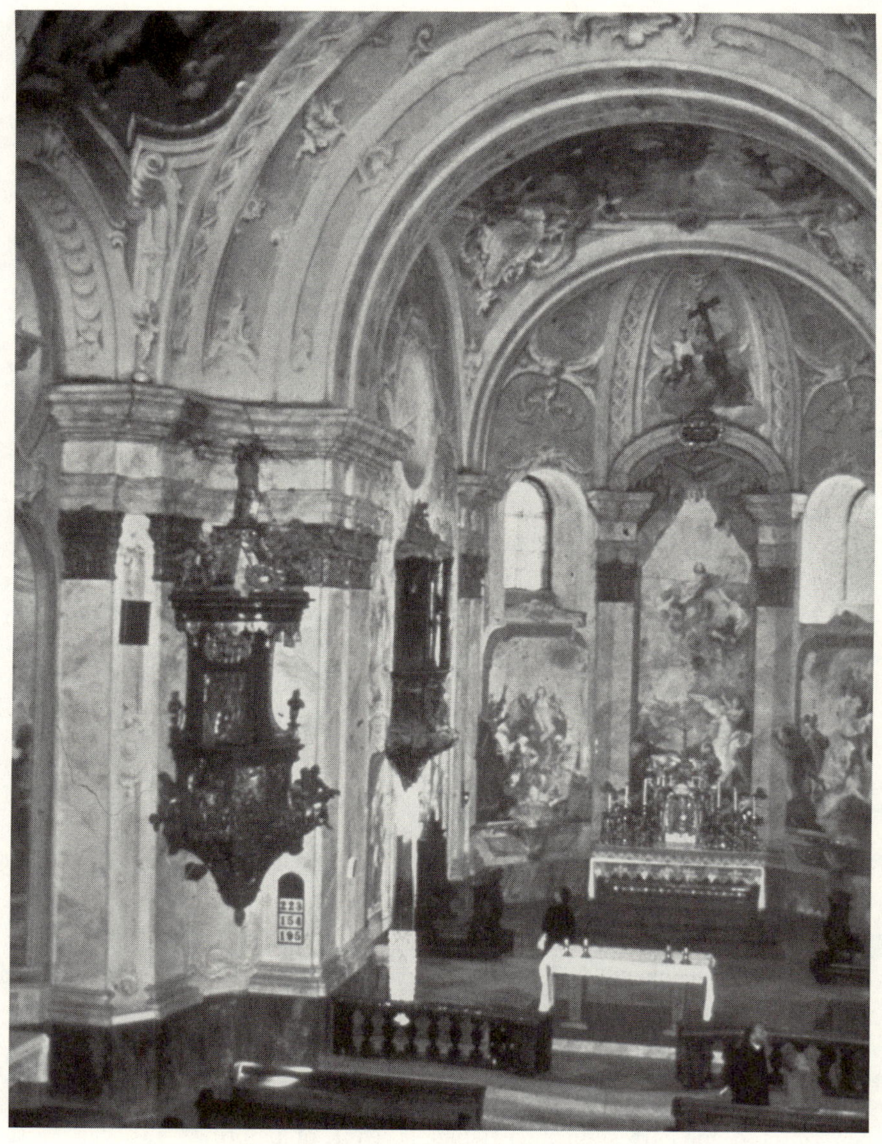

FIGURE 2. View of nave and apse, Parish Church, Sümeg, Hungary
(Photograph: Author's Archive)

Besides these issues, relating the experience of Maulbertsch's frescoes faces another large problem. Pictures like those in the Piarist church have been described as seeming to coalesce out of light and color, as if produced from a stream of colors loosened from their surroundings.[42] (See Plate 1.) This perception of color depends on the light in which the paintings are seen. Yet this experience is as difficult to comprehend as it is to communicate. It is often not easy to find a correct vantage point from which to view such works, and even harder to attempt to re-create or simulate the viewing experience involved in looking at a large expanse of paint: to do so one also often needs to move to take in the whole, and lighting conditions may change radically as one does. In any event, the experience can only be reproduced with great difficulty, because ceiling paintings have to be studied *in situ*; their experience cannot be easily simulated in a book, lecture hall, or classroom. The small compass of a book such as this can but scarcely evoke what is to be seen.

Photographic reproductions present further problems, whatever the technique used. This issue is a common problem in art history, although recent discussions seem to have obscured more than illuminated it.[43] Large questions are involved in photographing paintings on ceilings and walls: one way of taking pictures of frescoes is to control light artificially, or to use spotlights, but this may create results contrary to the experience that one has at the actual location under normal conditions. Remarkable differences may be seen in illustrations of paintings illuminated in artificial light versus those in natural light: a comparison of the huge differences in color, tone, and hue, not to mention overall effect, between different reproductions of the same ceiling taken with windows blacked out, and the church illuminated with spotlights, with those seen illuminated wholly or largely by natural light demonstrates the point.[44]

Questions of medium and condition also arise. Maulbertsch's wall paintings are usually done in varieties of fresco, but one of his earliest works was in marouflage, that is, oil painting on canvas attached to a ceiling (Figure 3). His wall and ceiling paintings employ a variety of techniques, including gilding, mentioned in his contracts and correspondence, which is visible on paintings' surfaces. Most often they are executed in what contemporaries called *Kalkmalerei*, to be discussed further below, employing pigments in a lime and water solution, as well as various other forms of painting *a secco*, on a dried surface. Studies of these issues have, however, not been based on a broad sample of the artist's own work, and some important data have not yet been published.[45] Restorations have been made of some of his easel and wall paintings, but care needs to be taken with them in any event.[46] Hence, while some of his frescoes, as for example his masterwork at

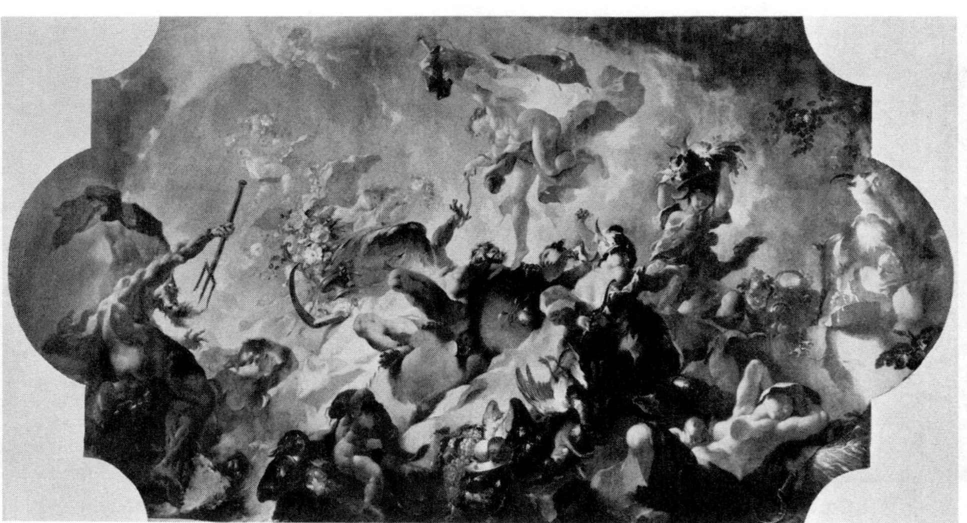

FIGURE 3. F. A. Maulbertsch, *Allegory of Time*, oil on canvas attached to ceiling of *Prunksaal*, c. 1750, Schloss Suttner, Kirchstetten, Lower Austria (Photograph: Bundesdenkmalamt, Vienna)

Kroměříž (Plate 3), seem to be in excellent condition, others have been restored; in some other instances, portions executed *a secco* (in such instances, probably with size or tempera) have either discolored, or dropped off, as has gold leaf, and this is visible even to the unaided eye. One result of the problems posed by accessibility, lighting conditions, and state of preservation seems to be that oil sketches and easel paintings have received a perhaps disproportionate amount of attention in the literature on the artist. Maulbertsch's oil sketches and smaller pictures may be seen more easily in museums. However, it must be emphasized that while he did altarpieces too, Maulbertsch was first and foremost a painter of ceilings and walls. Like other artists of his métier, he would prepare sketches and altarpieces during the winter time, and in the warmer months of the year, when the climate allowed for their execution, he would go on campaigns to complete the wall paintings for which he had contracted.[47]

Hence, while the concept of the oil sketch as an autonomous work of art (Plate 4) has become current and has been related to the work of the Austrian painter,[48] and some of Maulbertsch's oil sketches were made as such, emphasis on the oil sketch as an independent work of art is somewhat misleading, since the oil sketches that Maulbertsch and other artists of his time did are most often related to larger works (Figure 4). Although they may also have been sold as inde-

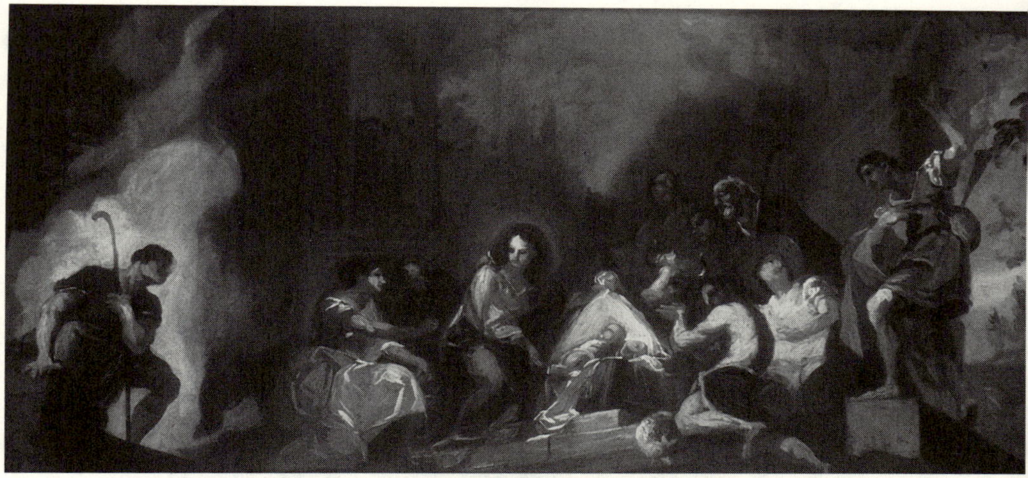

FIGURE 4. F. A. Maulbertsch (?), *Adoration of the Shepherds*, oil sketch (modello) for ceiling painting in Dyje, c. 1775, Národní Galerie, Prague (Photograph: Národní Galerie, Prague)

pendent works, oil sketches were primarily integral to an artist's working procedure and related to larger projects.[49] An oil sketch could represent a preliminary idea for part or all of a composition (called a *bozzetto*), be presented for approval to a patron (a *modello*), or serve as a record in the artist's workshop (a *ricordo*). Oil sketches could also serve several of these functions at different times.

Even though Maulbertsch's oil sketches are remarkable works in themselves, have long rightly gained praise, and do reveal his stylistic qualities, this book will therefore treat them, and his still less abundant drawings,[50] as revealing, but subsidiary. Some problems of attribution are thereby avoided.[51] More important, contemporary documents indicate that Maulbertsch called himself a painter of histories and frescoes; his smaller oil paintings, or drawings, were not what he would have regarded as his major efforts, nor should we consider them as such.[52] To reiterate: oil sketches possess qualities that are also seen in frescoes—more correctly wall paintings, as will be discussed further below—and frescoes remain his most important works, from the point of view of the time spent on them, their size, the pay Maulbertsch earned, and the prestige he gained. Even if oil sketches may reveal important aspects of Maulbertsch's art, they were preliminary to his larger projects, and in any case their qualities are writ large, as it were, in frescoes and altarpieces. Maulbertsch also frequently changed his ideas as he worked, and numerous pentimenti and much overpainting are seen in his finished easel and mural paintings.[53] Concentration on oil sketches does not speak for all the similar traits to be found in Maulbertsch's art, and begs the knotty question of how Maulbertsch's paintings were executed, anyway, even though many interpretations of his art have hinged on them. For all of these reasons frescoes—rather than oil sketches, or drawings, which moreover raise larger problems of attribution—are placed at the center of this book.[54]

Whatever its problems have been, the reception of Maulbertsch nevertheless opens up avenues for renewed consideration of his work. First, later reactions to his works represent responses to certain elements that do seem to be observable in Maulbertsch's paintings. Second, some of these may be related to and indeed stem from roots that were laid in the artistic theory, criticism, and practice of Maulbertsch's own time. Third, if taken in this way, as a guide to historical understanding, and then to Maulbertsch's relation to subsequent art, the later reception of his painting helps not only to situate the artist in relation to contemporaneous questions, but also to reorientate a view of the artist both in regard to his own time and in regard to his place in the history of art.

Two notions that appear in the literature on Maulbertsch inform the themes of this book. The first is a term that appears in various contexts in Maulbertsch criticism: "painterly." Feulner for instance speaks of Maulbertsch's brilliant boldness of painterly expression (*des malerischen Ausdruckes*).[55] Maulbertsch has been called "the most painterly of all Viennese painters."[56] This term derives from the language of formalist art history of the earlier twentieth century, made familiar in the work of Heinrich Wölfflin,[57] meaning in general free application of paint, or of the color carried by paint.

Eberhard Hempel tried to relate this critical assessment to the artist's historical context. He argued that Maulbertsch "was not an isolated artistic phenomenon; on the contrary his art represents only the finest flower of a universal painterly culture and could strike a responsive chord in many people."[58] This usage of the term is not entirely inappropriate or anachronistic, because the very qualities of paint handling, color, and composition that numerous scholars have noticed in Maulbertsch's work, and that are expressed by the term "painterly," have been singled out since Maulbertsch's own time, when his works called forth the first reactions from contemporary observers. Even the word "painterly" (*malerisch*), albeit not employed in exactly the same sense, can be found in eighteenth-century responses to Maulbertsch.

A further association of the notion of painterly is the way in which light is communicated by paint. Kokoschka's reaction to Maulbertsch comes to mind here. Kokoschka said that in his early youth in the Piarist church in Vienna, the luminosity of Maulbertsch's frescoes became a startling visual experience (*zum bestürzenden Seherlebnis*) to which he owed his point of view (*Blickrichtung*), his artistic conviction of the primacy of the light-filled spiritual in art (*des lichtvoll Geistigen in der bildenden Kunst*). Kokoschka's emphasis on "the inner fire of the colors of the painter of luminosity,"[59] his reaction to Maulbertsch's light as spiritual or intellectual, brings up another notion: "enlightenment."

More than metaphor is intended here. This book will explicate the meaning of "painterly enlightenment" in various ways, in the first instance in reference to the historical movement(s) of the Enlightenment(s) of the eighteenth century. Maulbertsch's relation to the Enlightenment has been a subject discussed by several art historians, and will be considered here; the idea that his painting itself may express enlightenment has also been advanced,[60] and that issue will also be addressed here. But the notion of "painterly Enlightenment"—that is, the relation of Maulbertsch's manner of painting to the questions of his age as dealt with in Enlightenment thought—has not been comprehensively explicated. This book will examine some of the meanings of "painterly Enlightenment" as a historical phenomenon expressed in and through Maulbertsch's art.

There is of course much more to say about Maulbertsch and his art, but in introducing this "original strangeling," these themes help to orient an interpretation to certain salient aspects of his work and its reception. First, however, it is necessary to review, in brief outline, how Maulbertsch developed as a painter and what his development might have to do with some central artistic issues related to various concerns of eighteenth-century art and society. Maulbertsch was born in 1724 in Langenargen on Lake Constance, the son of an obscure local painter, from whom he probably received his first, basic training. He came from an area known for its splendid ensembles of church decoration: sites such as Salem, Birnau, and even Weingarten are not far from his birthplace, and it is possible that they, or ensembles like them, as well as works by even more local artists, may have informed his early artistic experiences.[61] Since, however the Habsburgs held sway over territories extending through the Tyrol and Vorarlberg into parts of Swabia, and beyond, Vienna was both the center of power as well of culture for a broad region, and moreover Count Montfort, a local lord, had important relatives (including the Schönborns) in Vienna. In any event, Maulbertsch was to be found in Vienna by 1739; he was to reside there for the rest of his life.

In 1739 Maulbertsch was enrolled in the Vienna academy of art, then under the direction of Jakob van Schuppen (1670–1751), and he was living with the painter Peter Van Royen (or Van Roy; c. 1706–45). Presumably Maulbertsch was apprenticed to Van Royen; probably more important, he was a student at the academy until 1745, when it was closed, and then again when, after it was reopened, in 1749–50. Little is known, however, about his work until the later 1740s, or for that matter much else concerning his artistic activity until the 1750s.

Maulbertsch's first signed and documented paintings, datable from the later 1740s, are pictures with religious subjects. These early easel paintings are, however, hard to distinguish from the works of other artists who had been trained at the Vienna academy.[62] He is first notable on the public scene in 1750, when he won a prize at the academy for a painting of an allegory. If the painting that has recently been identified with this prize-winning work is correctly attributed, it nevertheless displays only a few elements that can be regarded as distinctive signs of what is known from his later style.[63]

Maulbertsch's earliest paintings closely resemble those of many other artists of his generation who were associated with the Vienna academy.[64] In the 1740s and 1750s aspiring painters in Vienna would have operated in an environment informed by the leading Viennese artists of the time, including Daniel Gran (1694–1757) (see Figure 30 in Chapter 2) and, for Maulbertsch particularly, Paul Troger (1698–1762; Figure 5) and Joseph Ignaz Mildorfer (1719–75; Figure 6), both of whom were professors at the academy in the 1750s. In addition to what he might have learned from them, Maulbertsch studied prints, notably by Rembrandt, as has long been suggested.[65] It has also long been suggested that he was influenced by Italian masters of the *settecento*; for knowledge of Italian painting he would not have had to travel to Italy, since many Italian paintings adorned churches and palaces in Vienna itself.[66] Venetian painting was particularly popular in Vienna, as it had become elsewhere in the Holy Roman Empire.[67]

How painters were trained in mid-eighteenth-century Vienna is in any case still not a well-investigated topic. Beyond inferences from prize-winning works, something of what and how students learned in the academy can be reconstructed from some of their drawings and from inferences from the works of those artists who were their professors. Instruction probably followed a standard procedure of making copies from other artists' works, and then drawing from the model, which was proposed in treatises that were respected in Vienna.[68] Drawings that were probably done at the academy in the period 1739–45 by Maulbertsch's contemporaries, notably Kaspar Franz Sambach (1713–95)[69] are executed in pen, with only the outlines of forms indicated, sometimes discontinuously; interior modeling is lacking (Figure 7). This manner may be associated with Troger's draftsmanship, itself informed by that painter's experience with Italian art.[70] Troger's drawings are probably also the source of a more graphic mode, in which a web of hatching and cross-hatching covers the figures, that

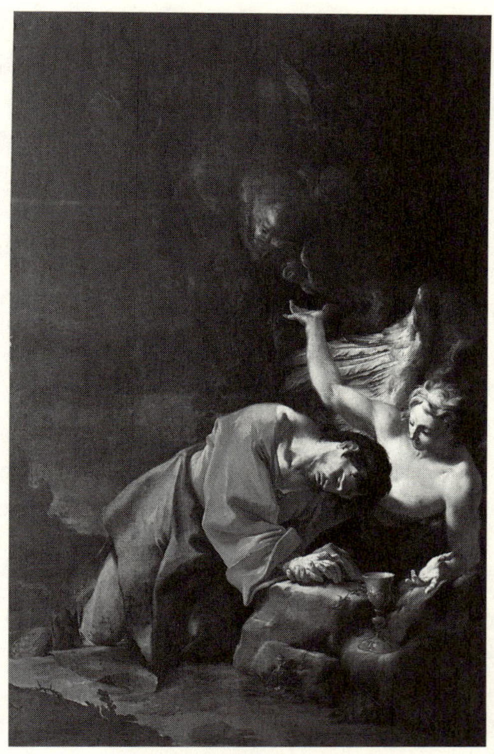

FIGURE 5. Paul Troger, *Christ on the Mount of Olives*, oil on canvas, c. 1750, Österreichische Galerie, Vienna (Photograph: Österreichische Galerie Belvedere Vienna)

is also found in the early drawings of another pupil at the academy in Maulbertsch's time, Johann Lukas Kracker (1719–79).[71] Troger's drawings were in any case readily accessible and were frequently copied by the younger generation of artists.[72]

Significantly, Viennese academic drawings of this sort display a vastly different mode of approaching the model than that which is associated with life drawing in contemporary France,[73] or for that matter with several contemporary Viennese sculptors. They also contrast with drawings from the life by Jakob Matthias Schmutzer (1733–1811), Maulbertsch's future father-in-law and director at the later Vienna academy, after it had been amalgamated in 1772 with the school for engravers Schmutzer had established in Vienna. Drawings from the model by Schmutzer, themselves derived from the practices of French draftsmanship, are done in chalk, and display an accurate mastery of anatomy, and in this they

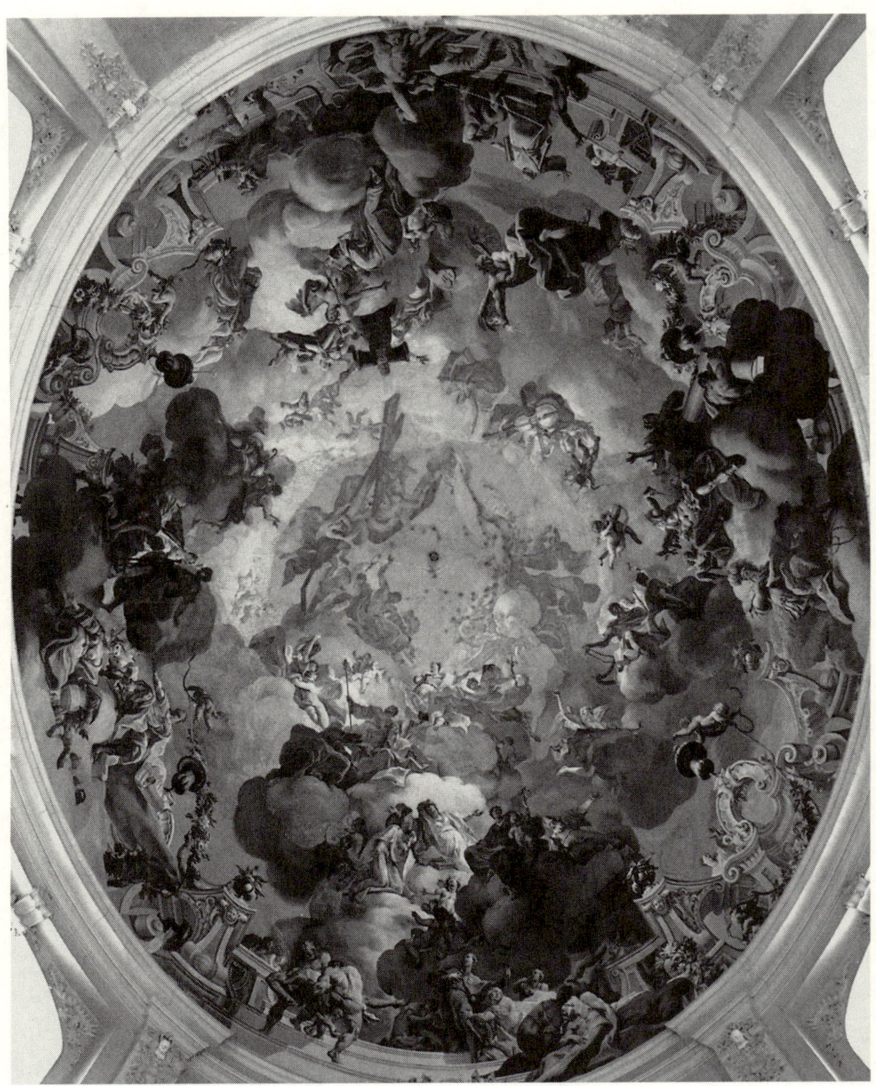

FIGURE 6. Joseph Mildorfer, *Holy Trinity and the Virgin with Typological Representations*, cupola painting, 1743, Parish and Pilgrimage Church of Our Lady, Hafnerberg, Lower Austria (Photograph: Bundesdenkmalamt, Vienna)

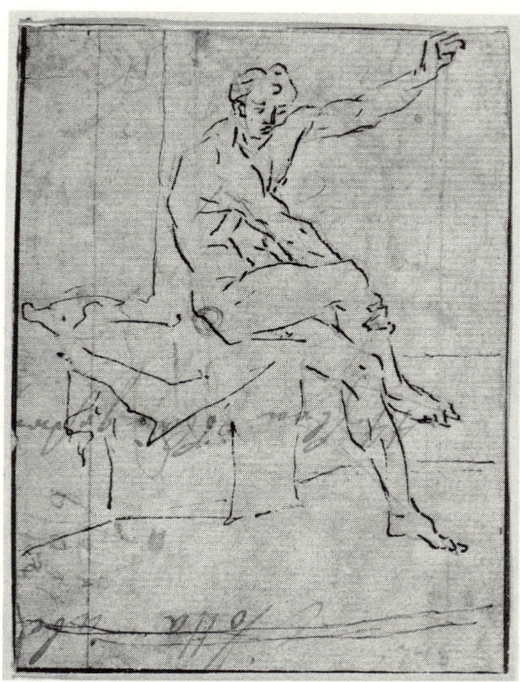

FIGURE 7. Kaspar Franz Sambach, *Academic Study*, pen and ink drawing, 1740s?, Szépművészeti Múzeum, Budapest (Photograph: Szépművészeti Múzeum, Budapest)

resemble studies from the life by professors of sculpture at the Vienna academy (Figure 8).[74] Yet such drawings stand in notable contrast with Troger's figure drawings, and thus presumably with what he would have taught (Figure 9).

Indeed, sheets by Troger of the 1740s (like Figure 9) are often drawn both with pen and with brush and wash on colored paper; rather than achieving a sculptural solidity of form, they produce strong contrasts of light and color, and are therefore closer to the effects desired in painting, for which they may often be preliminary designs. These drawings elongate bodies and distort the anatomy of their forms.[75] The approximation to painting again legitimates the appellation "painterly" for them. It is important to consider this sort of drawing as a possible source or model for Maulbertsch's draftsmanship, especially in the light of critiques of his drawing that were later made, for this was a standard in the milieu in which Maulbertsch matured as an artist. It seems reasonable to assume that Maulbertsch's drawing was later criticized not because he lacked basic skill in

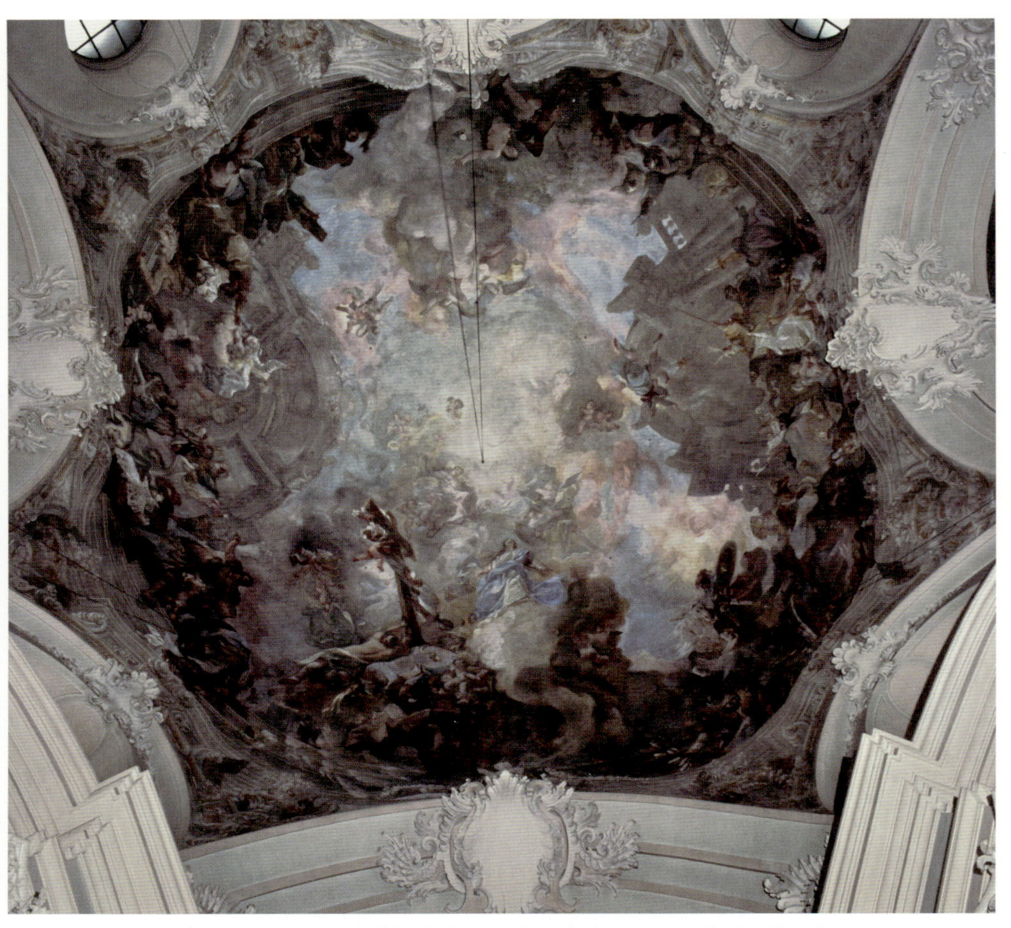

PLATE 1. *Assumption of the Virgin*, cupola paintings, 1752, Piarist Church of Maria Treu, Vienna (Photograph: Eduard Beranek)

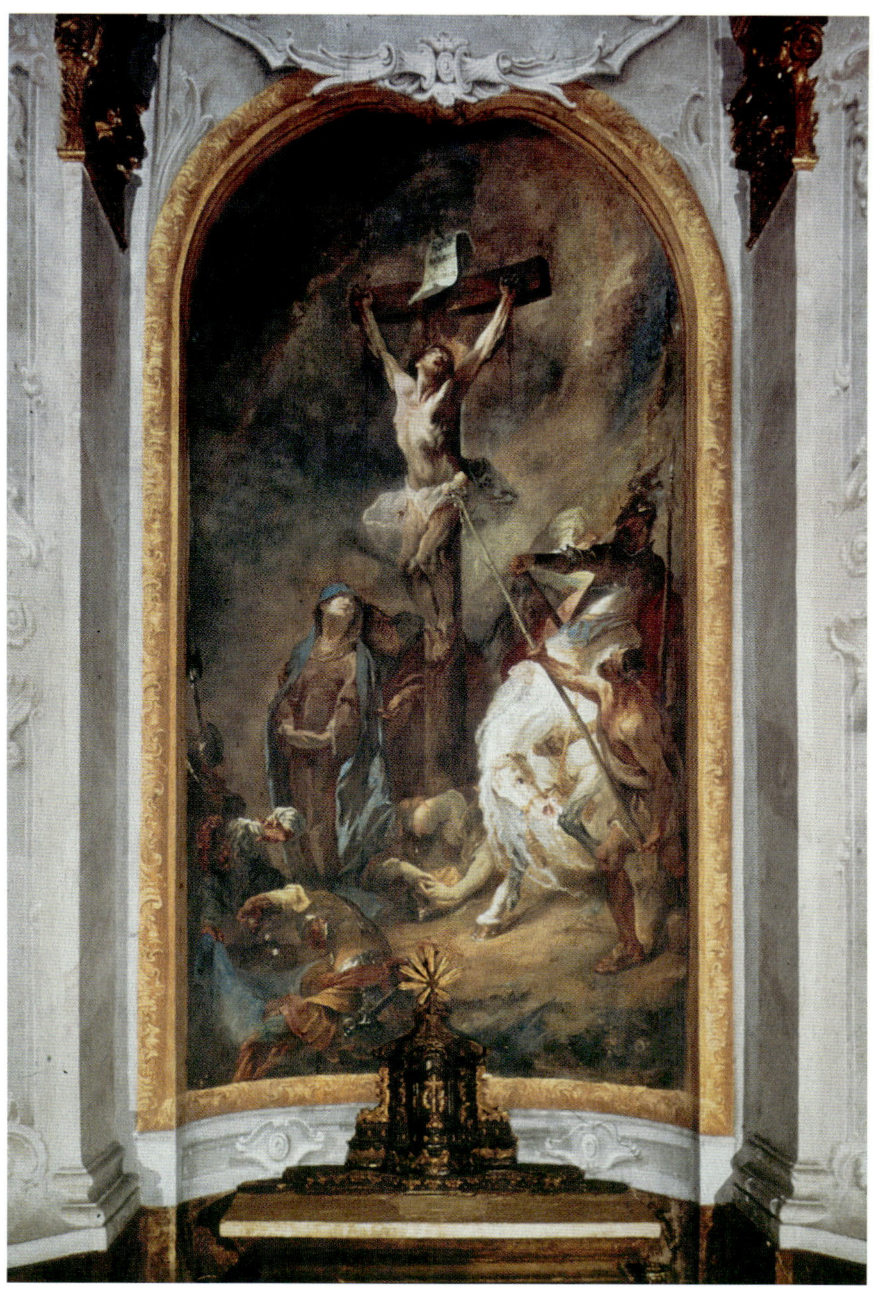

PLATE 2. *Crucifixion*, side altar, 1758, Parish Church, Sümeg, Hungary (Photograph: Károly Szelényi, Magyar Képek / Hungarian Pictures, Budapest)

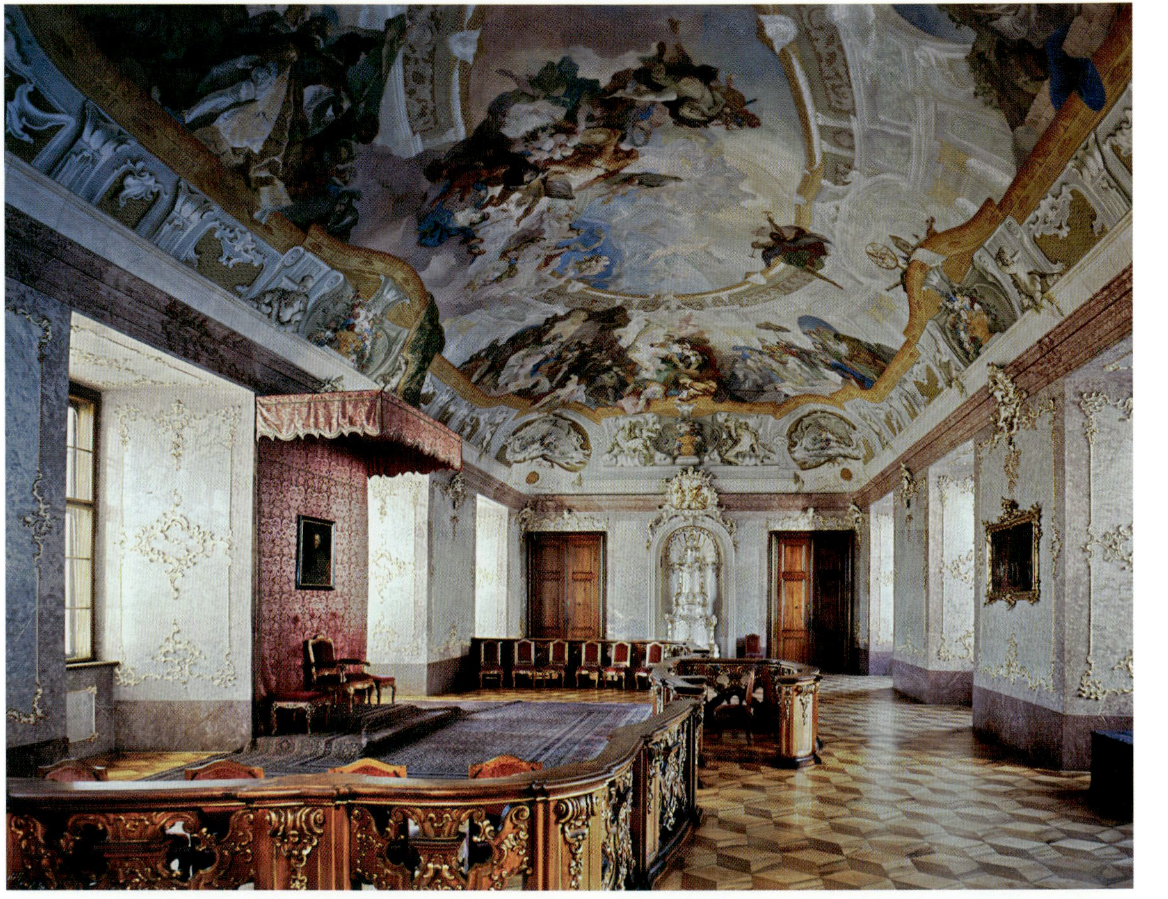

PLATE 3. General view of Feudal Room (*Lehensaal*), 1759, Palace of Bishop of Olomouc, Kroměříž (Kremsier), Moravia, Czech Republic (Photograph: Brno University, courtesy of Bishopric of Brno)

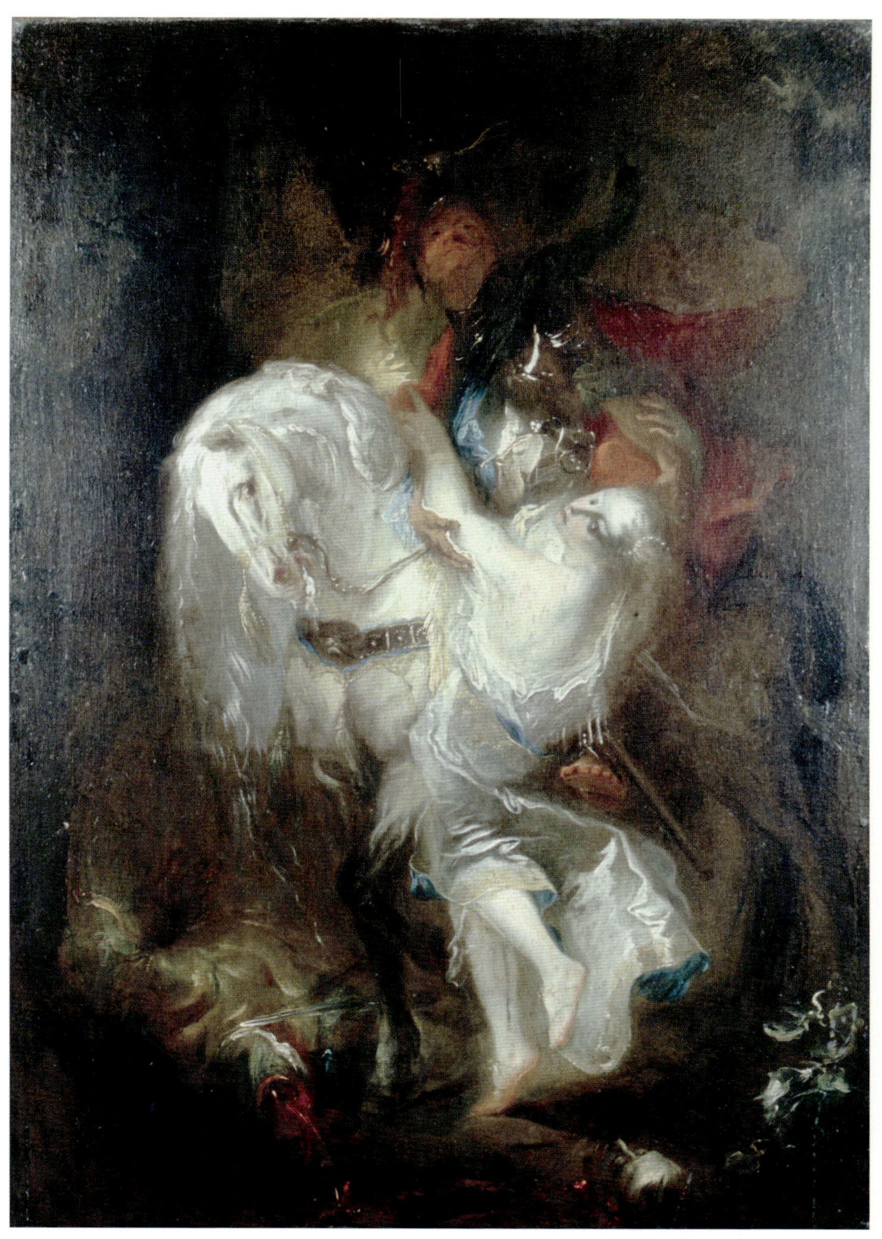

PLATE 4. *An Abduction*, oil sketch, c. 1759, Moravská Galerie, Brno (Photograph: Moravská Galerie)

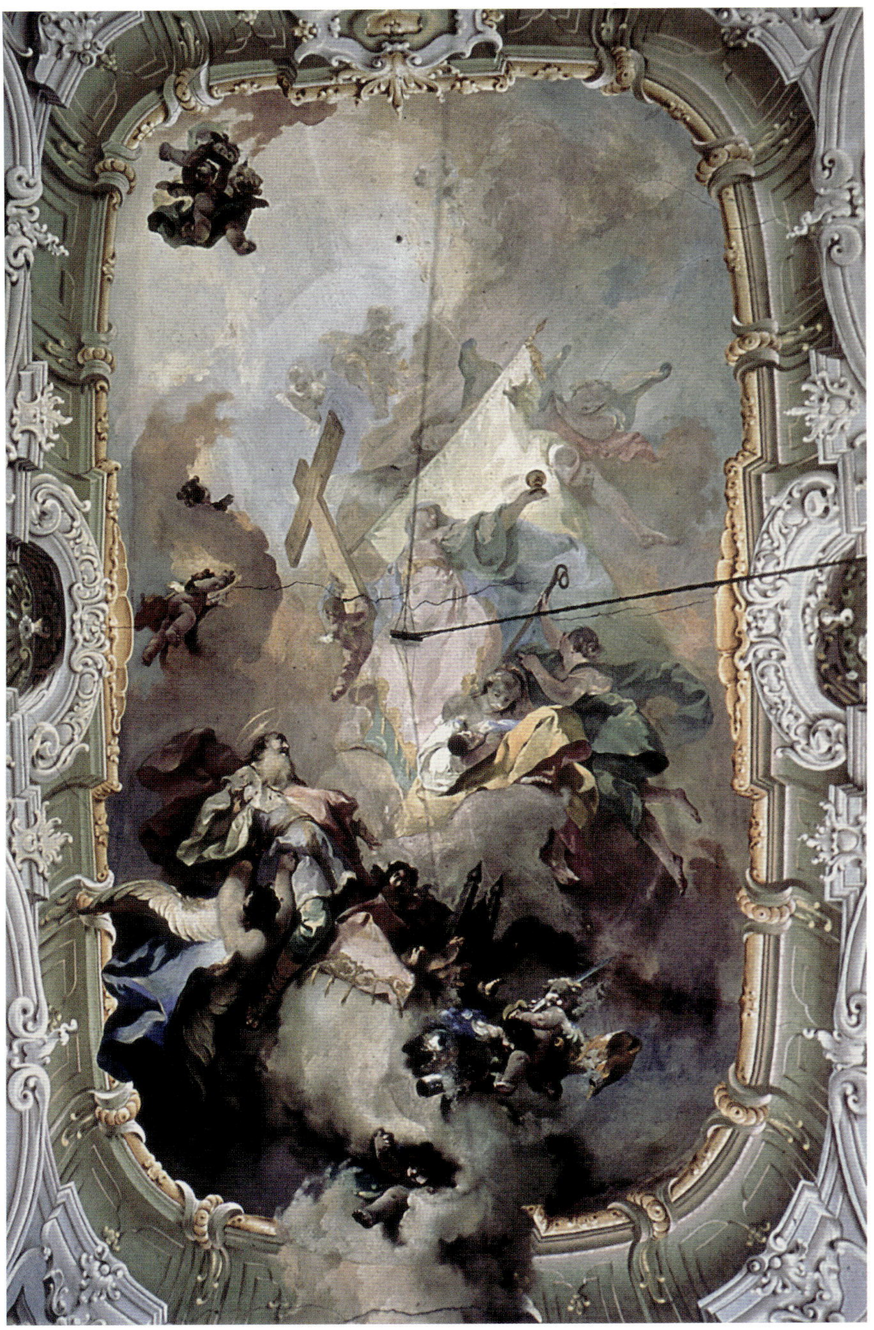

PLATE 5. *Glorification of St. Leonard*, chapel ceiling, 1754, Schloss Suttner, Ebenfurth, Lower Austria (Photograph: Eduard Beranek)

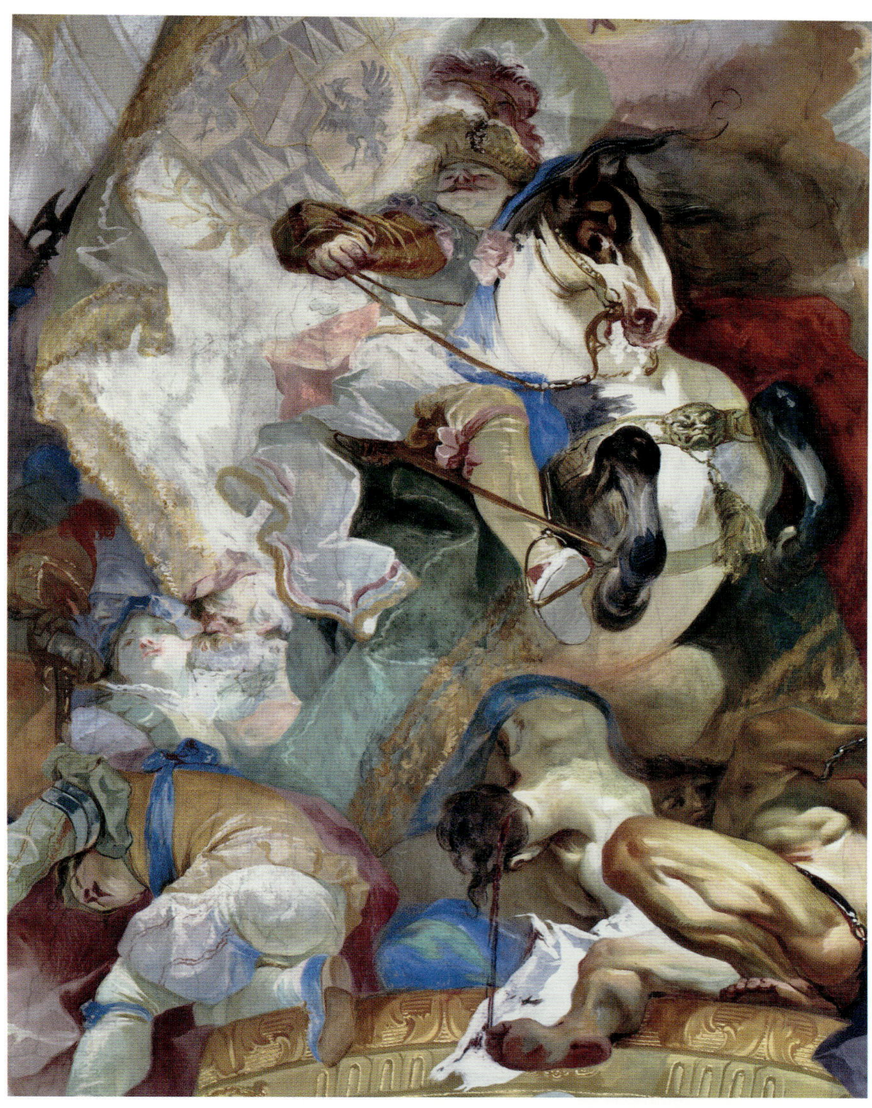

PLATE 6. Detail of ceiling painting, Feudal Room (*Lehensaal*), 1759, Palace of Bishop of Olomouc (Olmütz), Kroměříž (Kremsier), Moravia, Czech Republic (Photograph: Brno University, courtesy Bishopric of Brno)

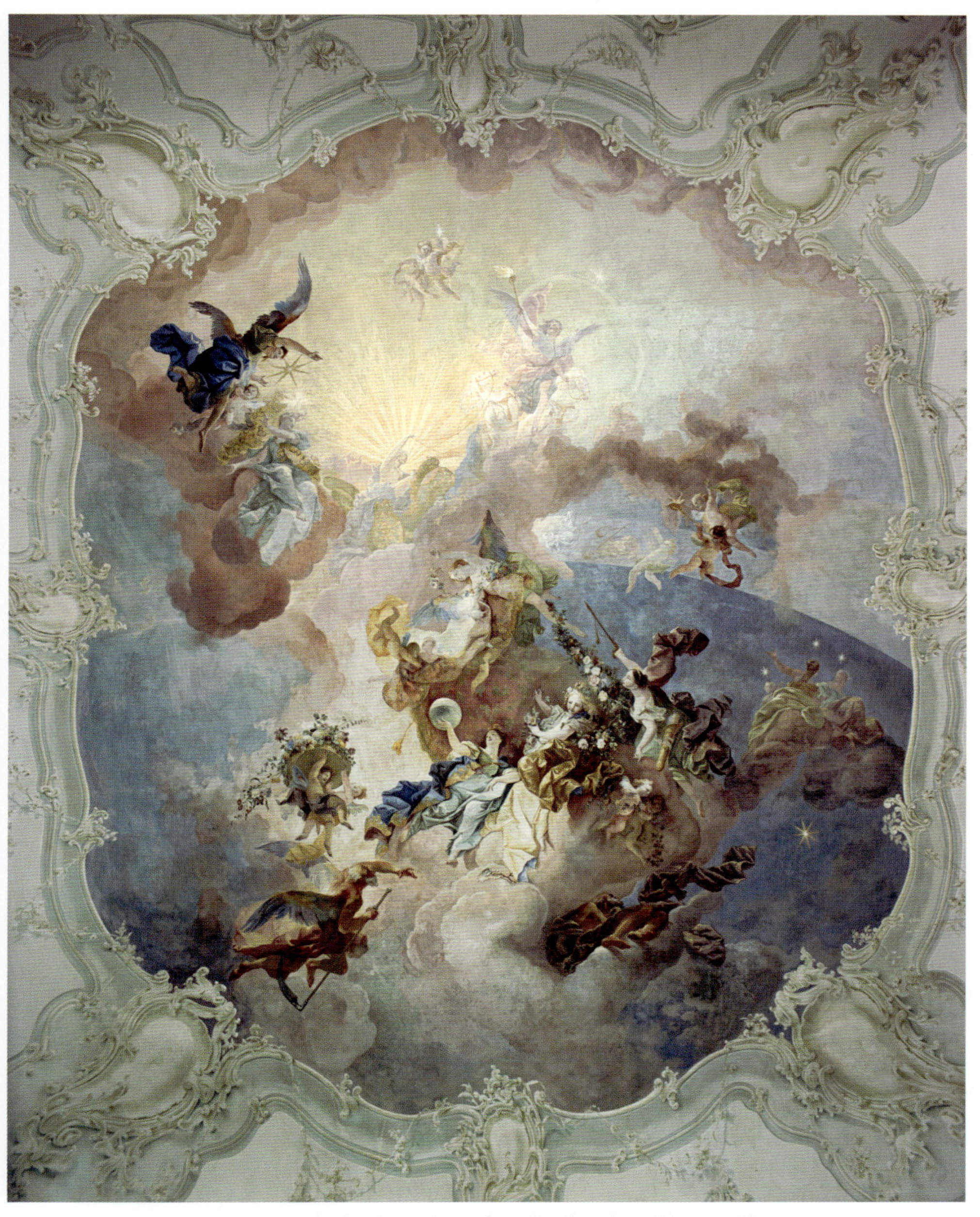

PLATE 7. *Triumph of Light*, ceiling of *Prunksaal*, 1765, Schloss, Halbturn, Burgenland (formerly Hungary) (Photograph: Eduard Beranek)

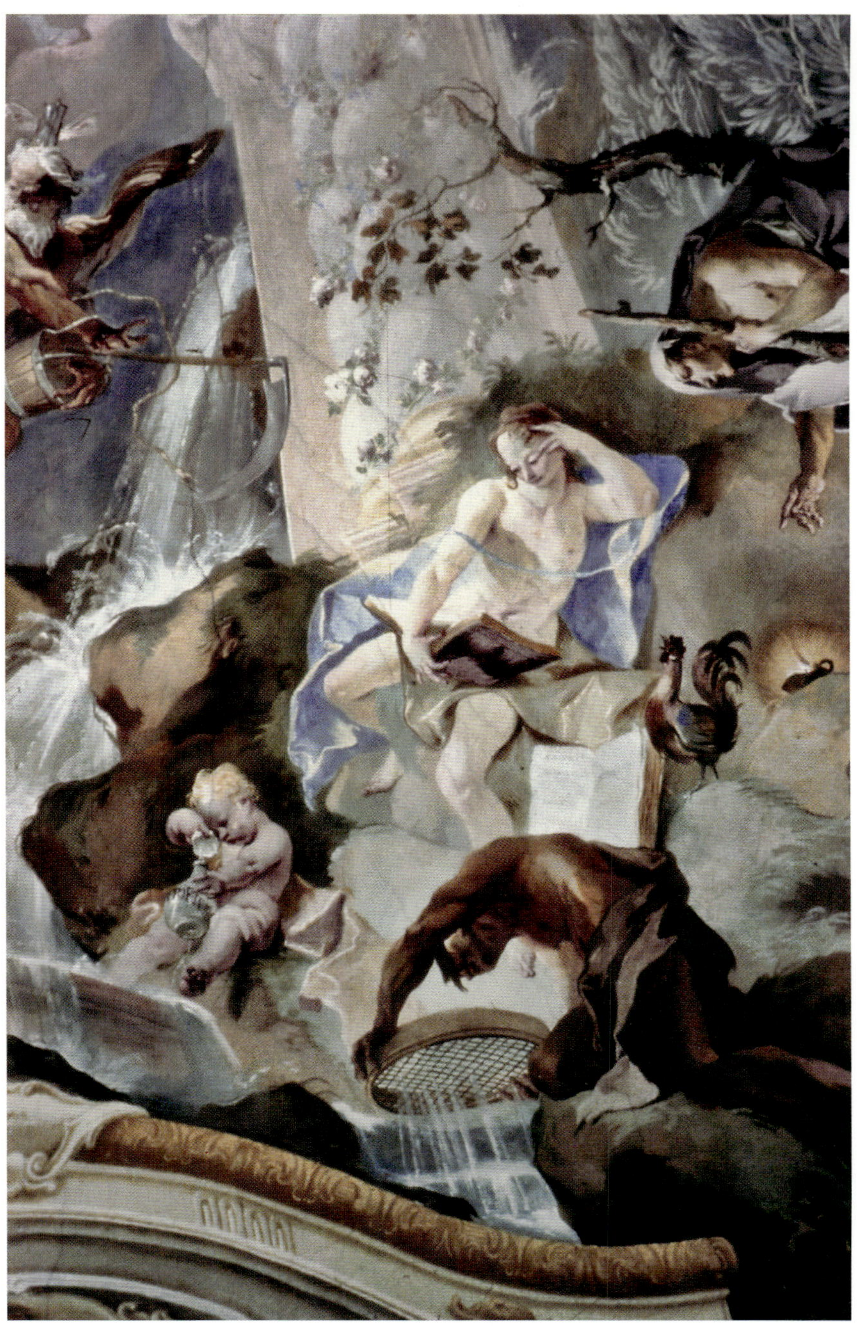

PLATE 8. *Progress and Fruits of Learning*, detail of library ceiling, 1760, former Barnabite Cloister, Mistelbach, Lower Austria (Photograph: Bundesdenkmalamt, Vienna)

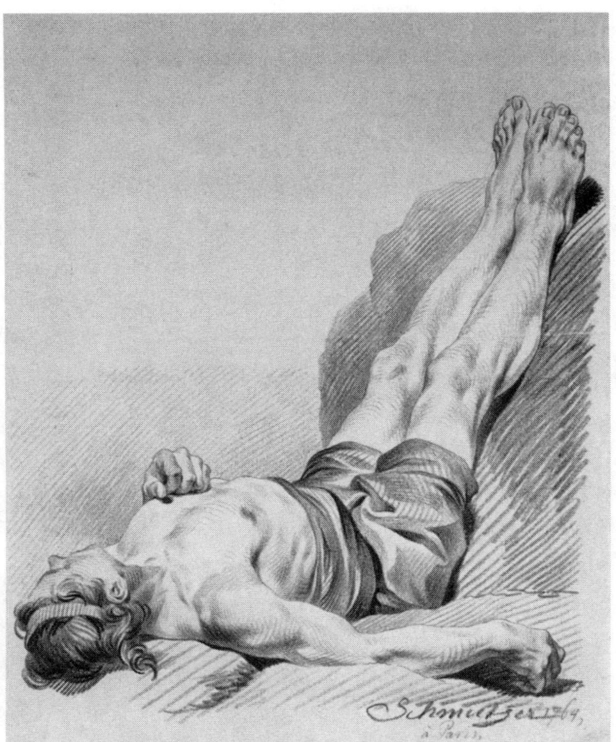

FIGURE 8. Jakob Matthias Schmutzer, *Academic Study*, black chalk drawing, 1764, private collection, New York (Photograph: Author's Archive; courtesy Susan K. Baker)

this medium, but because of the application of different criteria for draftsmanship.

In contrast with the classically inspired norms that came into favor in the later eighteenth century, the Trogeresque manner of draftsmanship can well be described as anticlassical; the term *Antiklassik* has in fact been used to designate the sort of painting that was represented by masters such as Troger, Mildorfer, and Michelangelo Unterberger (1695–1758) in mid-eighteenth-century Vienna.[76] Painting in this vein presents figures shown in bold contrapposto, strong foreshortening, and startling points of view. Such pictures often have bright accents of light and off-center compositions. Mildorfer's paintings in particular have been seen as possessing an expressive painterly style characterized by broad handling of the brush and bright colors.[77] This painting style effected a change

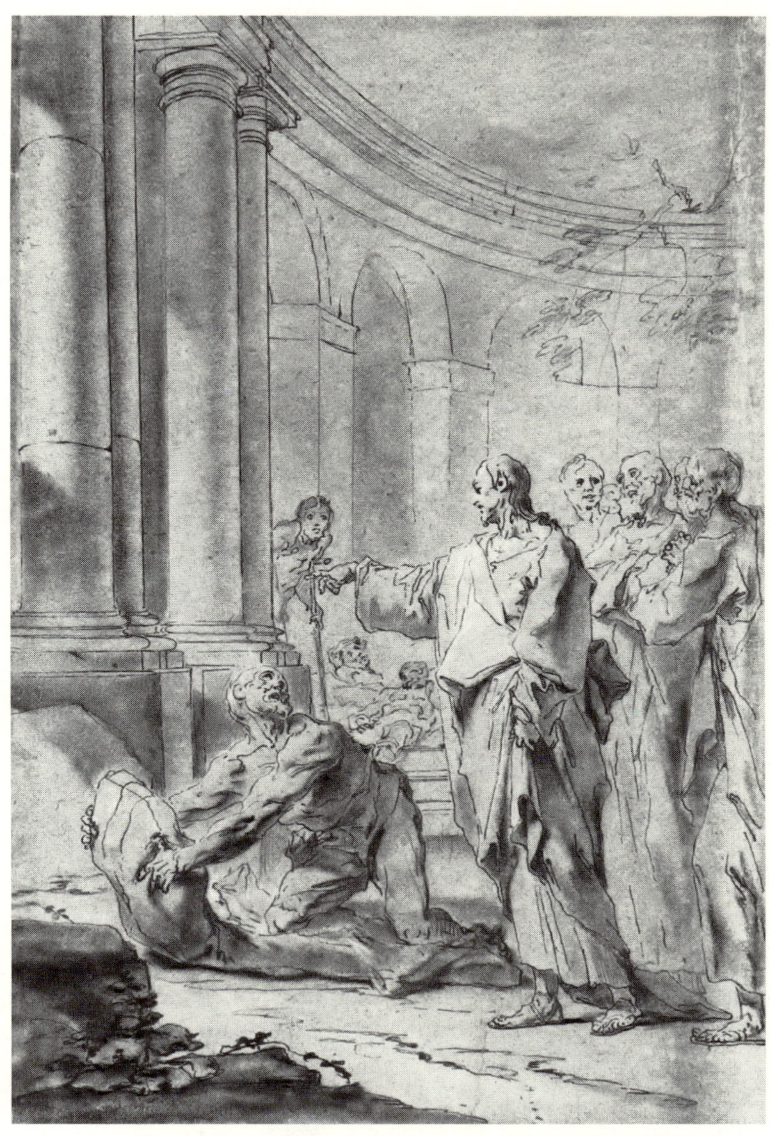

FIGURE 9. Paul Troger, *Christ Heals the Lame*, pen and ink and wash drawing, 1740s, Städelsches Kunstinstitut, Frankfurt (Photograph: Städelsches Kunstinstitut, Frankfurt am Main)

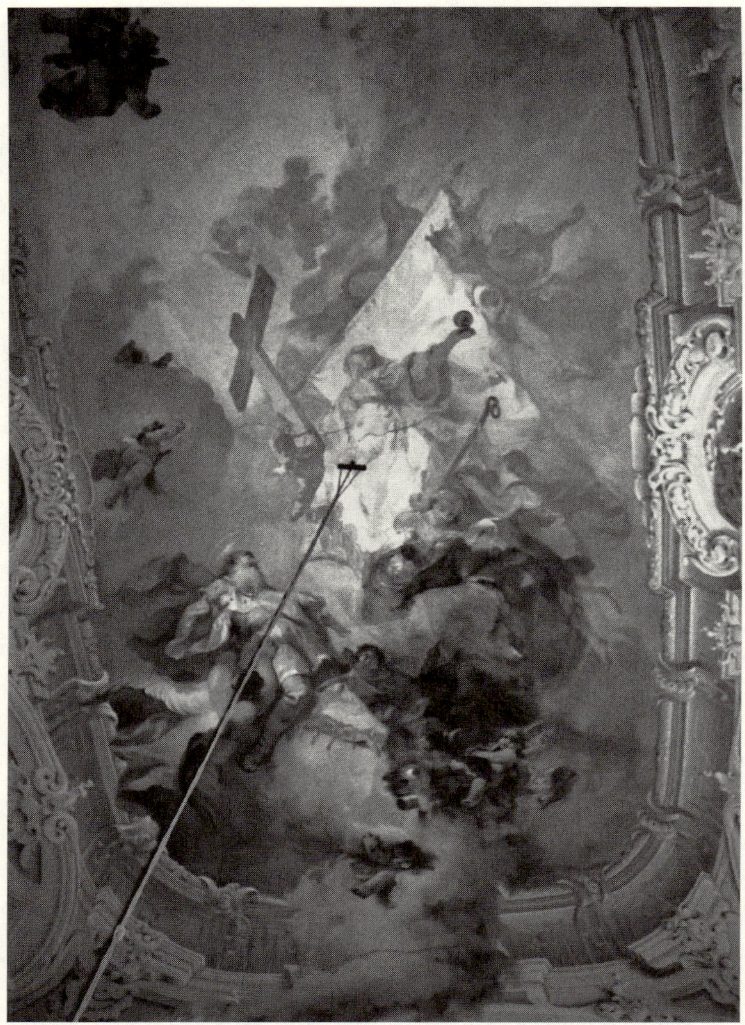

FIGURE 10. F. A. Maulbertsch, *Glorification of St. Leopold*, detail of ceiling, 1754, Schloss Suttner, Ebenfurth, Lower Austria (Photograph: Bundesdenkmalamt, Vienna)

in taste that influenced the formation of painters who studied at the Vienna academy in the 1740s and 1750s.[78]

Similar elements appear in Maulbertsch's earlier works, both in his drawings and in his oil paintings, and especially in the frescoes of the early 1750s that do reveal his distinctive touch. Comparison of forms in Maulbertsch's early ceiling paintings in Kirchstetten (Figure 3) and Ebenfurth (Figure 10 and Plate 5) of the first years of the 1750s to Troger's drawings of the 1740s (Figure 9) reveals many similarities. Among them are the approach to light, the anatomical distortions of figures, who are disproportionately tall and thin, and the elongation of arms and legs to the extent of anatomical impossibility to create emphases.

It has also been observed that compositional devices found in Maulbertsch's ceilings may derive from Mildorfer.[79] Like Mildorfer, Maulbertsch also paints characters charged with emotion, who often make frantic gestures and lack repose. They are packed in complicated, active, at times diagonally oriented compositions. Frescoes from the earlier part of his career exhibit bright, contrasting colors, and even sharp and acid tones, often with *couleur changeant* modeling, or shot draperies. Rapid changes of color, strong chiaroscuro, and startling light effects are also seen in Maulbertsch's pictures, in which there seem to be many sources of light. In them light fractures, rather than shapes, forms (Figure 11 and Plate 6).

Maulbertsch's first ceiling paintings were also quickly executed. The ability to work surely and was rapidly required especially in fresco, where only so much area of a wall or ceiling can be painted as remains humid in a day; what is applied in fresco must be put on the surface of plaster and sand before the water slaked with lime-based pigments dries. Corrections can be done only if the wall is chipped away, or additions are made *a secco*, using a dry binding agent for largely earthen pigments. The same need for celerity applies to the more standard practice found in Central Europe, where lime and water–based pigments were applied to a surface, often covered with a ground in true fresco, that had already dried. Like other great masters of mural media, Maulbertsch seems to have had this ability from the start, and his first efforts display his bravura execution.[80] He is said to have completed the ceilings of the smaller side chapels in the Piarist church in ten days (Figure 12). The freedom of handling, and technique, here and elsewhere throughout his career recalls handling of paint in oil painting; Maulbertsch's painting style will be discussed at greater length in subsequent chapters.

However questions of Maulbertsch's origins, technique, and condition may be resolved, from the first mural paintings the results are impressive. In the ones in the Piarist church, executed in 1752–53 (see Figures 1 and 12, Plate 1), Maulbertsch creates fireworks in paint; the Virgin ascends to heaven as if rocketing upward on a cloud. The whole is a burst of movement. Color seems to explode out of light and streams down from the ceiling.

This luminously colorful style launched Maulbertsch on his career as a mural painter. He worked in a related manner for the next decade and a half. While he painted his first frescoes in the Piarist church for an "honorarium" (*Gnade*),

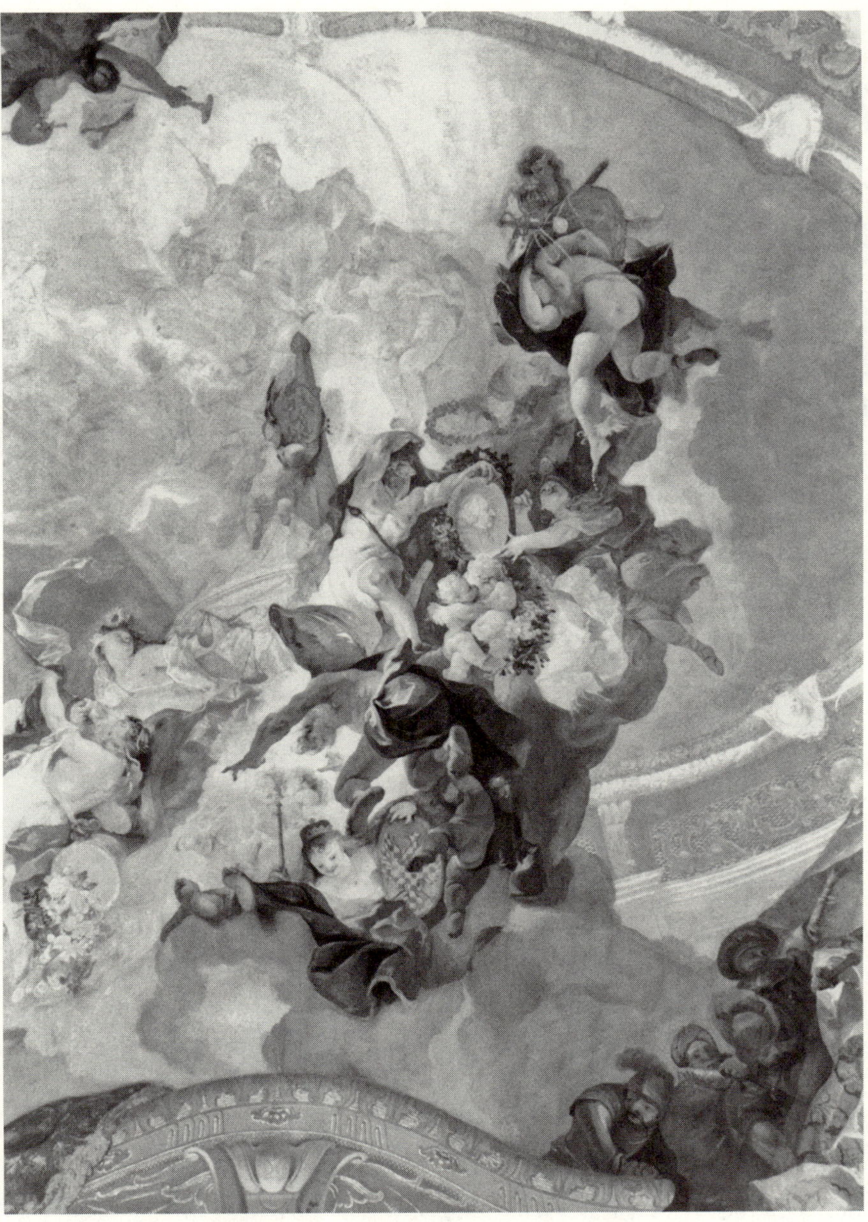

FIGURE 11. F. A. Maulbertsch, ceiling of Feudal Room (*Lehensaal*), detail, 1759, Palace of Bishop of Olomouc (Olmütz), Kroměříž (Kremsier), Moravia, Czech Republic (Photograph: Bildarchiv, Herder-Institut, Marburg)

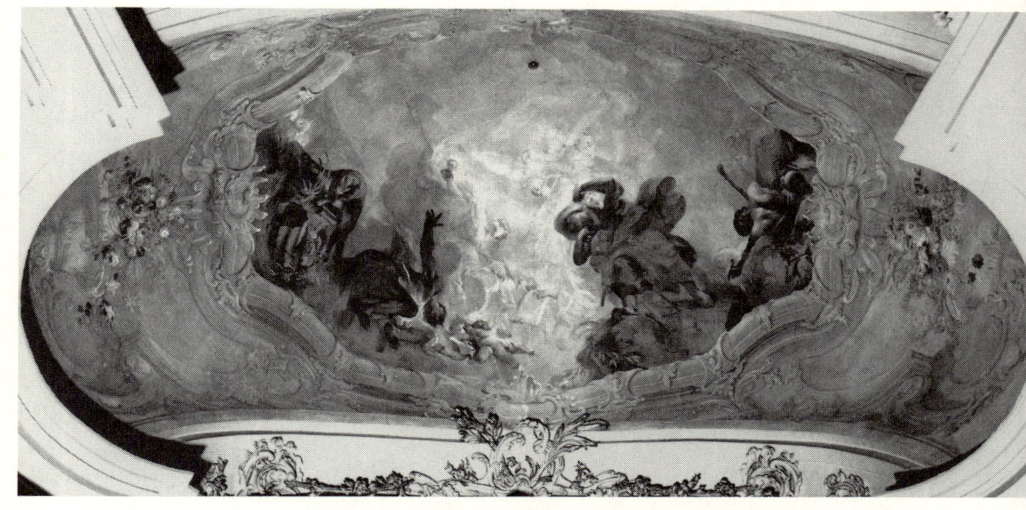

FIGURE 12. F. A. Maulbertsch, *The Good Shepherd*, ceiling of side chapel, 1753, Piarist Church of Maria Treu, Vienna (Photograph: Eduard Beranek)

he soon received commissions for his first wall paintings with a secular subject: these were painted along with the walls and ceiling of a chapel in a *Schloss* in Ebenfurth (Ebenfurt) for the Suttners (see Figure 10 and Plate 5), who had also employed him to do a painting in oil for the ceiling of their Schloss at Kirchstetten (Figure 3). The Ebenfurth paintings are remarkable, colorful works, which are, however, executed in a slightly different tonal mode from that of the Piarist church. But aristocratic patronage for secular projects, while some commissions were granted in later years, was not to become much of a source of employment for Maulbertsch. This may be because many noble residences had already been decorated earlier in the century.

In any event, in the first part of his career Maulbertsch received commissions mainly from religious orders, who were still prospering and expanding in the Habsburg lands. He worked for monasteries, monastic churches, and many orders, including the Piarists, Carmelites, Augustinians, Barnabites, and Jesuits (Figure 13), who were soon to be dissolved. He also maintained a lasting association with the Premonstratensians. Thus it was as a painter for religious houses that he became known.[81]

By the mid-1760s the series of extraordinary cycles of frescoes that Maulbertsch had painted in Moravia, Austria, and Hungary had evidently already gained for him considerable acclaim, since he attracted the attention of the imperial court. He received imperial commissions, at first for altarpieces, but then,

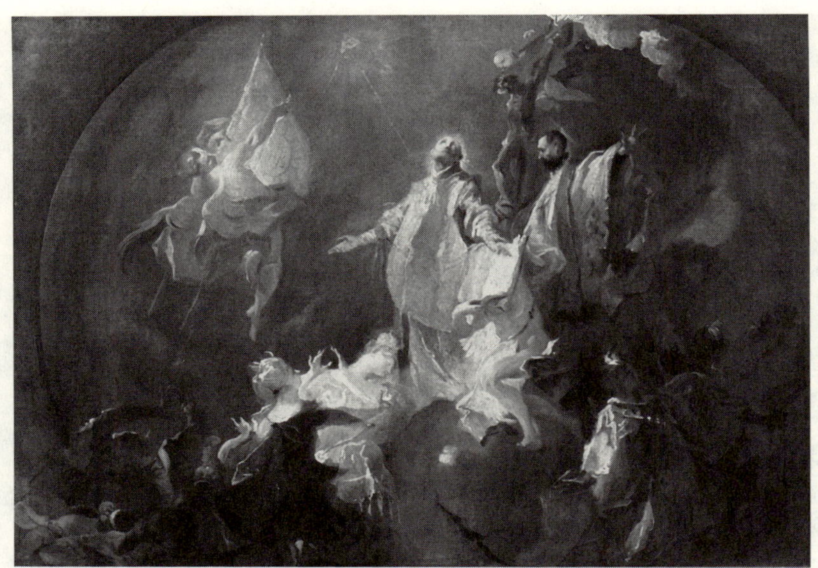

FIGURE 13. F. A. Maulbertsch, *Glorification of Sts. Ignatius Loyola and Francis Xavier*, oil sketch, c. 1760, probably for Jesuit Church in Komárno, Österreichische Galerie, Vienna (Photograph: Österreichische Galerie Belvedere Vienna)

from 1765 on, for ceilings, first in Halbturn, to be treated in chapter 2, next in the Vienna Hofburg in 1772,[82] and then in 1775–76 in Innsbruck. These imperial commissions, together with Maulbertsch's reception of the title of *Kammermaler*, and his completion of the ceiling in the chapel of St. Benno in the Court Church in Dresden (destroyed in 1945), mark the acme of his career, and signal that he had gained broad fame.

But these were also years that spelled fundamental changes in social and aesthetic conditions for the arts. Joseph II succeeded to the imperial title in 1765, and after his ascension as sole ruler in the Habsburg lands, with Maria Theresia's death in 1780, conditions for Maulbertsch's employment also were altered. Joseph II initiated the suppression of monasteries. Maulbertsch was as a consequence deprived of what had been some of the major sources of patronage for his work. Simultaneously, the taste for smaller, easel paintings, often with secular subjects, instead of large wall paintings, was also growing. Smaller, more intimate spaces characterized the sorts of rooms that were to be decorated, and this may be another reason why Maulbertsch did not decorate many residences. The needs of a growing middle-class market were also to be served. To a degree, Maulbertsch tried to meet this last demand, and painted some smaller pictures

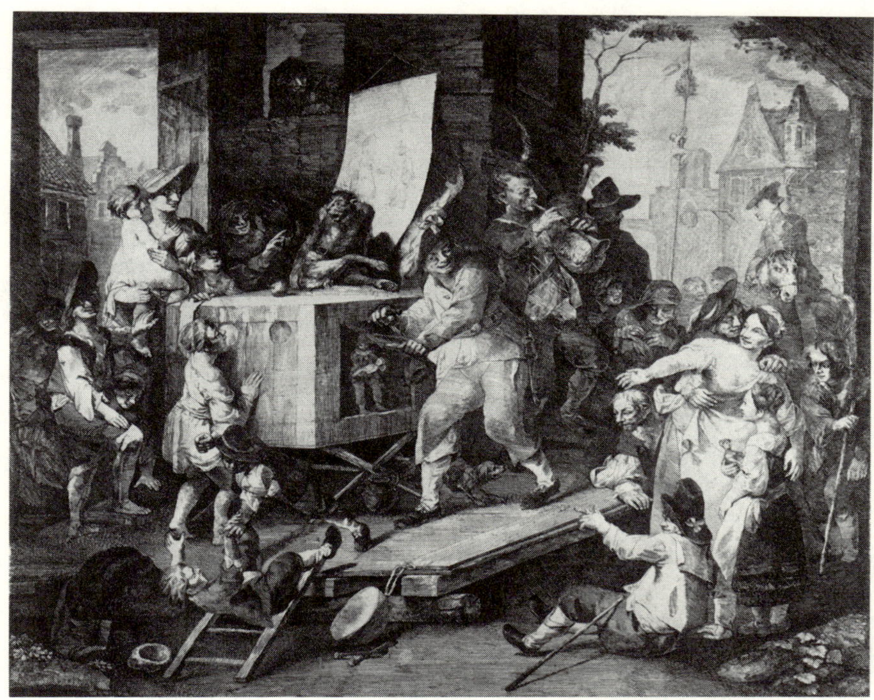

FIGURE 14. F. A. Maulbertsch, *The Peepshow Man*, etching, 1785, Szépművészeti Múzeum, Budapest (Photograph: Szépművészeti Múzeum, Budapest)

with genre (scenes of everyday life) or mythological subjects, and also made prints with similar subjects (Figure 14).[83]

Starting in the mid-1770s the major sources and hence locales of Maulbertsch's patronage moved. He had already worked for Hungarian prelates (for the bishop of Veszprem at Sümeg; for Cardinal Migazzi, bishop of Vienna and also of Vác, at Vác in 1770), but from the mid-1770s Hungary provided the major locus for his work. His chances to paint frescoes (and large altarpieces) came increasingly from Hungarian clerics, many of whom were also magnates. These Hungarian "princes of the church" have been called the last great patrons of the baroque, considered as the style of the time (Figure 15).[84]

The repopulation after the wars with the Turks, attempts at re-Catholicization (in the eighteenth century Hungary was half Protestant), and the ecclesiastical reorganization of Hungary created new bishoprics and opened many new possibilities for the arts. Maulbertsch gained from them, with commissions for Győr (Figure 16), Kalocsa, Pápa, Bratislava (in the palace of the Hungarian primate in what was then Poszony or Pressburg), Eger, and Szombathely. His last completed

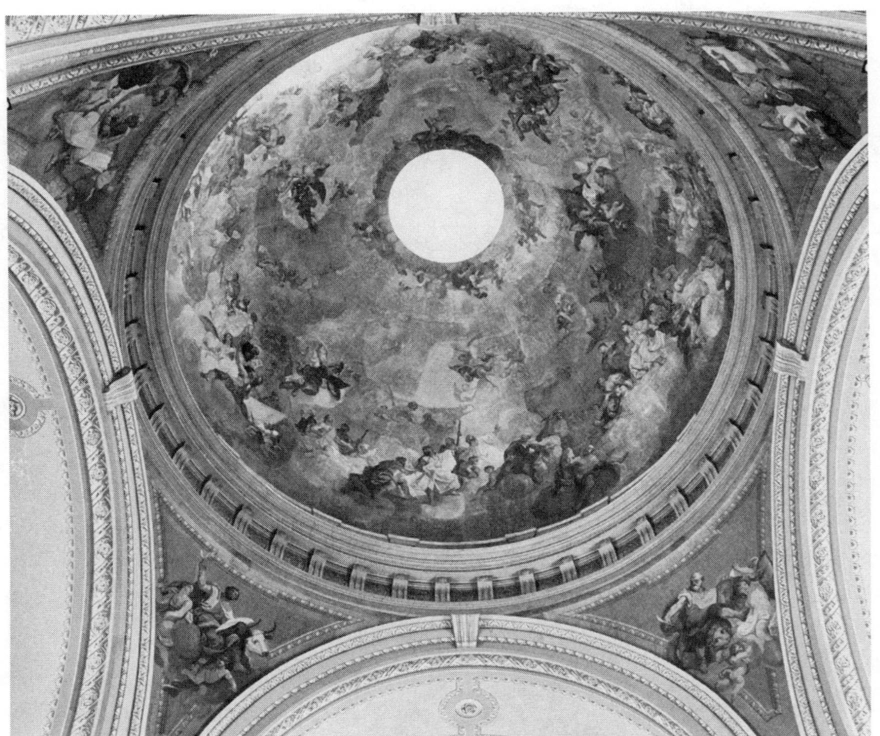

FIGURE 15. F. A. Maulbertsch, *Glorification of the Holy Trinity* (with four Evangelists in the pendentives), cupola, 1770–71, Cathedral, Vác, Hungary (Photograph: Károly Szelényi, Magyar Képek / Hungarian Pictures, Budapest)

fresco was however for the Premonstratensians in Prague, a place in which he otherwise left little (Figure 17).

The style of Maulbertsch's later works changed from circa 1765 onward. To put it briefly, his colors become clearer, his drawing tighter; his compositions are made more orderly. His ornament is modified, to decorative forms based ultimately on the antique. Questions abound about why this occurred: the issues will be discussed in Chapter 3.

By this time, he had begun to receive considerable critical attention, also to be discussed in Chapter 3. Beyond the many people who could have directly seen Maulbertsch's work in churches and public buildings, several descriptions of his paintings were published. They formed part of the development of a new public sphere for art as for other things in the eighteenth century. This public sphere has been defined as the growth of a reading public and its facilitation by the

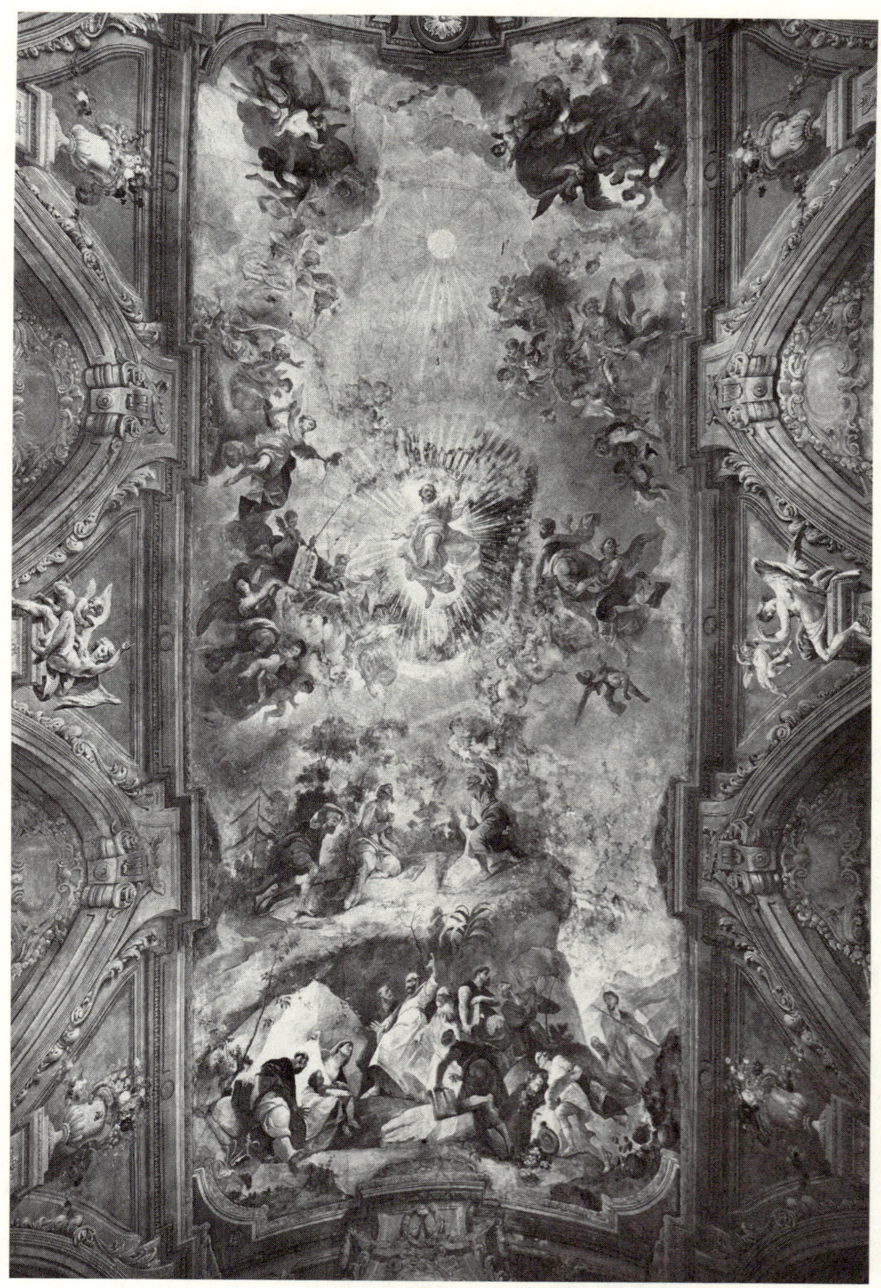

FIGURE 16. F. A. Maulbertsch, *Transfiguration of Christ*, nave ceiling, 1781, Cathedral, Győr (Photograph: Károly Szelényi, Magyar Képek / Hungarian Pictures, Budapest)

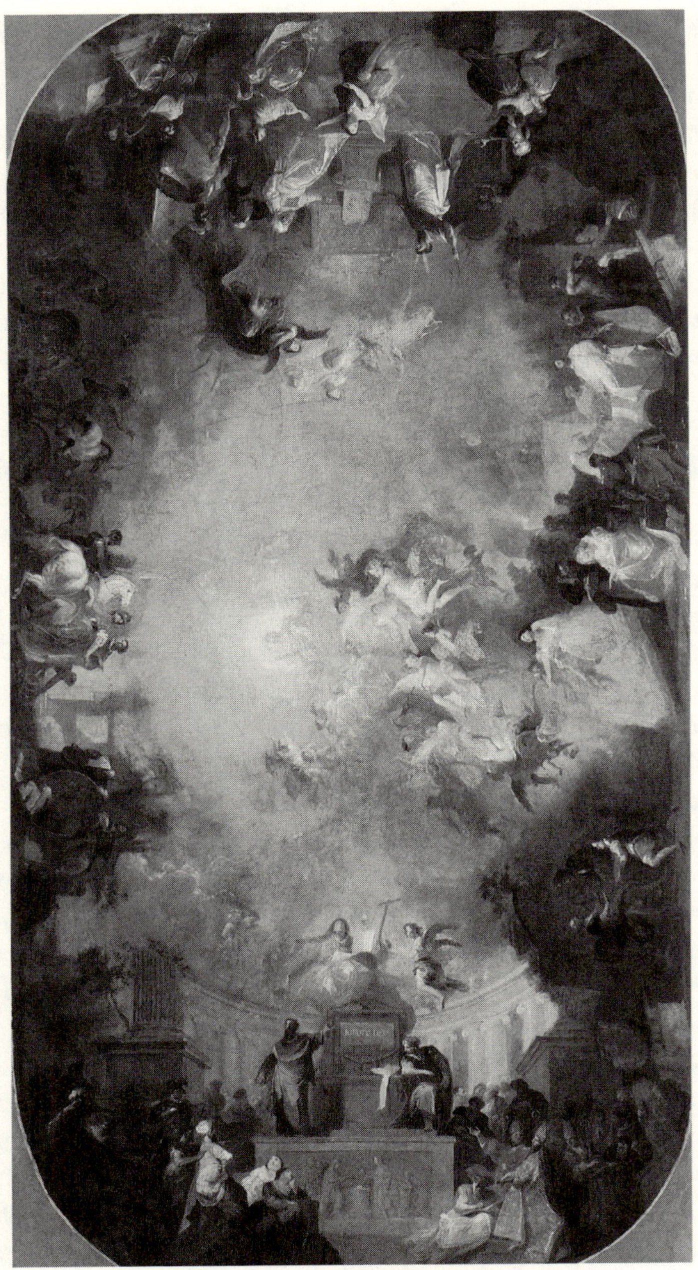

FIGURE 17. F. A. Maulbertsch, *Allegory of the Revelation of Divine Wisdom*, oil on canvas, modello for library ceiling, 1793–94, Premonstratensian Monastery, Strahov, Prague (Photograph: Premonstratensian Kanonie, Strahov, Prague)

publication of newspapers and periodicals. Mention and even criticism of Maulbertsch in such publications also more broadly increased the audience for his art. So did the display of his works in salons, another product of the new public sphere.[85] Furthermore, criticism of art may be associated with the critique of all forms of culture and society identified with the Enlightenment.

This takes us back to what may be meant by Enlightenment, in the sense of the historical movement of the eighteenth century. The Enlightenment may evoke the names of Voltaire, Denis Diderot, and Montesquieu, all writers and thinkers. There has been some tendency to restrict the notion of the Enlightenment to France, but this would be to ignore such major thinkers as Gotthold Ephraim Lessing and Immanuel Kant, and a host of other figures in Germany and elsewhere.[86] Nevertheless, while Diderot was one philosophe who of course wrote about paintings, Enlightenment thought, especially in its Germanic manifestations, is not usually associated with the visual arts. It has even been argued that the Enlightenment should be regarded primarily as a literary movement. The question is how Enlightenment concerns might also touch on the aesthetic response to Maulbertsch's work, and on how Maulbertsch may have made his own pictures in response to criticism and Enlightenment thought.

As we shall see, contemporary critics who responded positively to his appeal and made his works known to a broader part of the populace described his art as one that had a sure touch in expression and coloring. The ability to execute paintings quickly was valued in fresco painting, and Maulbertsch was praised for this quality, too. Other critics noted specifically that his color, and the pleasure this offered to the multitude, was part of the *Aufheiterung* of frescoes. Yet some of the very elements that were appreciated in Maulbertsch's art were also criticized by other contemporaries. For example, distortion of anatomy, fragmentation of form, dramatic use of draperies, color, and light were all features mentioned in discussions of his art, and all were disparaged by some.

In addition to the contradictory public response, many more contradictions may be found among aspects of the relation of Maulbertsch's painting to the Enlightenment. Contradictions exist between Enlightenment demands for discipline and control in obtaining moral ends for art and the painterly means used to express them; between what can be called baroque illusionism, employed in the dramatic scenography by which subjects were frescoed in churches, and the critique of such pictorial means as deceptive, which stemmed from demands for truth in expression; between what might seem a luxurious form of art, in that the exaltation of divine subjects often called for the use of gold to depict highlights, versus the increasing abandonment of such luxuries.

The concept of "painterly Enlightenment" epitomizes some of the paradoxes presented by the problem of the juxtaposing the different demands of the expression of new ideals in pictorial means. It sets in relief the crucial question of Maulbertsch's development as a painter. To sum up: his initial works, an art of colorful and emotive forms, ran up against the demands of attitudes shaped by Enlightenment critiques, which called for an approach shaped by reason, and decried aspects of Maulbertsch's art that did not seem to be consonant with such demands. Whether or not this was the sole or major cause for the noticeable change in his style, changes in taste related to Enlightenment aesthetic critiques caused Maulbertsch to fall out of favor, and he remained long forgotten by history. However, clearly matters did not end here: modernist artists and art historians renewed the response to the color, light, and beauty of Maulbertsch's work. Moreover, their response to eighteenth-century art is not simply to be regarded as anachronistic.[87] Some of the same characteristics had also led critics contemporary with Maulbertsch to praise his work, and these features have remained matters of concern since the eighteenth century.

This book will deal with several of these issues. On the one hand, it will try to find an appropriate language to interpret what Maulbertsch's painterly response to the Enlightenment may have been. On the other hand, it will try to show that some of the contradictions present in the critique of Maulbertsch's art result from the problem of making art that have remained concerns from his time to ours. The second chapter will handle the question of Maulbertsch's relation to the ideals of the Enlightenment, and the relation of his painting mainly to ideas and subject matter. The third chapter will consider the change in Maulbertsch's style in relation to Enlightenment debates on the arts. The final chapter will reexamine the central issue of his coloring and handling in relation to other discourses on the arts of the eighteenth century. While many writers have long linked Maulbertsch with nineteenth-century romanticism, it has not hitherto been adequately emphasized that many such visual elements that have been thought to be "romantic" were already discussed in a positive manner in eighteenth-century reflections on the visual arts. Maulbertsch's work can be related to these aesthetic ideals, as well as be associated with concerns of later art.

It may at first seem that Maulbertsch has a liminal position—whether one considers him geographically, historically, or art historically. However, tendencies in his art, and what can be appreciated in it, are not only the sum and culmination of his own particular painterly culture. They suggest that there is something more at stake in it: they illuminate the problems of making art in a time of change and crisis. Among the issues involved are making a meaningful didactic, or ethically charged, art that is to communicate to a widened public; considering the possibilities of new forms of symbolism; forming an artistic response to the creation of a critical public; and reconciling communication with aesthetic expression.

Many qualities may therefore be found in Maulbertsch (and in the critical response to him, too) that allow us not only to relate him to the history of his time, but also to answer the question why he may still have interest for us today. For the various contradictory impulses to be found in Maulbertsch's situation have in manifold forms remained in tension throughout much of the history of art since the eighteenth century. Maulbertsch is not only an artist whose situation dramatizes issues of the history of painting in his own time and place. His works continue to resound both in the aesthetic response their beauty evokes and in some of the fundamental, continuing, concerns of artistic creation that they illuminate.

TWO
Shades of Enlightenment

On 31 May 1765 Franz Anton Maulbertsch received a payment in the amount of 1,200 thalers for work completed at Halbturn, in a small villa-like Schloss near what was then the western border of Hungary. (It is now in Burgenland, Austria.)[1] With the aid of Joseph Winterhalder the Younger,[2] who was his assistant during the years 1764–68 but whose participation in this instance can not be distinguished from his own, Maulbertsch had painted the ceiling of the *Prunksaal* (also called the *Festsaal*; Plate 7 and Figure 18), the main reception hall, as part of the redecoration of 1765–67 that accompanied the rebuilding of the Schloss by the Viennese architect Franz Anton Hillebrandt (1719–97). Like Maulbertsch, Hillebrandt, who at the time was head of the *Hofbauamt* (the imperial building office), carried out many such projects in Hungary.[3] Halbturn was intended to be a summer seat for the royal court of Hungary; the court was then usually located in Bratislava (Pressburg/Poszony), where Archduchess Maria Christina resided; the archduchess was betrothed to Albert of Sachsen-Teschen, who was later to found the collection of graphic art now known after him as the Albertina. Maulbertsch's fresco at Halbturn is the first documented commission he received from the Habsburgs, who besides controlling the imperial throne also ruled Bohemia and Hungary.

Within a surrounding frame that simulated stucco decoration in what is now often called the rococo manner,[4] Maulbertsch depicted Apollo riding in the chariot of the sun. Preceded by a figure who carries a torch, and bathed in light himself, Apollo emerges from clouds veiling the morning star. Apollo proceeds through the circle of the zodiac toward the evening star on the other side of the

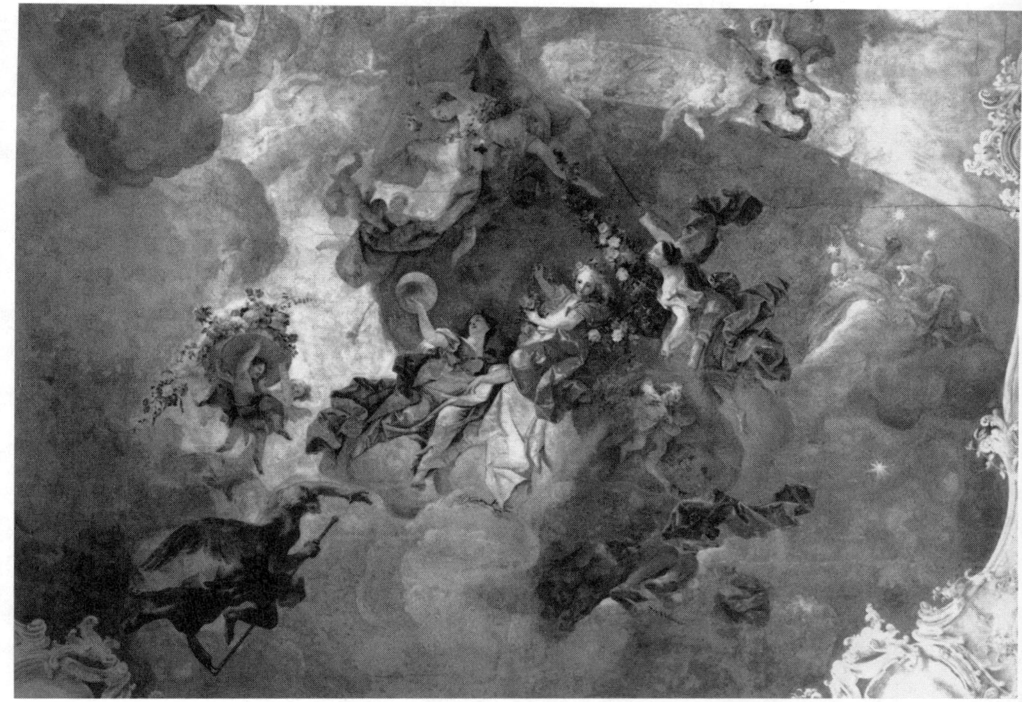

FIGURE 18. F. A. Maulbertsch, *Triumph of Light*, ceiling of *Prunksaal*, detail, 1765, Schloss, Halbturn, Burgenland (formerly Hungary) (Photograph: Bundesdenkmalamt, Vienna)

ceiling. Beneath him a group of figures swirls upward; this group includes putti carrying flowers and other figures with garlands. (See Figure 18 and Plate 7.) While complete agreement does not exist about the precise identification of the figures who accompany or greet the sun god—they have been variously interpreted as Aurora, Flora, the Horai, the Seasons—the figures below them are more easily identifiable. Saturn, a winged old man with a scythe may be discerned, along with Night, an old man in a cloak with an owl beside him, and Diana, identified as the goddess of moon with her crescent-adorned tiara.[5]

The basic meaning of the composition is keyed by another figure seated with a shell containing pearls and coral at her feet. She wears a crown composed of city walls, identifying her most likely as Ceres, or Terra, since she holds aloft a globe whose top is illuminated. This detail suggests the contrast of light above with darkness below: the composition is so divided between personifications of light and darkness.

Depictions of Apollo in the chariot of the sun are common in ceiling paintings of the seventeenth and eighteenth centuries, in the Habsburg lands as elsewhere. Several drawings by Johann Michael Rottmayr datable to 1704–7 that were probably intended for the Liechtenstein Garden Palace in the Rossau (now the Liechtenstein Museum in the Ninth District, Vienna) had already presented this theme at the beginning of the eighteenth century.[6] Among many other paintings of the subject, frescoes were also executed prior to Maulbertsch by other important Austrian masters such as Daniel Gran in the Schwarzenberg Palace in Vienna in 1723 and in the Hunting Schloss at Eckartsau in 1732, and by Paul Troger in 1739 in the imperial staircase at the Benedictine Abbey at Göttweig in Lower Austria.[7] Closer to Halbturn, a fresco with similar theme could be seen in a Schloss that is located on the way from Vienna to Halbturn at Mannersdorf, which F. M. Haberditzl considered to be a prototype for Maulbertsch.[8] But frescoes of the 1690s by Carpoforo Tencalla that are also located relatively nearby in Hungary, in the Esterházy Schloss in Kismarton, now Eisenstadt, Burgenland, represent a similar subject. Still another work with a similar scene that is located not far away from Halbturn in Hungary and that was painted approximately at the same time as Maulbertsch's picture is a work by Basilius Grundmann on the ceiling of the main hall in Schloss Eszterháza in Fertőd, another Eszterházy residence.[9]

As a favored theme for secular salons and for representative rooms in cloisters, the appearance of Apollo in his chariot has been regarded as referring to all sorts of meanings pertaining to light and fire, and is thus open to a variety of readings. Among the sorts of significance that the scene may bear, Wilhelm Mrazek has tabulated natural explications, in relation to the seasons of the year, the times of the day, dawn and dusk, and the like, as well as more religious, philosophical, or allegorical types of significance.[10] Another sort of significance is suggested at Göttweig (Figure 19), where Emperor Charles VI is personified as Apollo, thereby transforming the theme into a political allegory of the secular apotheosis of the sun-emperor—who as pretender to the Spanish throne, for which the War of Spanish Succession had been fought, could claim to rule as far as the sun shines.[11]

At Halbturn the emphasis on flowers suggests spring or summer, however. The appearance of Apollo approximately in the sign of Leo, as in other examples where Apollo rides through the part of the zodiac occupied by the summer signs, also links the scene with summer.[12] This association is reinforced by the bright coloration, tending toward pale pastel tones: these could appear on a bright, warm day in the countryside. Another fitting detail for the location of the fresco in a summer or country residence is the emphatic depiction of Diana as goddess of the hunt: her identification as such is stressed by the spear she carries and

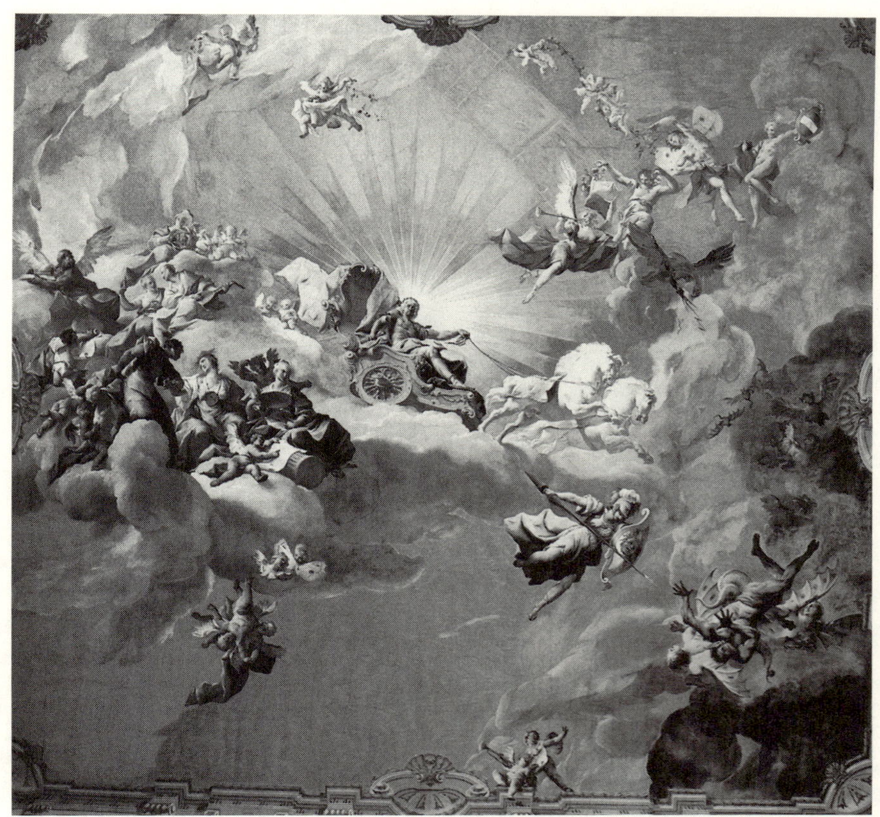

FIGURE 19. Paul Troger, *Triumph of Apollo* (with Emperor Charles VI as Apollo), ceiling of imperial stairway, detail, 1739, Benedictine Abbey, Göttweig, Lower Austria (Photograph: Bundesdenkmalamt, Vienna)

the quiver she wears, that may also be related to the probable use of the Schloss for the courtly recreation of hunting.

The summer months are of course also those with the most daylight. The bright, luminous colors of Maulbertsch, and even the similarly toned grisaille surround, indicate that the depiction of the dawning day at Halbturn represents the bringing of light to the world (personified as Terra). Maulbertsch's figures at the top of the composition seem to explode from light. As the symbolism of the lighting of the globe held by Terra suggests, the composition of the whole emphasizes the coming of light, which must be the main theme.

Ceilings long carried the connotation of the heavens, and they were therefore connected with the realm of light in fresco painting of the seventeenth and eighteenth centuries. The contrast of dark and light antedates its particular association with the age of Enlightenment, to be defined first as the cultural, political, and cultural tendencies that from the eighteenth century onward have been called *Aufklärung*, the Enlightenment, or *le siècle des Lumières*.[13] As Edward Maser noted in his account of one of the precedents for Maulbertsch, namely some of Rottmayr's designs, the theme of the victory of light (or intelligence) over darkness (or ignorance) was very popular in Europe already at the beginning of the eighteenth century.[14] The general theme of the triumph of light, with or without the appearance of Apollo, appeared in earlier works by Maulbertsch, including a canvas of the early 1750s mounted on the ceiling of Schloss Suttner at Kirchstetten in Lower Austria. (See Figure 3.) Mrazek, while recognizing that the same theme of the triumph of light is represented in the Halbturn fresco, added that it also had general allegorical connotations here: the contrast of light and dark at Halbturn represents polar contrasts, of the male-female, Apollonian-chthonic, heavenly-earthly.[15]

This reading has, however, been contested. While setting light against darkness, Maulbertsch avoids polarizing them.[16] Instead of sharp contrasts, he suffuses the whole composition with light; transitions to darker areas are nuanced. Hence to another interpreter, the work seems free of moralizing elements or of apotheosis.[17]

Yet Maulbertsch's characteristically subtle treatment of the imagery is appropriate for the setting: although the painting is in the main room of the Schloss, the building itself was not intended for formal occasions, and complicated allegories would not have been suitable. Nevertheless, the subtle relation of the coloring of Maulbertsch's fresco to its lighting and the resultant dissolution of its forms in light may be seen differently, as an expression of the inherent meaning of the theme. To sum up: as Bruno Bushart has stated, if one wanted to translate the word "Enlightenment" into the language of painting, the result could be a picture of the kind seen at Halbturn.[18]

In fact, at the time that it was painted, the Halbturn fresco may easily have been so read. For while the triumph of light had been regularly depicted in ceiling paintings from the early eighteenth century, and the theme may be interpreted in many ways, representations of light against darkness, and of the coming of light, were visualizations of a central concept of Enlightenment.[19] By 1765 associations of the theme with the Enlightenment would have been hard to avoid: by this time the depiction of sunrise had become what Georg Christoph Lichtenberg called, albeit with a touch of irony, the most common allegorical symbol of the Enlightenment. Recent scholarship has confirmed Lichtenberg's opinion.[20]

The interpretation of the Halbturn fresco introduces the subject of this chapter—the problem of relating Maulbertsch and his painting to the Enlightenment, considered as an age, or a movement, current, or tendency in eighteenth-century European (and American) culture, in relation to its social circumstances. Many points of contact between Maulbertsch and aspects of the Enlightenment exist. Yet, as the difficulties in pinning down a specific interpretation of the imagery or relating themes at Halbturn to the way they are handled in paint may have suggested, the question of Maulbertsch and Enlightenment is not so simple. The meaning of Maulbertsch's paintings, their relation to the intentions and ideas of his patrons, their possible relation to the Enlightenment, and the relation of Maulbertsch's means of expression to such subjects have indeed received varying, at times contradictory, interpretations.

Maulbertsch's association with the Enlightenment is a theme that has engaged art historical scholarship for at least half a century. Among an older generation of scholars who were involved in the revival of interest in the artist, Klára Garas seems to have been first to consider the question at some length. Garas mused whether Maulbertsch merely executed the complicated programs that others had designed, or had a direct hand in carrying them out and putting them together: she assumed the latter.[21] Pavel Preiss took Garas's arguments further, affirming that Maulbertsch espoused the goals of the Enlightenment, even in his earlier works.[22] Bruno Bushart's comments about Halbturn have been quoted above, and in another, earlier essay, he stated that some of Maulbertsch's frescoes, like that at Halbturn, were imbued with the spirit of the Enlightenment. Although Bushart has subsequently elaborated some of the difficulties of dealing with the problem of Maulbertsch and the Enlightenment, in a more recent essay he ended offering a portrait, quite literally, of Maulbertsch as "*Aufklärer*," or a figure of the Enlightenment.[23]

A book by Karl Möseneder is the most extensive treatment of the question of Maulbertsch and the Enlightenment.[24] Here Möseneder develops subjects that had been adumbrated by Bushart and Preiss,[25] and by Möseneder himself in another essay,[26] one related to the "Catholic Enlightenment" and "Reform Catholicism." This is revealed chiefly in Maulbertsch's ceilings for libraries, paintings at Louka (Figures 20 and 21), and Strahov (see Figure 17), and by Winterhalder's in the library at Geras.

However, in a book-length study of the late Enlightenment in Moravia, as well as in several essays, Jiří Kroupa has treated the same paintings as has Möseneder, but has offered different interpretations for them. While he has related the paintings once in Louka to aspects of the secular Enlightenment in Moravia, he has

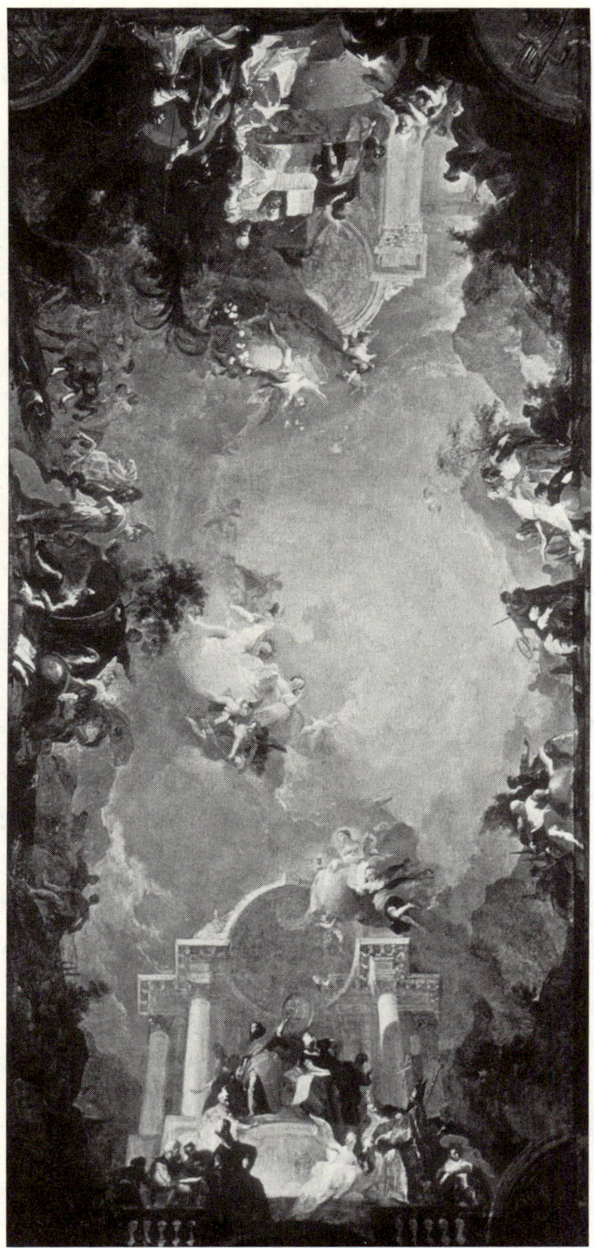

FIGURE 20. F. A. Maulbertsch, *Triumph of Divine Wisdom*, oil on canvas, study (modello?) for library ceiling, c. 1777, Premonstratensian Abbey (destroyed), Städtische Kunstsammlungen, Deutsche Galerie, Augsburg (Photograph: Department of Art and Archaeology, Princeton University)

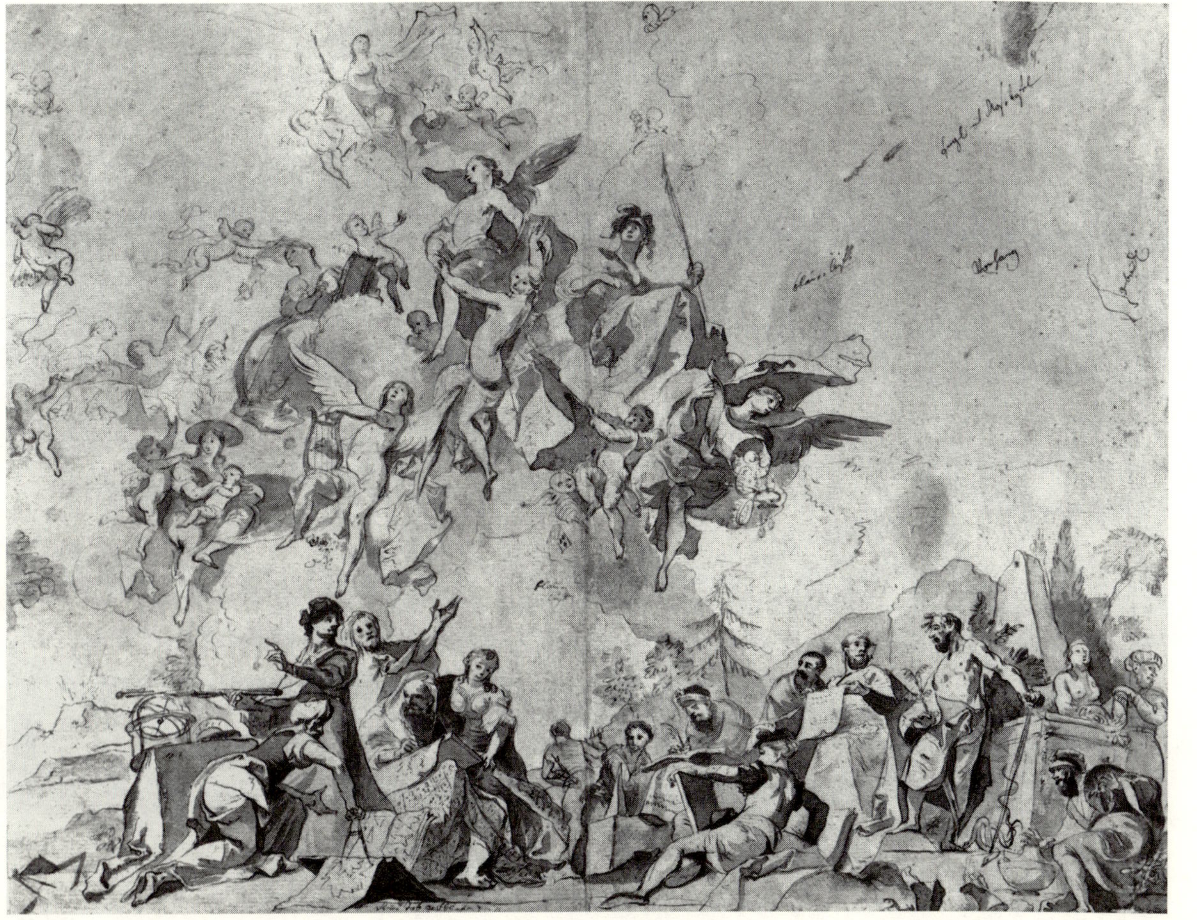

FIGURE 21. Joseph Winterhalder the Younger, pen and wash drawing, copy of Maulbertsch's ceiling in library, Louka, Moravská Galerie, Brno (Photograph: Brno, Moravská Galerie)

called the paintings in Strahov and Geras examples of the opposite pole to Enlightenment.[27] Several other scholars who have concentrated on independent easel paintings and prints by the artist have also adduced a different sort of Enlightenment from that emphasized by Möseneder, associating them with secular ideals, although not necessarily with themes discussed by Kroupa. Instead, works by Maulbertsch have been linked with "Enlightened despotism."[28]

Whatever the interpretation advanced, Enlightenment thus looms large in the continuing interpretation of Maulbertsch's work. But what sort of Enlightenment? The variety of answers evokes another question from Maulbertsch's own time: what is Enlightenment? This is of course the query that Immanuel Kant addressed in a famous essay, "*Was ist Aufklärung?*" His answer is expressed in the maxim *sapere aude* (dare to know): Enlightenment is "man's freedom from self-imposed tutelage." Kant's response was, however, but one of several of those published initially in reply to a question raised in a contemporary Berlin periodical; many other writers responded differently.[29] In northern Germany alone, a number of other contemporaneous German intellectuals, including Moses Mendelssohn and Christoph Martin Wieland, offered their own, diverse ideas about Enlightenment. While it might in general be said that the notion of Enlightenment stands for a current of thought or cultural movement that believed that the application of reason and understanding would lead to the betterment of the human condition, and that progress was possible and evident in human history, this was not the sole definition.

The Enlightenment may indeed be more familiar from its French manifestations in such figures as Voltaire, Diderot, Rousseau, and many others, but Kant, Moses Mendelssohn, Christoph Martin Wieland, and many other contemporaries evince its presence in the German-speaking world, and similar tendencies and activities existed all over Europe.[30] Not only in Berlin and other places in Germany, but elsewhere in Central Europe, many expressions of Enlightenment existed, to which it is difficult to give a common definition. Scholars have accordingly come up with numerous ways of defining the Enlightenment.[31] Seen historically, confessional, regional, and national expressions abounded. They articulated different ideas, and appeared in different times and places, and were thus presented in many different forms.[32] Hence in Austria, as elsewhere, since the eighteenth century itself scholars of the period have arrived at varying definitions for the phenomena associated with the movement, or movements, called Enlightenment.

Within the Habsburg lands one could encounter a variety of forms of Enlightenment in Vienna alone, where Maulbertsch resided. It has been said that in Vienna different versions of the Enlightenment coexisted that inspired, tolerated, overlapped, or fought with each other. The different versions that crossed paths there have been identified with an Enlightenment ordered by Joseph II (what is commonly called "Enlightened despotism"); a bourgeois Enlightenment, related to middle-class thinkers and the literature they engendered;[33] an antique Enlightenment, one oriented toward Johann Joachim Winckelmann and the rage for classical antiquity; a natural historical Enlightenment, related to scientific inquiry; and a Freemasons' Enlightenment.[34] To these may be added a "Catholic Enlightenment," related to church reforms.

However it may be defined, the Enlightenment was by no means the only prevalent current of thought in eighteenth-century Europe, and certainly not in the Habsburg lands. While forms of Enlightenment may have diverged from and even contradicted each other, other contemporaneous cultural tendencies cannot easily be comprehended by the notion of Enlightenment. One need only think of the literary movements contemporary with Maulbertsch that are known as *Empfindsamkeit* and *Sturm und Drang*. Other currents ran strongly against the Enlightenment, since not just clerics, but lay intellectuals did not all share in the project of the Enlightenment, of whatever form. Johann Georg Hamann is but one prominent thinker who in contrast with Kant stood in opposition to the Enlightenment. Many others, including Johann Gottfried von Herder, offered critical, or divergent opinions of the Enlightenment. Hence we now embrace the idea that a "Counter-Enlightenment" also existed.[35]

The problem of definition—along with the multiplicity of cultural forms—has consequences for understanding how eighteenth-century art might be related to the Enlightenment. While arguments for connections between the Enlightenment and art have often been diffuse, recently more attention has been paid to the problem. In any event, many different sorts of artistic expression may be connected with the Enlightenment.[36]

The eighteenth century saw the birth of aesthetics as a form of philosophical discourse, the origins of a modern history of art, and the rise of art criticism. Yet aestheticians and art critics of the eighteenth century conceived of the aims of art in a several ways, while they of course could hold overlapping or multiple beliefs. To be brief: some thinkers argued that art was something that was to be defined according to its forms, that it was noble, because it was symmetrical, or because it revealed inherently harmonious qualities of proportion, that corresponded to ideals of rational judgment, and thus followed Enlightenment precepts of reason.[37] Others thought the aim of art was to embody beauty, and that could be achieved through what might be revealed in certain ideal forms (as in those of antiquity).[38] Still others thought the aim of art was to serve an educational or ethical aim, to better mankind: in this Friedrich Schiller's ideas were anticipated.[39] And still other Enlightenment thinkers advanced the ideal that art should serve, as could philosophy, in the reconciliation of religion and reason.[40]

These diverse, competing Enlightenment views of art could have had, and in some cases did have, an impact on both the content and the form of artistic imagery. Not the least of such competing views, which also affected Maulbertsch, was the contest between religious and secular concerns. This contest raised a larger problem in the Habsburg lands concerning the relation of the "Catholic Enlightenment" or "Reform Catholicism" to secular manifestations of Enlightenment, and particularly the policies of the Habsburgs, especially Joseph II.

Clergymen and especially abbots in the Habsburg lands, like the Abbé Sieyès in France, and not just laymen, could be associated with Enlightenment ideals or institutions of a secular sort. Among them were Maulbertsch's patrons at Královo Pole and Strahov. The Carthusian abbot of Královo Pole, Athanasius Gottfried, an art lover who owned twelve oil sketches by Maulbertsch, shared the taste of Enlightened circles, including those around Maria Theresia's chancellor Wenzel Prince Kaunitz and around the society of Hessen-Hombourg in Brno, an important early Enlightenment society.[41] The Premonstratensian abbot Wenzel II Mayer, Maulbertsch's patron at Strahov in Prague, was a member of a Masonic lodge.[42]

Nevertheless, contrary to some older historical interpretations, secular Enlightenment tendencies in the Habsburg lands, while at times in alliance with the "Catholic Enlightenment" or "Reform Catholicism," are to be distinguished from them, and secular and Catholic tendencies ultimately clashed. Fundamental problems subtend the relation of secular to "Catholic" versions of the Enlightenment. If the Enlightenment represented the "rise of modern paganism,"[43] as one powerful interpretation has it, how could this movement be expressed inside the church? How could an ideology that proclaimed the virtues of reason and the ideals of classical antiquity be reconciled with the demands of faith and the forms of Christianity? And even if it may now seem that this interpretation of the Enlightenment is incomplete, because there were many versions of Enlightenment thought, including those associated with the Catholic Enlightenment, how could the claims of reason be reconciled with the belief in revelation? Finally, how could the fundamentally different views of nature, and also human nature, that were held by secular and religious thinkers, who posited different notions of perfectibility versus redemption, be made compatible?

Hence a disposition to reform the Roman Church, or to express sympathy for some Enlightenment notions, did not mean that a clergyman was in favor of all aspects of any particular Enlightenment program; in fact, depending on the situation or the issue, prelates who supported the reform of the liturgy or education, and who might be regarded as sympathetic to some ideas of the Enlightenment, could become committed foes of other secular state programs. When the reforms initiated by secular authority during the reign of Emperor Joseph II (especially on his own after the death of Maria Theresia in 1780) threatened ecclesiastical authority and even the institutions of the church, including cloisters, attitudes were in general transformed. This is exemplified most notably by the change of course taken by Cardinal Christoph Anton Migazzi, who was Maulbertsch's patron for frescoes at Vác: Migazzi began as an ardent supporter of the reforms of education, the church, and other institutions that were introduced during the reign of Maria Theresia, but he became an implacable opponent of Joseph II's measures.[44] Hence Maulbertsch could at first have been aligned with prelates like Migazzi who were initially connected with the Catholic Enlightenment and who then, after state policy toward the church had changed, assumed what might be called an increasingly reactionary attitude.

In any event, Maulbertsch was directly involved with major personalities, some of whom have been mentioned, and tendencies that may be associated with the Enlightenment in the Habsburg lands. In carrying out his commissions, he thus would often have encountered, directly or indirectly, the problem of expressing Enlightenment values in art. As an artist, he would have had to deal directly with the problem of how to express often abstract ideas in painted images. This chapter considers some of these complications.

Maulbertsch and the "Catholic Enlightenment"

An overview of the issues may well begin with Maulbertsch's connection with the "Catholic Enlightenment." A fresco Maulbertsch painted in 1778 on the ceiling of the library of the Premonstratensian monastery at Louka (Bruck, or Klosterbruck) near Znojmo (Znaim) in southern Moravia provides what may be recognized as one of the clearest expressions of Enlightenment iconography in all of his oeuvre.[45] While the frescoes at Louka do not survive, a modello by Maulbertsch (Figure 20) and a copy drawn by Winterhalder (Figure 21), taken together with an extensive *Historische Erklärung der Kalckmahlerey in Freßko* written by the abbot Gregor Norbert Ritter von Korber, who probably supplied the program to

Maulbertsch, allow for a reconstruction of its appearance, and an extensive interpretation of its content as an Enlightenment project.

In a burst of light in the center of the composition, eternal wisdom may barely be discerned. Around it are personifications of the desire to learn, the spirit of tolerance, force, reason, sensitivity, genius—virtues that lead man to wisdom. Depictions of classical exemplars are paralleled to representatives of the Old and New Testament. The composition has been read as suggesting the progress of man from his rough origins in nature—from early origins, seen in the company of cavorting centaurs, through the inspiration of natural theology and the development of the sciences, above all through the revelations of the Scriptures, to wisdom and literally to the light.

Man progresses through what Korber specifically calls the Enlightenment (*Aufklärung*) of faith. Korber says that man is led according to the "light of nature," which is the origin of the sciences; the growth of the knowledge of this source, and of the necessarily related duty to nurture and give expression to that knowledge, is the "purpose" of Maulbertsch's painting.[46] If the oil sketch gives a fair indication of the final painting, the actual execution of the picture, in which figures seem to rise from relatively dark areas of paint to relatively bright ones—with wisdom the brightest burst of light—might suggest that Maulbertsch has also found a way of expressing this imagery by means of the composition, that is, through the distribution of light.

The theme of divine wisdom commonly encountered in baroque ceiling paintings (one thinks of Andrea Sacchi's famous painting in the Palazzo Barberini in Rome) thus seems to be recast here into a message of the increase of wisdom through Enlightenment.[47] The program of the painting, as expressed in Korber's description, with its apparent overtones of toleration, its paralleling of Christian and pagan thinkers, and its emphasis on the light of nature that guides all human progress, may also call forth more general impressions of the movement of the Enlightenment. The presentation of the general message of the progress of humanity to Enlightenment through Faith on the ceiling of a monastic library thus seems to support the description of Maulbertsch's composition as an image of a special kind of "Catholic Enlightenment."

The combination of this sort of Catholic rationalism, belief in human progress, and historical examples was also appropriate for library decoration.[48] During the eighteenth century, the increase of wisdom was a common theme in paintings in Central European libraries, as it was in libraries elsewhere; the subject adorned the ceilings of many monastic libraries.[49] In fact, the ceiling of another library that Maulbertsch painted more than a decade before, in 1760 in the

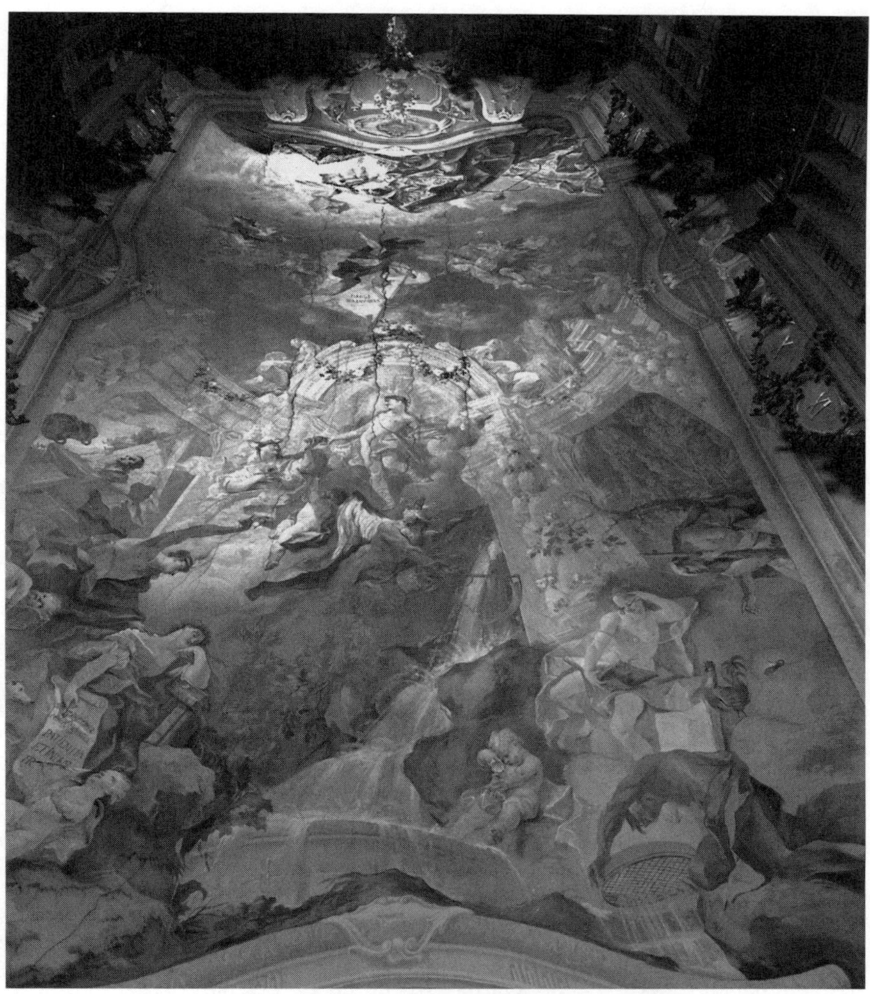

FIGURE 22. F. A. Maulbertsch, *Progress and Fruits of Learning*, library ceiling, 1760, former Barnabite Cloister, Mistelbach, Lower Austria (Photograph: Bundesdenkmalamt, Vienna)

Barnabite cloister at Mistelbach, appears to anticipate the general idea of the painting at Louka, although not its details (Figure 22 and Plate 8).[50] The marriage of virtue with knowledge or learning (*connubium virtutis ac scientiae*) presented at Mistelbach is also traditional to library decoration.[51] The contrast in Mistelbach between personifications of *impatientia* and *negligentia* with those of *patientia* and *industria* is echoed in similar representations in the library of the Premonstratensian abbey at Louka, although the ceiling there substantially elaborates the theme of wisdom gained through the union of faith and reason or learning.[52]

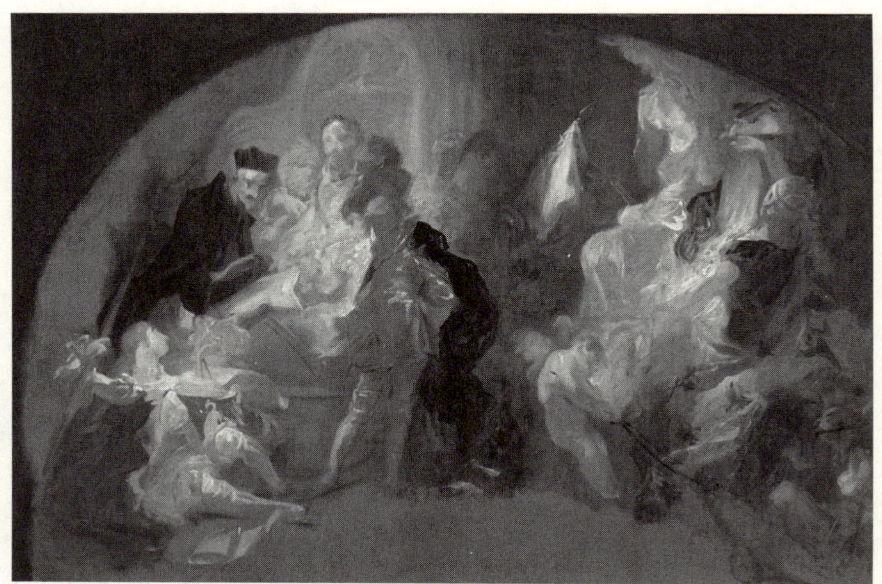

FIGURE 23. F. A. Maulbertsch, *Allegory on Education* (with St. Joseph of Calasanz), oil on canvas, 1750s, Österreichische Galerie, Vienna (Photograph: Österreichische Galerie Belvedere Vienna)

An oil sketch that was executed probably a couple of years earlier, in the 1750s, may also be associated with Catholic allegories of education. (See Figure 23.) While its meaning is not completely clear, this small painting shows St. Joseph of Calasanz, the founder of the Piarist Order for whom Maulbertsch had painted the cupola of the Church of Maria Treu in Vienna in 1752–53, and for which church he again worked in 1759–60, as well as in the Piarists' cloister in Vienna in 1761. The Piarists were an order deeply committed to education. They also advanced studies of philosophy and the natural sciences in the Austrian and Czech lands.[53] Hence this picture may be read as expressing the theme of the virtues of education dear to the Piarists; in particular the sketch was perhaps connected with plans for the decoration of the refectory of their Vienna cloister.[54]

Much as the Enlightenment in general emphasized the importance of education, education was central to Catholic reform programs in the eighteenth century. In the Habsburg lands as elsewhere dissatisfaction was expressed with the Jesuits and their domination of teaching, which led to a "revival of interest in the work and ideals of the earlier Counter-Reformation, with its emphasis on parish work and improved education."[55] When the Jesuits were ultimately expelled from the Habsburg lands, the Piarists took over much of their role in education. Like other supporters of the new movement for educational reform, the Piarists were moreover acquainted with the New Philosophy of the late seventeenth and the eighteenth centuries, as exemplified by the works of such philosophers as Leibniz and Christian Wolff. Their activities and those of other prelates and orders involved in educational reform complemented the efforts of the state authorities, who also implemented a program of school reform.[56] However, in the Habsburg lands education in the church, beyond the level of the parish schools, meant in particular the production of an educated, Enlightened clergy who would be able to communicate the teachings of the church, not the production of an educated bourgeoisie, what was later called the *Bildungsbürgertum*.[57]

The larger program of Reform Catholicism in Central Europe, in which many religious orders played a part, drew strength from numerous sources, including Jansenism,[58] and, more important for considerations of the visual arts, the writings of Ludovico Antonio Muratori.[59] Muratori's *Della regolata divozione de' cristiani* advocated a drastic reduction in public religious observances, feast days, and monastic orders, and emphasized a concentration on the mass, and a greater concern for practical Christian charity. This book, which has been called "a manifesto of enlightened reform-Catholicism," went through twenty German editions, eight of them published in Vienna alone.[60] The first of these Viennese editions appeared in 1757, the year in which Cardinal Migazzi succeeded Johann Joseph von Trautson as archbishop of Vienna.[61] Migazzi was an advocate of Muratori: in 1759 he stirred up a controversy when he recommended the works of Muratori to one of Maria Theresia's daughters.[62] In the same year the publication of another edition of Muratori's work in German translation as *Die wahre Andacht des Christen* caused a conflict between Migazzi, who praised it, and Jesuit censors from the University of Vienna, who tried to block its appearance. Migazzi's favorable judgment of Muratori in this case was then published as a laudatory preface to the 1762 edition.[63]

Maulbertsch can be brought into proximity with these figures at this time. In 1757, when the first Vienna edition of Muratori appeared, Maulbertsch was engaged by F. A. Marxer to paint frescoes on the ceiling of the church at his residence in Lower Austria at Heiligenkreuz-Gutenbrunn; Marxer was suffragan bishop (*Weihbischof*) of Vienna under Migazzi. (See Plate 9.) Later, in 1770–71, Migazzi himself employed Maulbertsch to paint the ceiling and apse frescoes in Vác (Plate 10).

But there were additional kinds of church reform in the Habsburg lands, with which other patrons of Maulbertsch at this time were involved.[64] Prominent among them was Márton Pádanyi Biró, bishop of Veszprem.[65] Biró supervised

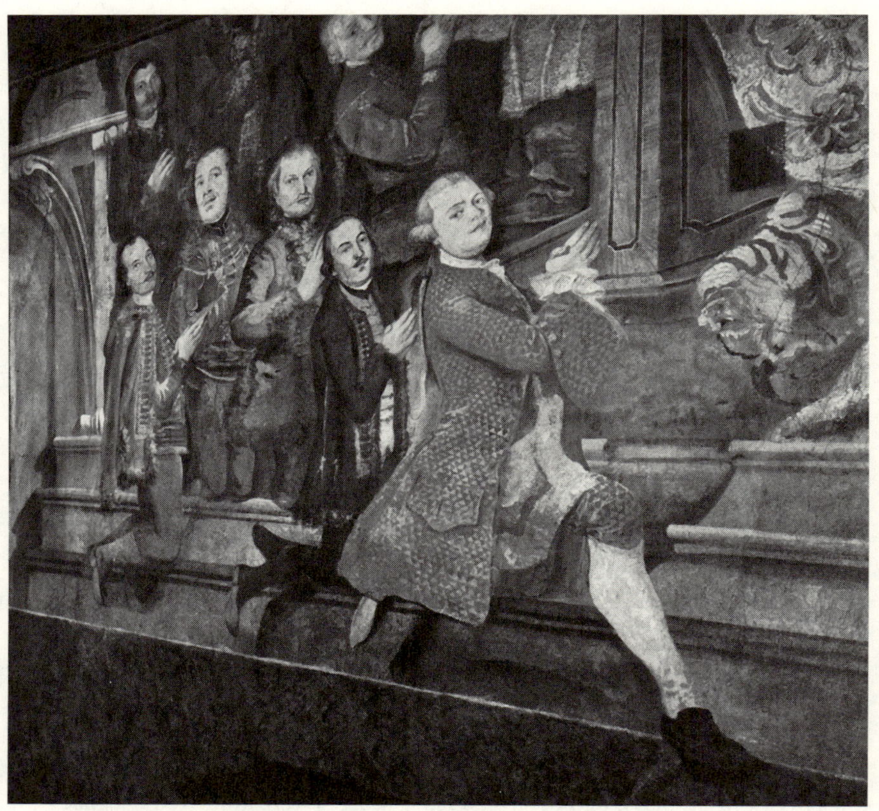

FIGURE 24. Workshop of Maulbertsch, detail of choir ceiling with portraits of Márton Pádanyi Biró and probably Maulbertsch (front right), 1758, Parish Church, Sümeg, Hungary (Photograph: Károly Szelényi, Magyar Képek / Hungarian Pictures, Budapest)

a significant reorganization of his diocese, which among other things involved the construction and decoration of many churches, including the one at Sümeg, where Maulbertsch was active in 1757 and 1758. Biró was closely involved with the arts in his diocese, was probably responsible for the design of the inscriptions for the paintings of the side altars at Sümeg, and was most likely closely involved with the conception of the program of the church.[66] (See Figure 24 and Plate 19.)

Protestants are estimated to have constituted half the population of Hungary at this time, and in the western areas belonging to his diocese Biró struggled to win them back to the Roman Church, or to suppress them. Calvinism, the predominant type of Protestantism in Hungary, was promoting its own form of ecclesiastical architecture.[67] In this light the extensive decoration of the church at Sümeg can be regarded as an emphatic reaffirmation of the visual expression of faith in the face of the anti-iconic doctrines and alternative practices of Protestantism. Thus both the program and the very fact that the cycle is so extensive can be seen to be in line with what have been described as Biró's Counter-Reformation tendencies, also evident in the repressive measures he took against Protestants. However, such tendencies, while ones of Catholic Reform, were at odds with beliefs in toleration that were increasingly being expressed at the time[68] and accordingly out of step with Enlightenment.

Furthermore, the subjects of the frescoes that Maulbertsch painted for his patrons at Sümeg, Heiligenkreuz-Gutenbrunn, and Vác belong to the tradition of the Counter- (or Catholic) Reformation. They represent the Virgin, her life, the Passion, and the glorification (and invention) of the true cross, as befits the relic of the cross that was preserved at Heiligenkreuz-Gutenbrunn. So too for that matter are the representations of the glory of the Virgin in the Piarist church in Vienna.[69]

In its view of the use of imagery, eighteenth-century "Reform Catholicism" was not far from the Catholic (i.e., Counter) Reformation of the sixteenth century. Muratori's texts on the veneration of images very much recall the arguments of the period of the Council of Trent. Indeed in his *Lettere ai segneri sulle Missioni* he cites the key text of the Twenty-fifth Session of the Council of Trent, which in 1563 decreed the appropriate attitude to be held in regard to veneration of the images of Christ, Mary, and of saints. Their images were approved because they had a spiritual and didactic function: to lead to the veneration of the prototypes they represented. In *Della regolata divozione de' Cristiani*, Muratori also summarized these arguments, adding the traditional defense that while imagery was necessary for the ignorant, images were not to be adored as idols.[70] Needless to say, these ideas are hardly what we usually think of in connection with the Enlightenment.

Muratori, however, expressed other ideas relevant to the visual arts that did have contemporary resonance. He admonished that the *wahre Andacht des Christen*, the true devotion of the Christian, was to be directed inwardly rather than to sensuous representations or theatrical rites. Muratori laid special emphasis on the interior of the church, into which one should lead back a populace that had fallen away from true devotion.[71] He wrote a rhetorical treatise in which he weighed in against the use of sublime mode and in favor of the dignity of popular eloquence in preaching in churches—and directly suggested that church interiors should not be elaborately decorated. In this tract, published in Latin translation in Augsburg in 1757, Muratori condemned the sublime rhetorical mode

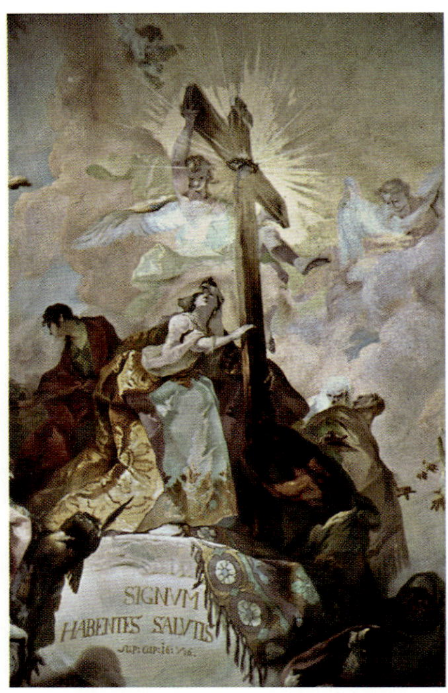

PLATE 9. *Glorification and Invention of the True Cross*, detail of nave ceiling, 1757–58, Parish and Pilgrimage Church, Heiligenkreuz-Gutenbrunn, Lower Austria (Photograph: Bundesdenkmalamt, Vienna)

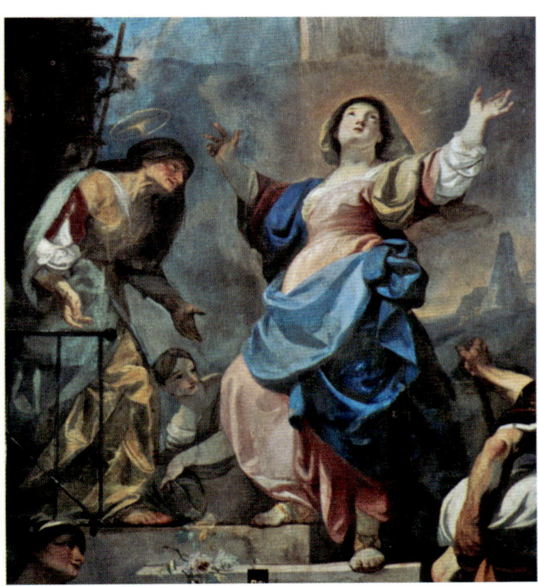

PLATE 10. *Visitation*, high altar mural, 1770–71, Cathedral, Vác, Hungary (Photograph: Károly Szelény, Magyar Képek / Hungarian Pictures, Budapest)

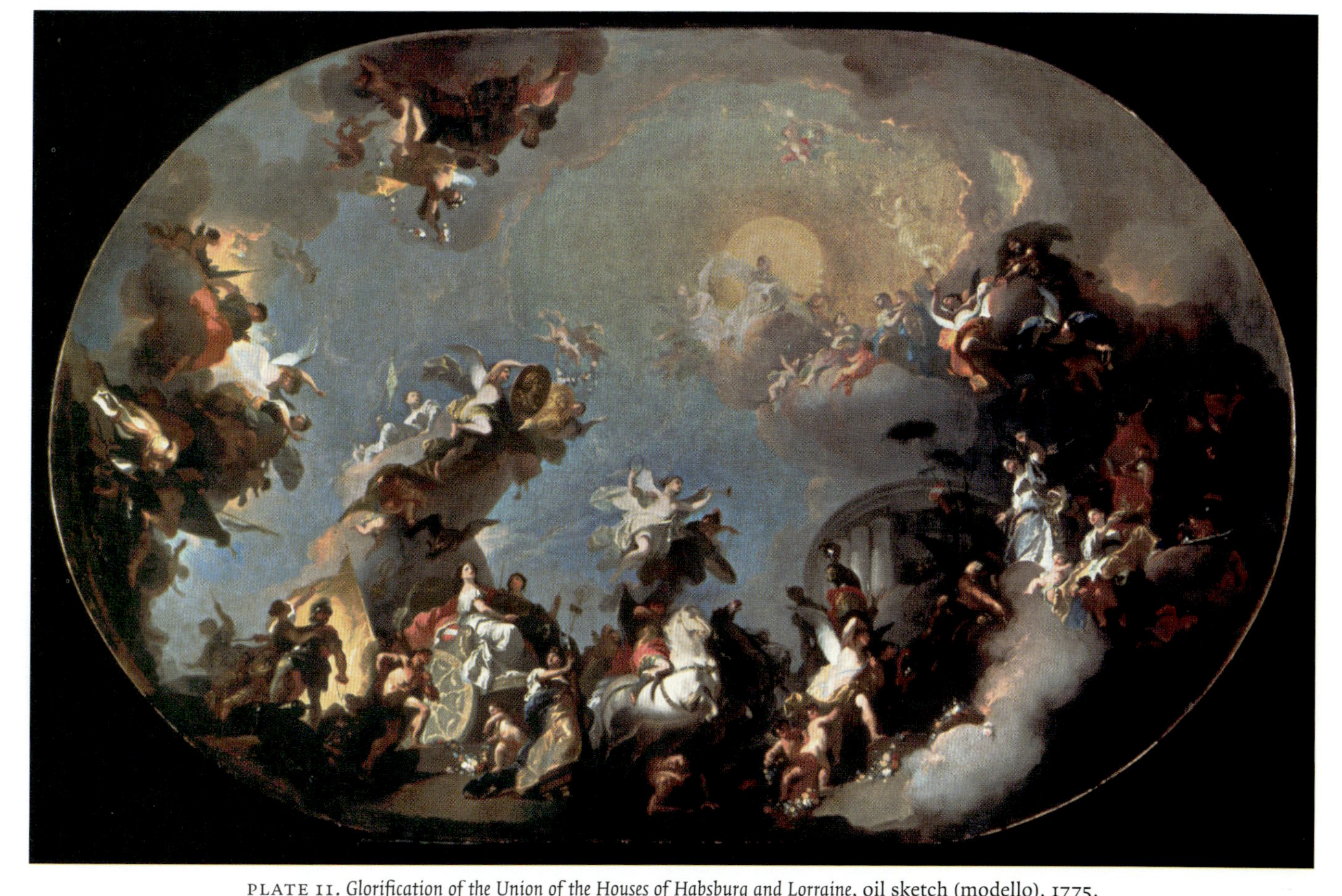

PLATE 11. *Glorification of the Union of the Houses of Habsburg and Lorraine*, oil sketch (modello), 1775, J. Paul Getty Museum, Los Angeles (Photograph: The J. Paul Getty Museum, Los Angeles)

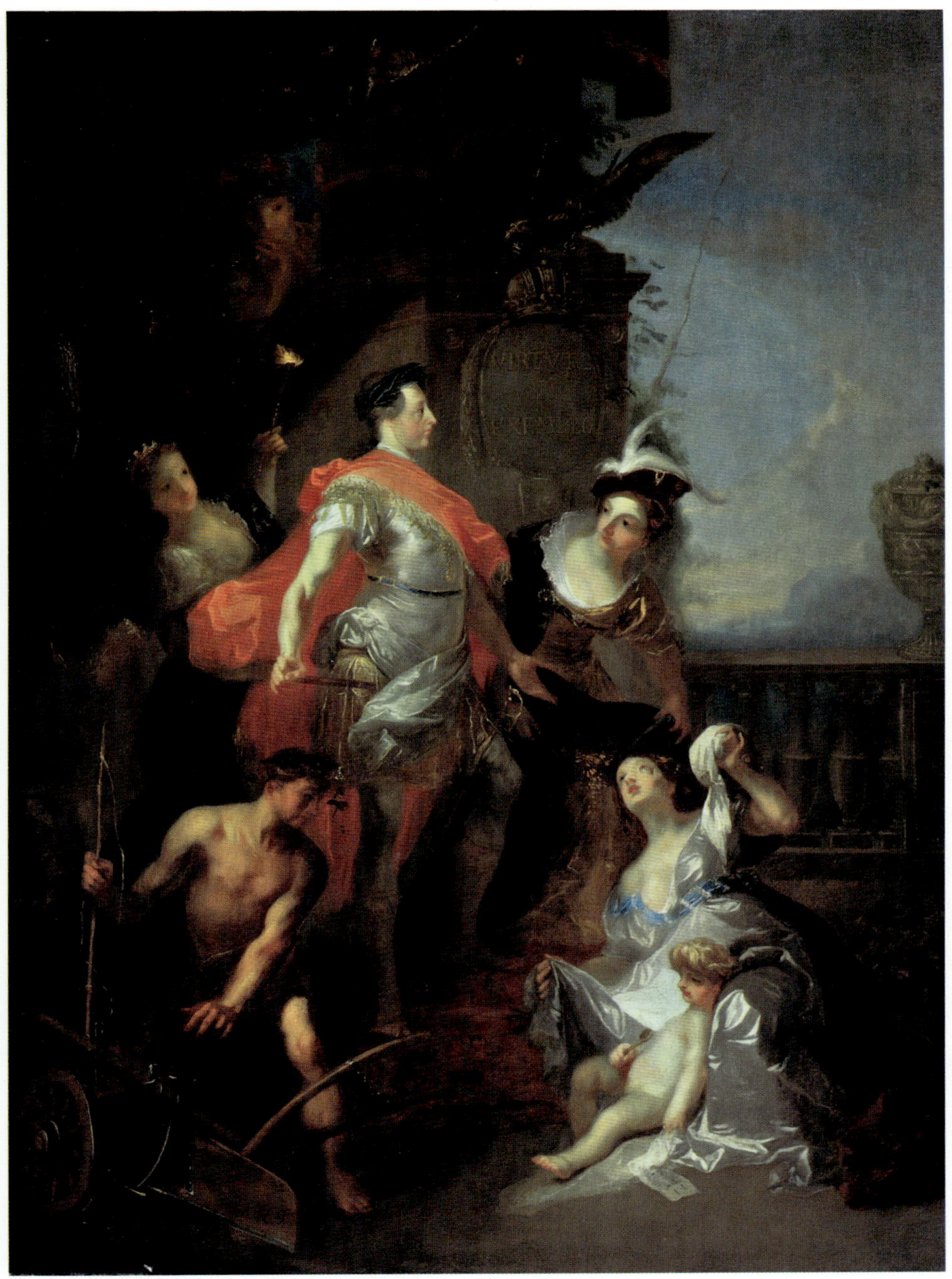

PLATE 12. *Glorification of Joseph II*, 1777, oil on canvas, Österreichische Galerie, Vienna (Photograph: Österreichische Galerie Belvedere Vienna)

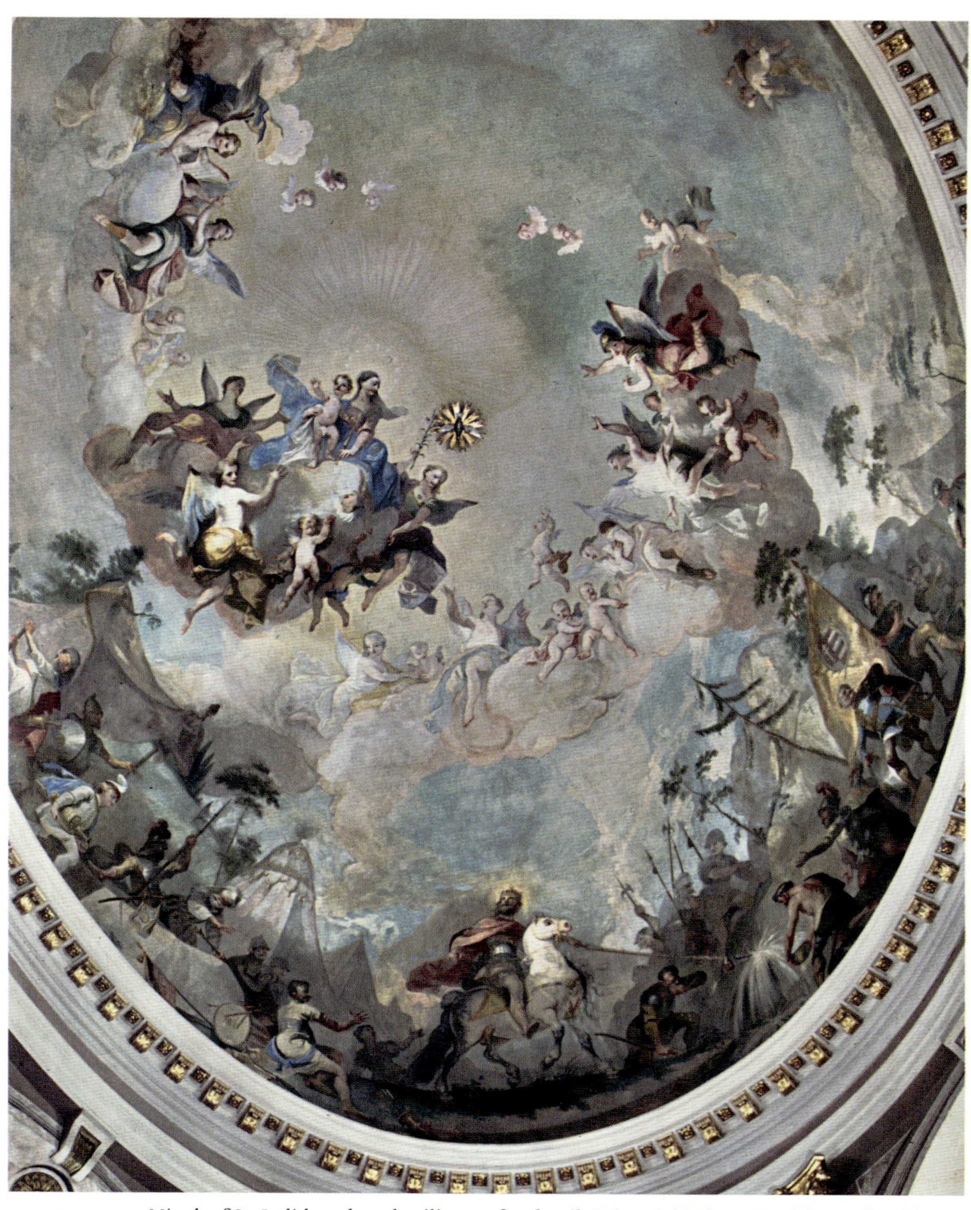

PLATE 13. *Miracle of St. Ladislas*, chapel ceiling, 1781, detail, Primatial Palace, Bratislava, Slovakia (Photograph: Courtesy Institute of Art History, Slovak Academy of Sciences [Ustav dejin umenia, Slovenská akadémia vied])

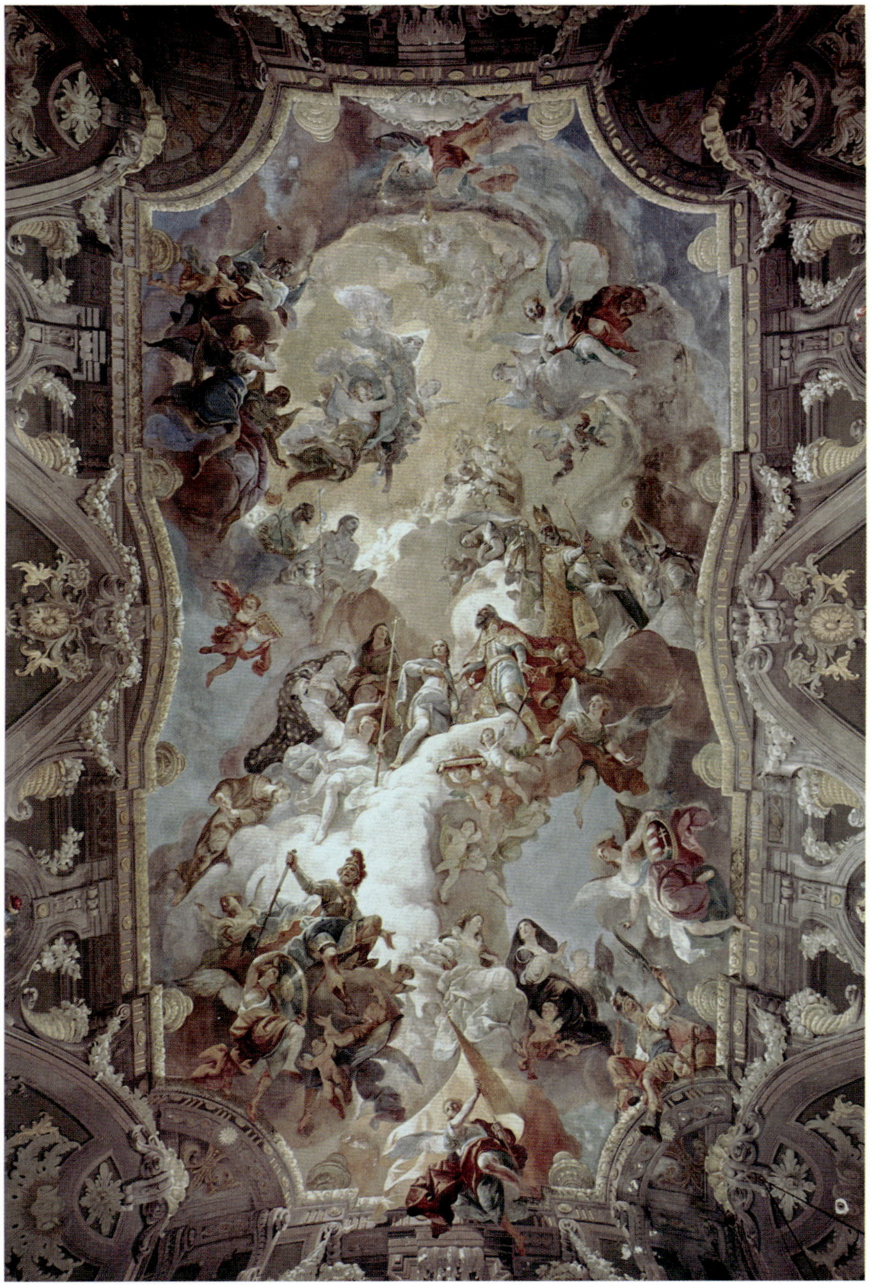

PLATE 14. *Glorification of the Saints of Hungary*, presbytery ceiling, 1773, Cathedral, Győr, Hungary (Photograph: Károly Szelény, Magyar Képek / Hungarian Pictures, Budapest)

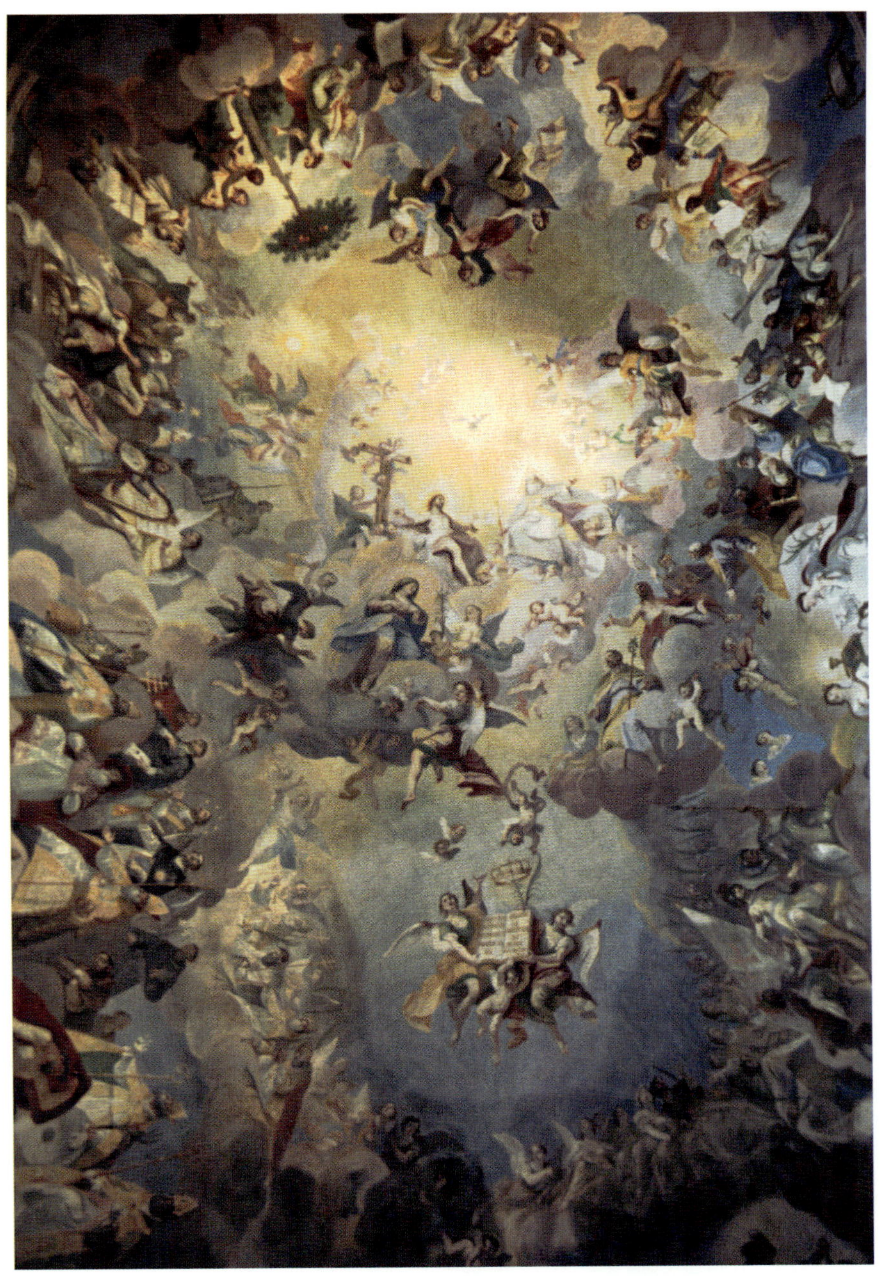

PLATE 15. *All Saints*, ceiling of former chapel, 1793, Lyceum, Eger, Hungary (Photograph: Károly Szelényi, Magyar Képek / Hungarian Pictures, Budapest)

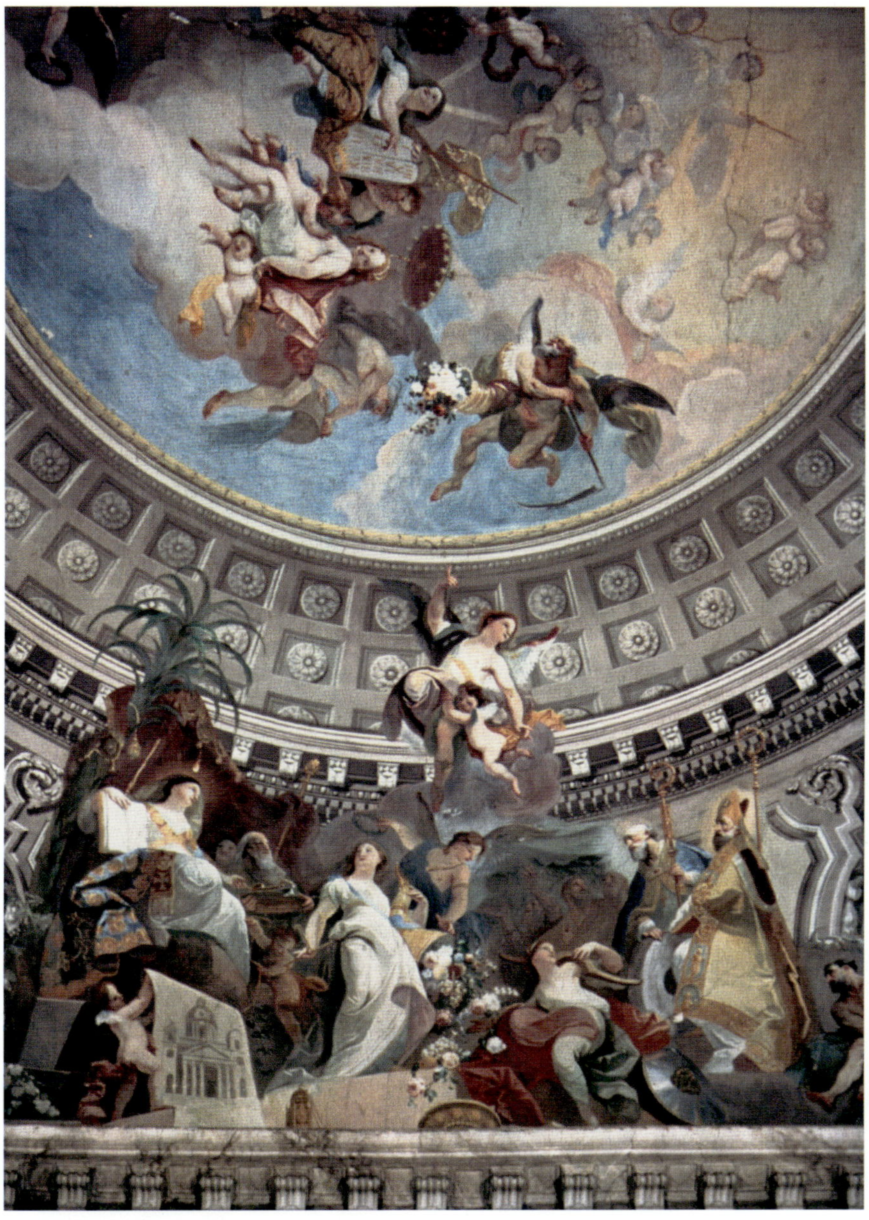

PLATE 16. Detail with Saints Martin and Quirinus and other personifications, ceiling of *Prunksaal*, 1783, Bishop's Palace, Szombathely, Hungary (Photograph: Károly Szelényi, Magyar Képek / Hungarian Pictures, Budapest)

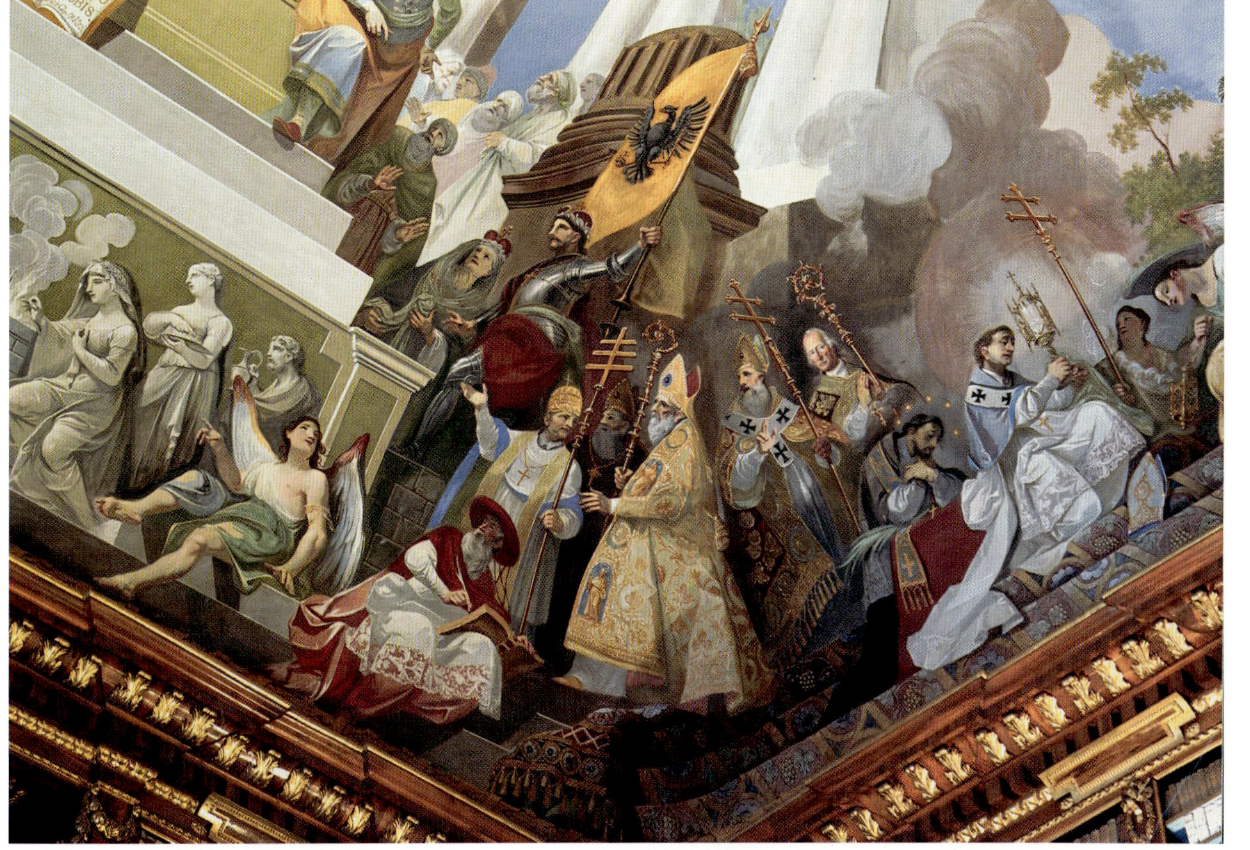

PLATE 17. *The Revelation of Divine Wisdom*, detail of saints, including saints of Bohemia with portrait of Abbot Wenzel Mayer, library ceiling, 1794, Premonstratensian Abbey, Strahov, Prague (Photograph: Premonstratensian Kanonie, Strahov, Prague)

(*genus dicendi*), saying that it was like licentious ornament (*ornamentorum luxuries*) in architecture, which the prudent would condemn with laughter.[72]

Important conclusions were drawn from such arguments. A pastoral brief promulgated by Archbishop Trautson in 1752, the year in which Maulbertsch began painting in the Piarist church in Vienna, was one important response. Like Muratori, Trautson decried those who were more given to venerating saints and the pictures of them rather than putting their faith in the merits of Christ.[73] Similarly, in a pamphlet concerning the veneration of images (*Unterricht über die Verehrung der Bilder*) published in 1762, Migazzi warned against the excessive use of "visual aids" in popular devotion.[74]

The demand for purer, simpler forms of expression that Muratori voiced stimulated a widening chorus that called for a departure from magnificence and rhetoric in churches. This was one of the sources leading to an electoral decree in Bavaria that promoted the preservation of "pure and regular architecture" and the consequent elimination of all "superfluous stucco and ridiculous ornaments" in favor of "noble simplicity."[75] A pastoral letter issued in 1782 by Hieronymus von Colloredo, archbishop of Salzburg, that was later generally disseminated by Emperor Joseph II in the Habsburg lands, advocated something similar. It decreed that unnecessary decoration (*unnötiges Zierwerk*) was to be removed from churches, and that purity (*Reinlichkeit*) was to be preserved in them. This stricture was enforced in a general ordinance of 1784 that made majestic decorum, simplicity, order, and purity the ruling principles in the interior decoration of churches.[76] A decree issued in 1786 limited churches in Lower Austria to three altars with their decoration, and determined that all other superfluous images and altarpieces should be removed.[77]

The art historian Karl Möseneder has called the parish church in Slavkov u Brna (Austerlitz), finished by 1791, a perfect realization of the Reform Catholic tendencies outlined above (Figure 25). This church was built by J. F. Hetzendorf von Hohenberg, who had earlier collaborated with Maulbertsch in the decoration of the Augustinian church at Korneuburg (Lower Austria; see Figure 50), on the lands of Wenzel Prince Kaunitz in Moravia. Möseneder also regards this church as an example of tendencies that explain why grisaille was increasingly used in Maulbertsch's art. Through his reading of a contemporary reaction to the church, he considers the church at Slavkov a "monument of tolerant iconography," of the approximation of Reform Catholicism to Protestantism in the desire for a clear, legible, and contained expression of beliefs.[78]

But the artistic and architectonic consequences of Muratori's ideas as an expression of Reform Catholicism do not lead in this way toward their fulfillment

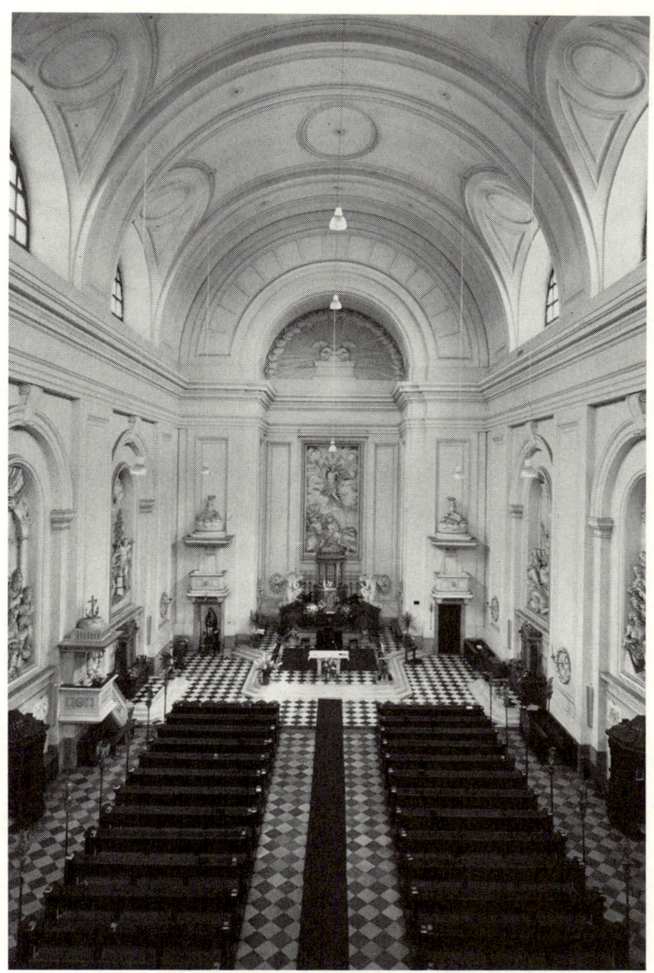

FIGURE 25. J. F. Hetzendorf von Hohenberg, Parish Church, Slavkov u Brna (Austerlitz), interior, 1780s (Photograph: The National Institute for the Protection and Conservation of Monuments and Sites Regional Unit at Brno; courtesy Bishopric of Brno)

in Maulbertsch. While the Slavkov church might seem to fit what Muratori and other critics of ecclesiastical magnificence and exalted rhetoric were advocating, what resulted would have created difficulties for any painter, not to mention Maulbertsch. For these reasons Möseneder's reading runs into problems. Where is there any place for painted decoration (including grisaille) in this building? The church at Slavkov is notably austere, its walls left pure white. It lacks paintings on its ceilings or walls; in fact it lacks any painted altarpieces or devotional images, as distinct from sculpted ones, altogether. If this building represents what Reform Catholicism was aiming at, where could a place be found for a painter like Maulbertsch?

Hans Rudolf Füßli, who has already been met in this book, indeed drew the conclusion that there was no such place. Chiming in with other voices of the later eighteenth century, Füßli criticized the "mere works of decoration or magnificence in fresco" (*blossen Zier- und Prachtwerken in Fresko*), and, specifically relating them to the Viennese scene, said they demonstrated the decline of painting that had been brought about by painters like Maulbertsch, whom he specifically mentions. Füßli summarized what had subsequently happened to church decoration as follows:

> . . . in the hereditary lands [the *Erblanden*, meaning those lands such as Austria above and below the Enns that had become the direct hereditary possessions of the Habsburgs] and chiefly in Vienna, the simplification of public worship, and the decrease in the all too numerous altars, and in the overloaded decoration in churches, along with the secularization of many cloisters, has very much diminished the kind of painting that almost entirely occupied history painters up to this time, and the so-called modern taste in the interior decoration of houses and palaces has also finally made rare history paintings on ceilings, which, fundamentally considered, are only unnatural depictions.[79]

Moreover, another noteworthy feature of the church at Slavkov can also not be connected with the beliefs of many of Maulbertsch's more orthodox Catholic patrons, and thus raises the further question if the church really corresponds to an ideal of Reform Catholicism. Pulpits are present in the Slavkov parish church for both Protestant and Catholic liturgical purposes. Although Möseneder does not remark on it, their presence amounts to an obvious expression of toleration, not just in iconography, but in practice. At first an inference might be that, as has been said, Reform Catholics "opposed intolerance and persecution of non-Catholics, because they considered Christian benevolence and rational persuasion to be more effective and appropriate means for maintaining and spreading the Catholic faith."[80] While the prominent presence of pulpits appears to meet the demand that the word of God be easily accessible in a church, the presence of a pulpit for Protestant practices goes beyond the needs of Catholic reform. It is highly unlikely that without external pressure any orthodox Catholic reformers of the eighteenth century in Central Europe would have gone so far as to encourage sharing a Catholic church with Protestants.

This matter is put in greater relief when one considers that two major patrons of Maulbertsch who were associated with Reform Catholicism would have been adamantly opposed to any such tendency. Bishop Biró actively persecuted Protestants in his diocese. While the stance of Cardinal Migazzi was, as we have seen, more complicated, he too was opposed to such tendencies to toleration, especially when they did not serve, or were critical of, the church or its interests. Migazzi headed a faction that was opposed to *Der Mann ohne Vorurtheil* (The Man without Prejudice, 1765–67) a weekly journal that among other things pilloried prejudices, and tried to have its editor, Joseph von Sonnenfels, prosecuted; Kaunitz characteristically supported Sonnenfels and the more tolerant aims against attacks made even by men who, during the 1760s before attitudes had hardened, might be considered "Reform Catholics."[81]

The presence of the pulpits in the Slavkov church resulted from the wishes of the patron Kaunitz, who in many ways may be associated with the Enlightenment.[82] Kaunitz was moreover one of the imperial courtiers who, along with Joseph von Sonnenfels and Joseph Freiherr von Sperges, had contacts with Maulbertsch. These figures are, however, not identified with Reform Catholicism, but with the politics of Josephism (or Josephinianism—most simply, the movement or state reforms associated with Joseph II). And the relationship of Josephism to Reform Catholicism is fraught.

Maulbertsch, Secular Enlightenment, Josephism, and Its Opponents

While the relation of Reform Catholicism to Josephism is a matter for continuing debate, a brief summary of the major positions may be offered.[83] An older interpretation argued that Reform Catholicism is consonant with Josephism.[84] It certainly seems true that "what became known as Josephism did not begin as an attack on the Church by the state" but out of internal movements to reform the church.[85] Joseph also shared in what has been termed a Jansenist emphasis in religious matters, but also laid emphasis, as did Muratori, on true devotion (*wahre Andacht*).[86] Migazzi, while later a fierce opponent, has even been regarded as an important forerunner of Josephism.[87] At any rate, the church and the state at first clearly worked together to effect the reform of education in the Habsburg lands.[88]

This consonance perhaps resonates in the similarities that are to be found in two allegories on education that Maulbertsch painted probably in the 1750s:

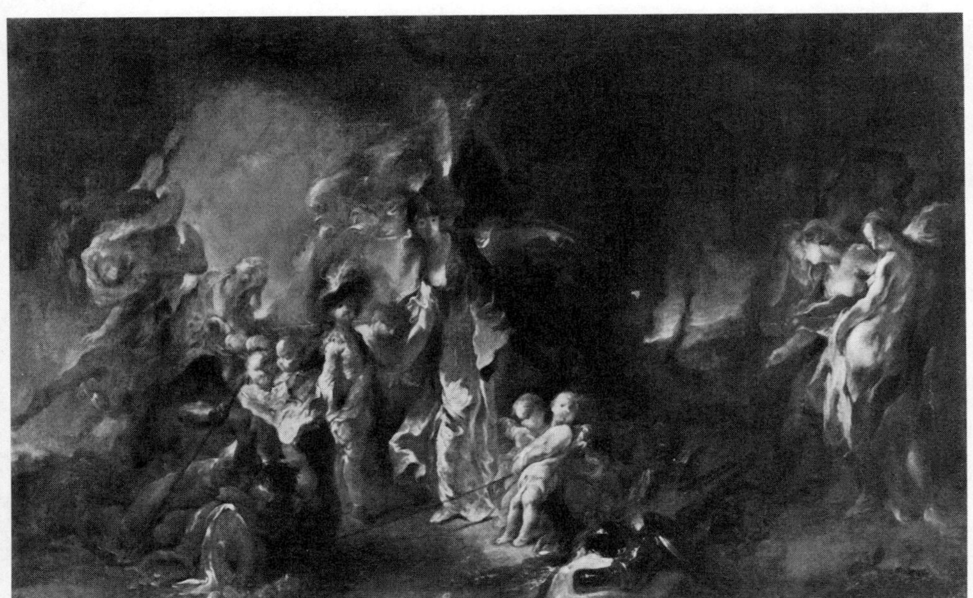

FIGURE 26. F. A. Maulbertsch, *Allegory on Education*, oil on canvas, c. 1760, Národní Galerie, Prague (Photograph: Národní Galerie)

both depict Catholic and secular views of the importance of education, hence rational progress, in society. The one, already mentioned, is an allegory on education that emphasizes the presence of Joseph of Calasanz, the founder of the Piarists (Figure 23). The other is an allegory on education, probably of a nobleman: in it the three Graces accompany Minerva, the goddess of wisdom (Figure 26). The latter work has been read as a reflection of the pedagogical ideas of Sonnenfels, according to which the aristocrat should dedicate himself to science, literature and art.[89]

Nevertheless, reforms that were not in the interest of Rome were already enacted during Maria Theresia's lifetime, and some of the most important measures that Joseph II effected during the 1780s by no means coincide with the aims of the "Catholic Enlightenment." These measures had drastic consequences for the Roman Church, and in fact directly for some of the figures and monuments associated with Maulbertsch. Joseph II moved to put the church under state control, and to have the church provide "pure and rational religious service," clearly not what Muratori would have had in mind. Student priests were to be trained in state seminaries from 1783 onward. This move, like several other Josephist reforms, stirred widespread opposition, especially in Hungary.[90]

The most drastic change Joseph promoted was to close numerous monasteries that did not seem to serve necessary social or parochial functions. Among them were several churches and cloisters that had housed works by Maulbertsch, including the Premonstratensian cloister at Louka. The buildings there were used for secular (including military) purposes, and soon Maulbertsch's frescoes fell into decay. The charterhouse at Královo Pole was also closed, and Abbot Gottfried left the clergy; Maulbertsch's paintings in the Chapter House and in a side chapel at Královo Pole have also suffered. In response to state-directed reforms and Erastian policies (advocating state control over the church), even clergymen who had supported a certain measure of change, such as Migazzi, gradually turned against Josephism.[91] The broadening divergence between Josephist policies and Reform Catholicism should thus provoke further reflection on the differences between the principles underlying their programs, and hence on the content and purposes of art meant to serve the church, versus that sponsored by the ruler, and consequently on the meaning of the Enlightenment for art.

The ideas that Kaunitz, Sonnenfels, and Sperges expressed concerning education and the arts, and especially the role of the arts in the service of the state and society, were not the same as those held by most contemporary churchmen about the role of art in the service of religion. The notion that the state and its institutions could play a beneficent role in society did not lead to the same ends as the Catholic Enlightenment. The aims of these counselors were definitely secular in orientation. For example, as counselor of Maria Theresia, before he played a similar role for Joseph, Kaunitz stressed the importance of the contribution of the fine arts to the development of industry and hence the economy through the creation of a population that was educated in the arts. Sonnenfels believed similarly that the arts had a positive affect on society. These beliefs took form in the establishment of the *Kupferstecherakademie* (Academy of Engravers); this institution stood under the protection of Kaunitz, with Sonnenfels as its secretary, and Sperges as its *präses*, or president.[92]

Maulbertsch was associated with these men and the new institution, as he had been with the older imperial academy of art with which it was soon merged. In 1770 he submitted an allegory on the fate of the arts (Figure 27), to be discussed further in the next chapter, and became a member of the Kupferstecherakademie. Later he served as a professor in the new academy. In another allegory, probably from the mid-1780s, he represents the academy's granting of prizes—prize competitions remained one of the chief educational tools of the new academy. This painting has been interpreted as a reflection of the Enlightenment's opti-

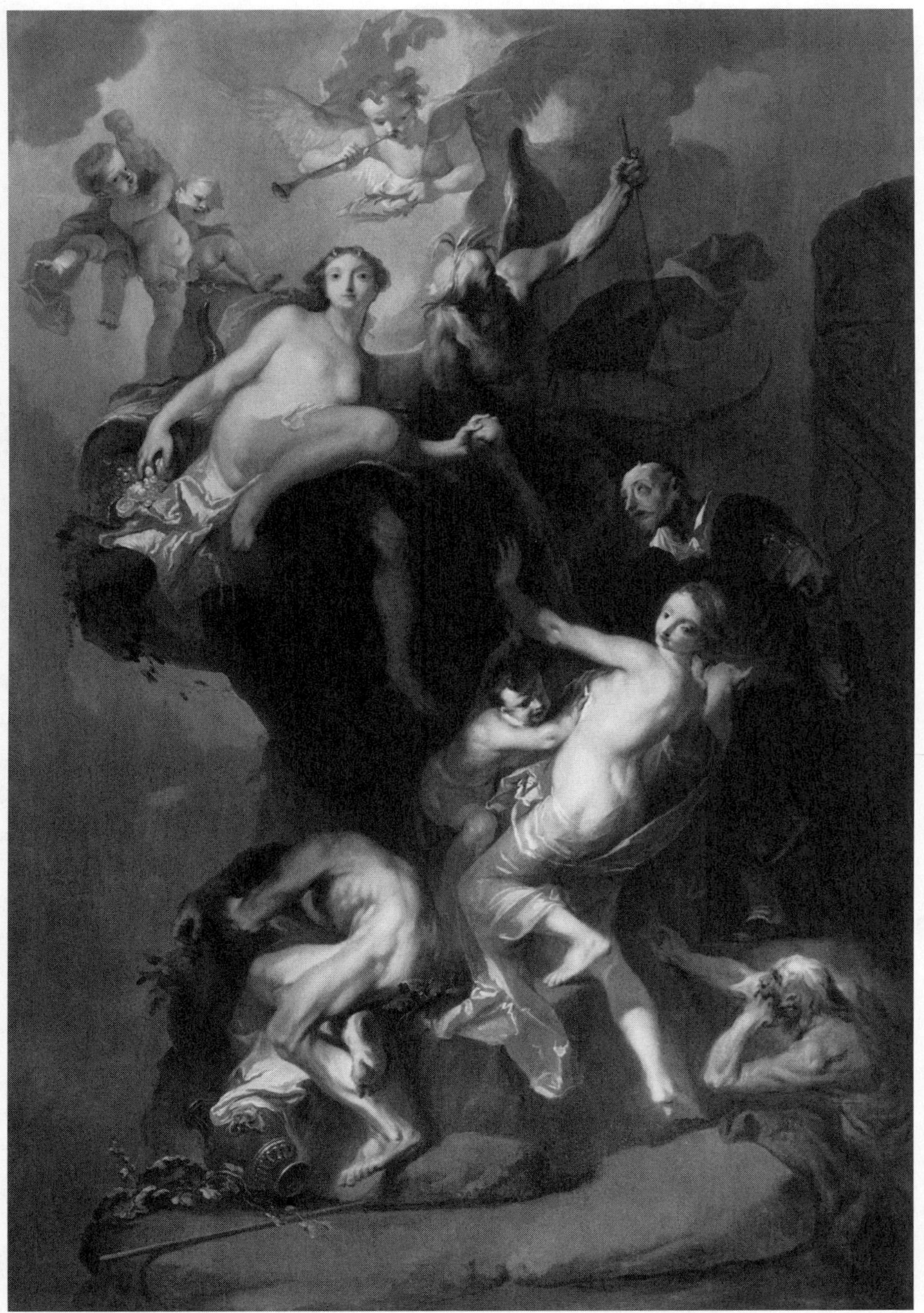

FIGURE 27. F. A. Maulbertsch, *Allegory on the Arts*, oil on panel, 1770, Akademie der bildenden Künste, Vienna (Photograph: Gemäldegalerie der Akademie der bildenden Künste, Vienna)

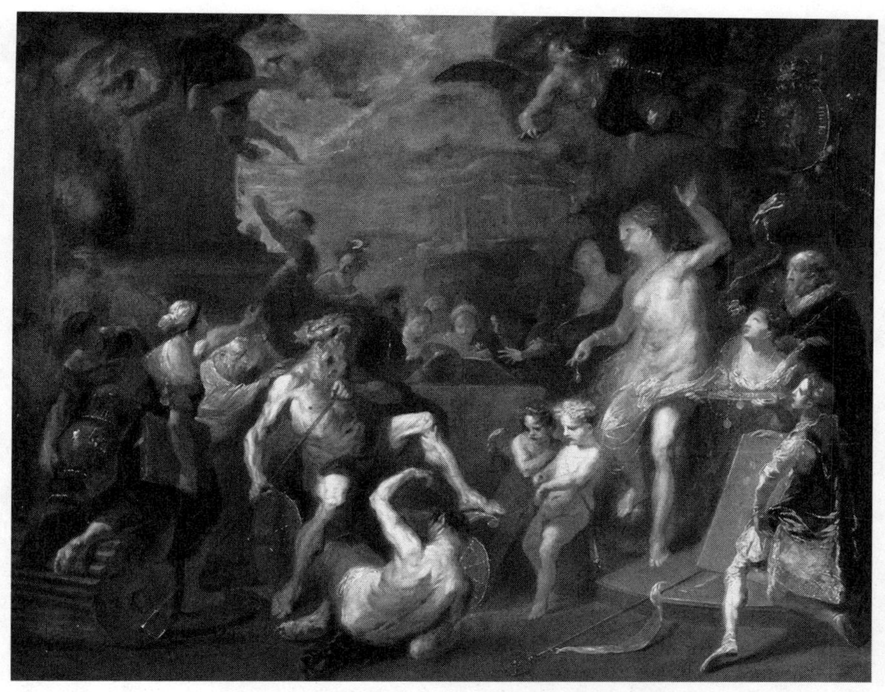

FIGURE 28. F. A. Maulbertsch, *Allegory on the Granting of Prizes at the Academy*, oil on panel, 1786, Österreichische Galerie, Vienna (Photograph: Österreichische Galerie Belvedere Vienna)

mistic view of progress, an expression of the belief that true art triumphs over its enemies (Figure 28).[93]

Josephism and Reform Catholicism also did not concur in the end about the role of religion and the place of the Catholic Church in society, not only in relation to questions of education, but also in regard to other issues. While both Reform Catholics and the imperial camp may at first have agreed about the need for educational or even to a degree about ecclesiastical reform, the emperor's approach appears to have been that religion and the church had a place in society simply because they were necessary props of it; yet the state, not the pope or his representatives, was to be supreme in ecclesiastical affairs. While religion might be regarded as essential to the service of the state, its goals and institutions were not indispensable. This is another reason why when the emperor began to implement Erastian policies, prelates such as Migazzi, who had initially been inclined to support church reform, broke with imperial programs.

Some obvious outcomes of imperial policy clearly indicate a signal difference between Josephism and Reform Catholicism. Not only the Jesuits, who had also patronized Maulbertsch in his earlier career, but, as noted, many other orders, including ones for which he had worked, were closed by imperial decree. Some anticlerical attitudes that were inherent in Josephism are expressed in an engraving by Franz Xaver Palko the Younger. Albeit extreme, it shows the Masons as the only ones who shed light on the true path that leads to the true church, directed by St. Peter and the emperor; nuns and monks, in contrast, search for earthly gold (Figure 29).[94]

Paintings executed by Maulbertsch for the imperial court also present a significantly different iconography, and different relation to the Enlightenment, from those he did for church patrons. Maulbertsch's association with the imperial house began in the same year, 1765, that Joseph II became emperor and coregent with his mother, and this succession signaled the arrival of new trends. Maulbertsch's first documented works for the Habsburgs were connected with monarchical representation. At the behest of Maria Theresia he celebrated, on the ceiling of the Hungarian Court Chancellery, the queen (*recte* king) of Hungary founding the Order of St. Stephen.[95] In 1769 he restored Daniel Gran's frescoes in the imperial library, now the National Library in Vienna, where the complicated program sums up learning.[96] This painting notably delivers a much different message than that found in Maulbertsch's other library ceilings. Instead of divine wisdom, the imperial house is portrayed as protector of learning (Figure 30). Another message of absolutist virtue is suggested in the design Maulbertsch made in 1769 for the title page of a codex of law, the *Supplementum Codicis Austriae* published in 1777 (Figure 31). This image celebrates Maria Theresa with figures of Abundance, Justice, and Wisdom: it strongly resembles similar allegorical glorifications of Louis XIV of France.[97]

The treatment of distinctively Enlightenment themes in works done by Maulbertsch for the imperial house is consequently also different from subjects in ecclesiastical settings. The ceiling paintings that he executed in 1775–76 in the *Riesensaal* of the imperial Hofburg in Innsbruck indicate this difference clearly (Figure 32). Maria Theresia herself seems to have taken an interest in their composition: in a letter of 29 April 1775 she indicated that she was going to communicate with Maulbertsch, and that two medallions were her invention.[98] Although it is not certain what these inventions were, the program of the larger pictures was devised, and published, by Freiherr von Sperges.[99] The central allegory, first imparted in a beautiful modello (Plate 11), represents the happy union of the Houses of Lorraine and Habsburg. In the spandrels of the composition are demonstrations in grisaille of the military prowess of the Habsburgs at Vienna

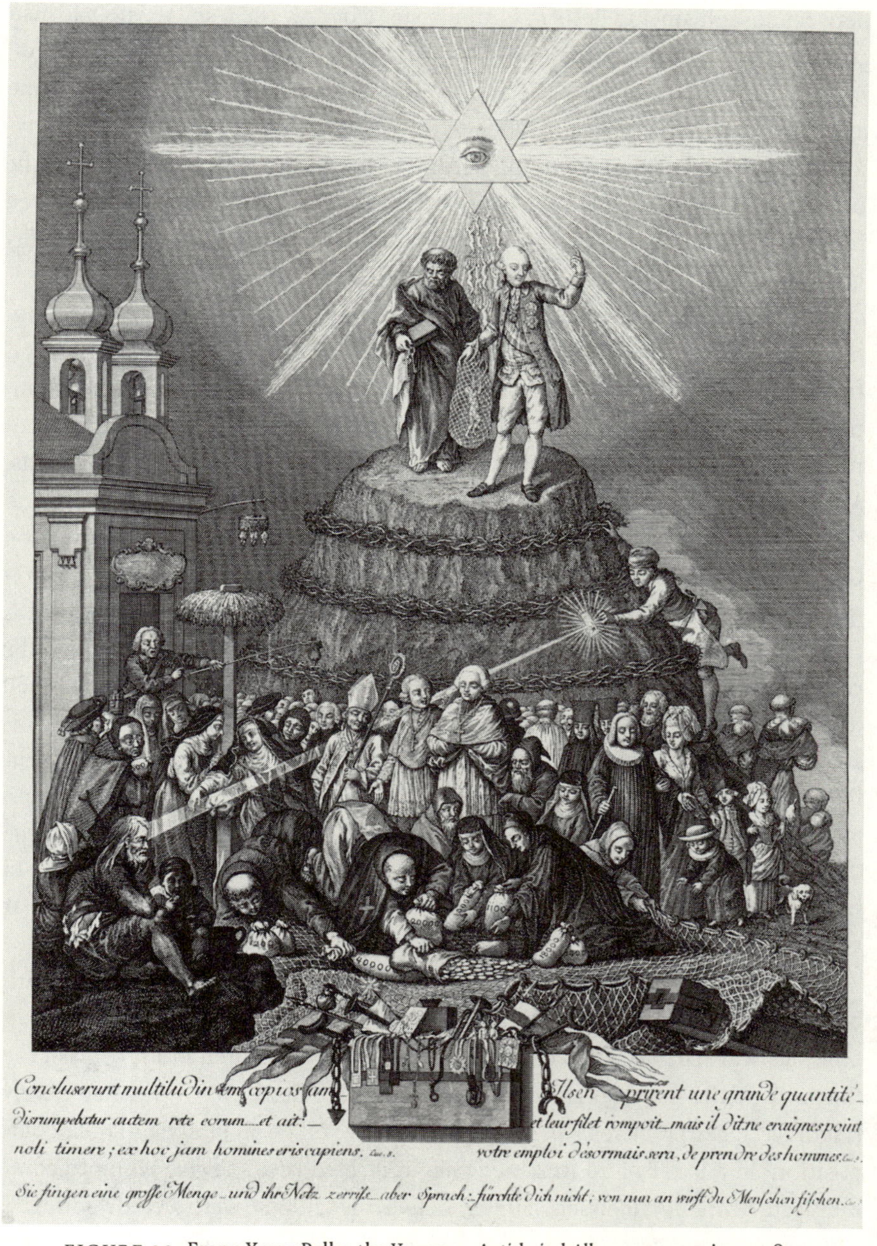

FIGURE 29. Franz Xaver Palko the Younger, *Anticlerical Allegory*, engraving, 1783, Szépművészeti Múzeum, Budapest (Photograph: Szépművészeti Múzeum, Budapest)

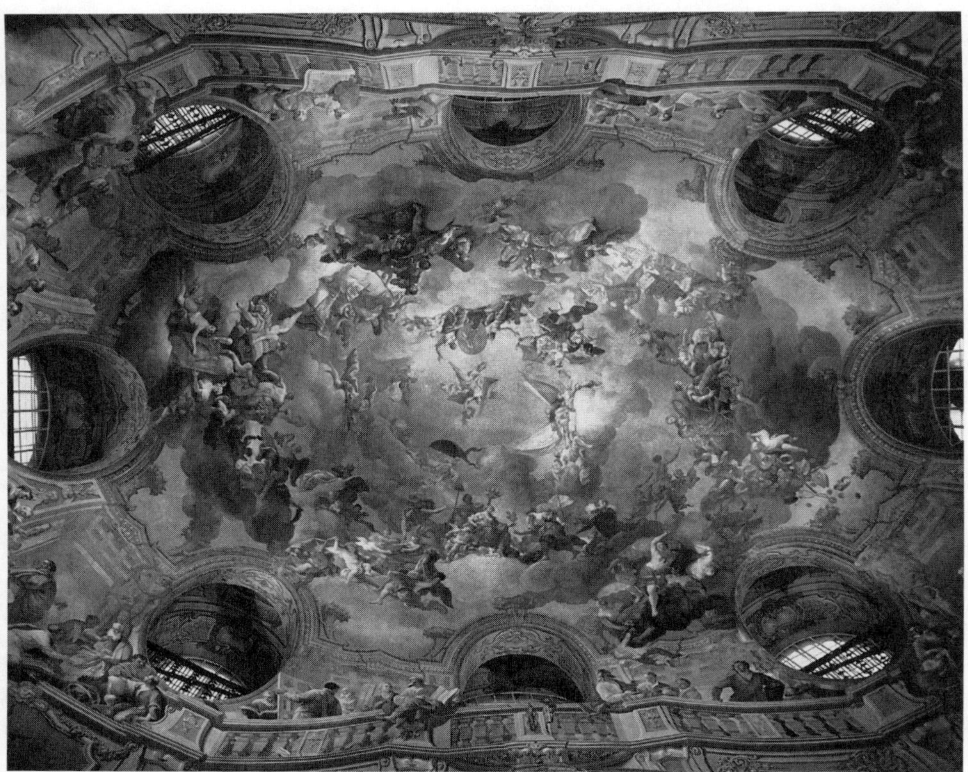

FIGURE 30. Daniel Gran, restored by Maulbertsch, *Allegory of Learning*, cupola of *Prunksaal*, Österreichische Nationalbibliothek, Vienna (Photograph: Bundesdenkmalamt, Vienna)

and Buda, while other frescoes show in color the natural wealth of the Tyrol, whose capital was Innsbruck. The industrious people of the Tyrol are smiled upon by Ceres and Pomona, as the Tyrol brings forth all kinds of products (Figure 33); Mercury favors its commerce. Maulbertsch thus combines a central scene displaying an allegorical theme that trumpets imperial absolutism, with subsidiary depictions containing naturalistic vignettes of human activity. These scenes moreover seem to represent Enlightenment ideals, in particular what has been called a characteristic belief in the intense delight in nature's bounties and man's productive energy.[100]

The message of what may be called Enlightened absolutism presented by the Innsbruck paintings suggest something more specific: they also express physiocratic ideals as they were interpreted in Austria.[101] Physiocracy is the school of political economy most familiar from the formulation of François Quesnay,

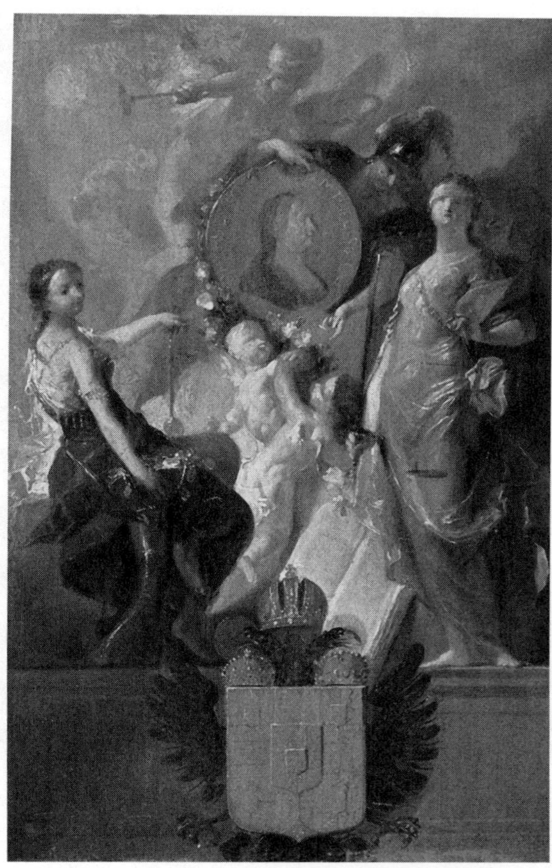

FIGURE 31. F. A. Maulbertsch, *Allegory on Maria Theresia*, oil sketch for engraving, 1769, Österreichische Galerie, Vienna (Photograph: Österreichische Galerie Belvedere Vienna)

who maintained that society should be governed according to an inherent natural order. Nature—along with the land—is the basis of wealth. In this case the natural order and the wealth that flows from it are seen to flourish under the benevolent reign of the Habsburgs. This sort of physiocratic ideology was expressed in another allegory that Maulbertsch presented the following year at the academy exhibition of 1777 (Plate 12).[102] This work celebrates a famed incident that occurred in 1769, a date inscribed on the plow in the picture: on a journey from Brno to Olomouc in Moravia Joseph II jumped out of his carriage at Slavikovice to take a plow from a peasant and push it. The description of the painting given when it was exhibited refers to it as an allegory of fertility, personified by

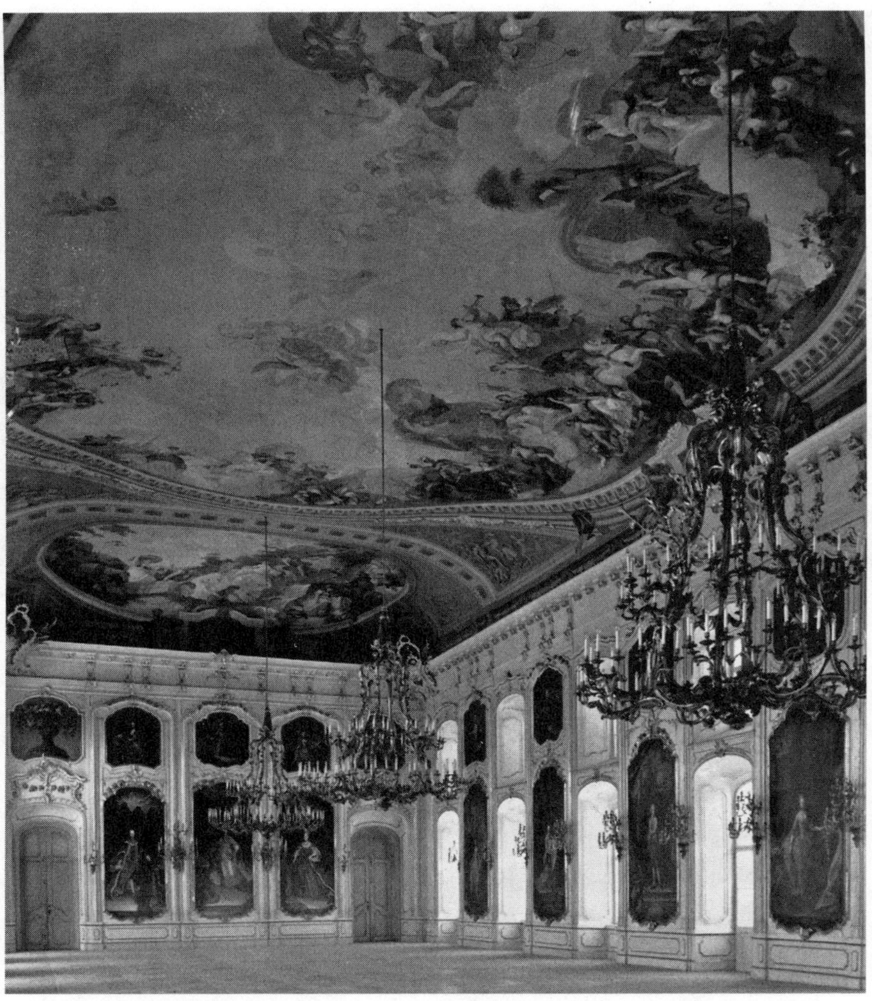

FIGURE 32. F. A. Maulbertsch, *Riesensaal* with ceilings depicting Allegory of the Union of the Houses of Austria and Lorraine, and Treasures of the Tyrol, 1775–76, Hofburg, Innsbruck, Tyrol (Photograph: Bundesdenkmalamt, Vienna)

the figure (of Ceres?) on the right who holds grain in her cloak, and is meant to flourish through the enlightened rule of the emperor, as suggested by the figure with the torch on the left. The reclining woman against whom leans a child with spoon in hand, and next to whom rests a card with the date 1772, refers to the end of a famine in Moravia, caused by successful agricultural policy, personified by the bewreathed, unclothed man, probably a peasant, with the plow. The depiction of Joseph II in Roman military costume, and in profile, with its recollec-

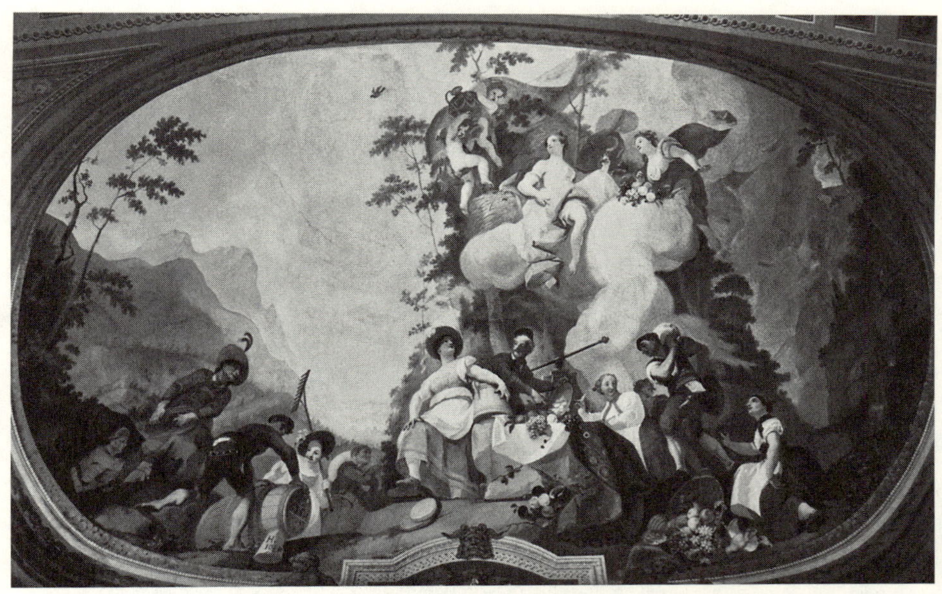

FIGURE 33. F. A. Maulbertsch, *Treasures of the Tyrol*, ceiling of Riesensaal, 1775–76, Hofburg, Innsbruck, Tyrol (Photograph: Bundesdenkmalamt, Vienna)

tions of traditional dynastic portraiture (the imperial crown and imperial eagle above him), maintain the traditional image of an absolute ruler, however. The whole thus suggests an image of the enlightened despot carrying out the physiocratic principles that benefit his state. This theme is echoed finally by an allegory for which Maulbertsch was paid in 1792, but is dated probably close in time, the 1780s, to that of the allegory on the distribution of prizes at the academy; it depicts a similar theme: the happy and fruitful reign of provinces of Galicia and Lodomeria under Habsburg rule (Figure 34).

The physiocratic doctrine that is expressed in such images was especially favored by rulers who claimed to possess absolute power, because of the doctrine's assumptions about natural law. In serving the national interest, the emperor could thus be seen as carrying out the decrees of natural law. To this end he would necessarily clear away accumulations of artificial, man-made law, since they choked progress.[103] Specifically, such principles provided the basis for the introduction of the tax reforms based on taxation of land in the Habsburg territories.[104]

These policies provoked widespread resistance, especially in Hungary. Clerics were demonstrably opposed to the policies behind them. Migazzi, for example, had already spoken out against Sonnenfels's idea that the wealth of a state was

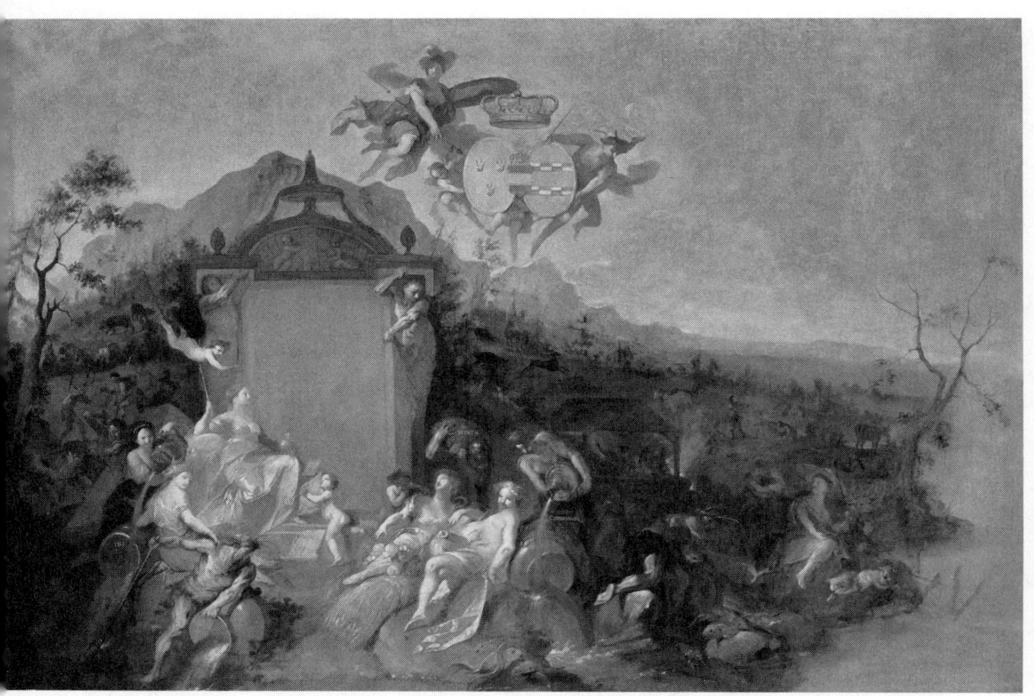

FIGURE 34. F. A. Maulbertsch, *Allegory on the Habsburg Reign in Galicia and Lodomeria*, oil on canvas, c. 1790, Österreichische Galerie, Vienna (Photograph: Österreichische Galerie Belvedere Vienna)

based on its population.[105] Obviously proponents of Josephist policies held a different view of the way wisdom had been revealed in nature from that offered at Louka. One might even imagine that the idea of clearing away man-made institutions was realized in the closing of monasteries.

Although there is no evidence that Maulbertsch would have taken such an extreme position, and, indeed, he ultimately worked for patrons who opposed Josephism, he does seem to have done more than just execute commissions for the imperial court: he appears to have sympathized with aspects of the Josephist program. In 1785 Maulbertsch produced his own etching on the Joseph II's *Edict of Toleration*, the edict that granted religious freedom to Protestants and Jews (Figure 35). In this etching, for which there is no evidence that he had received a commission, Maulbertsch presents his theme through the use of historical figures, and traditional, as well as new personifications. These new forms include Reason Triumphant (*ratio triumphans*). Maulbertsch thus suggests that in the enlightened era of Joseph II, Reason has triumphed, and toleration reigns.[106]

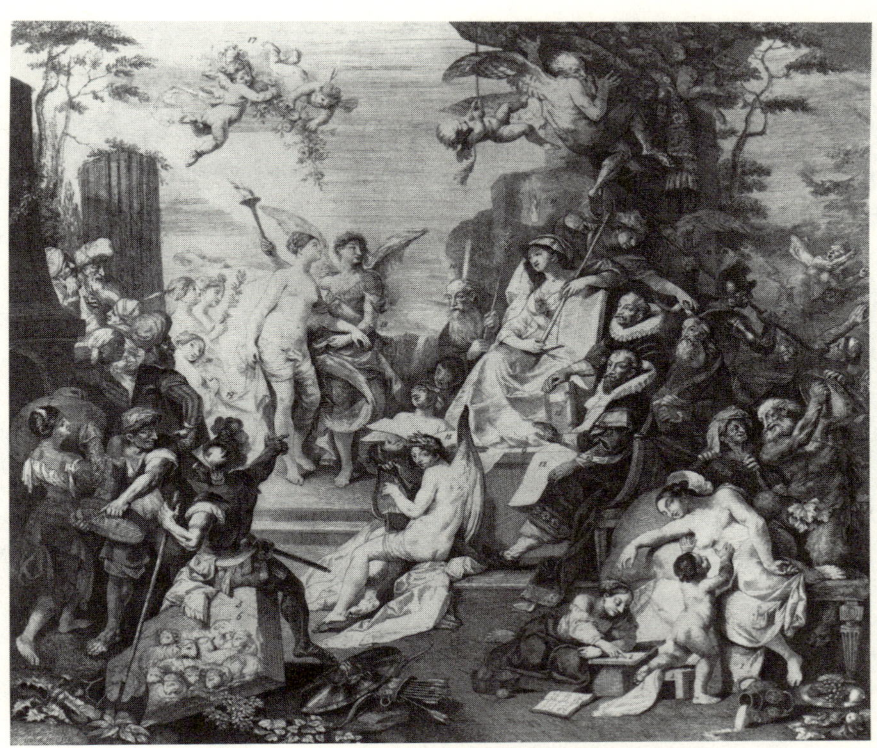

FIGURE 35. F. A. Maulbertsch, *Allegory on the Edict of Toleration (Das Bild der Duldung)*, etching, detail, 1785, Graphische Sammlung Albertina, Vienna (Photograph: Graphische Sammlung Albertina)

In contrast, several of the works that Maulbertsch executed for his ecclesiastical patrons in the 1780s and 1790s can be read as manifestations of resistance to Joseph's reforms. This is particularly the case with paintings done for prelates in Hungary, for whom Maulbertsch worked especially in the last part of his career.[107] Hungarian resistance to Josephism grew for various reasons, including the imposition of German as an administrative language in Hungary, Joseph's refusal to be crowned king of Hungary, and the transferal of the symbol of the kingdom (and source of authority), the crown of St. Stephen, to Vienna. Ultimately opposition led to revolt.[108]

The emphasis on local or national saints and scenes from their lives in Maulbertsch's paintings seems particularly pointed at a time when the emperor claimed to be serving the nation,[109] but acting against the interests and aspirations of those magnates who thought they spoke for it in Hungary. In 1781 Maulbertsch painted the story of St. Ladislas's striking water from a rock for the ceiling of the chapel of the Bishop's Palace in Bratislava (Plate 13). This work depicts the royal saint wearing the crown of St. Stephen, the symbol and source of power of the Hungarian king, which was then in fact kept in Bratislava; it also displays soldiers unfurling the flag of Hungary. It was done for the Cardinal Primate of Hungary, Joseph (József) von Batthyány, who was the leader of opposition to Josephism in Hungary. In the same year Maulbertsch painted for Bishop Ferenc Zichy of Győr the same subject, along with that of the founding of the church at Győr, on the walls of the nave of the cathedral there. On the ceilings above was painted the glorification of Hungarian saints (Plate 14).

In 1792–93, with the aid of Martin Michl, Maulbertsch painted a depiction of all the saints for Bishop Károly Eszterházy on the ceiling of the chapel of the Lyceum (Lyzeum) at Eger, but mainly noticeable are Hungarian saints (Plate 15). This painting was done during a period of conflict with imperial authorities, and the contract for this ceiling Maulbertsch signed on 25 September 1792 specified the presence of saints of the realm (*Hailige dises Raichs* [i.e., Hungary]). All were to be depicted with their royal (meaning Hungarian) emblems (*alle mit ihren Königl[ichen] Zeichen*). The contract also called for the painting of one angel carrying the Hungarian Patriotic or Patriarch's cross (*Patriotischen, oder Patriarchs Kreuz*), and another with a banner with the Hungarian arms visible (*Ein anderen Engl mit den Raiches Fane worauff die Hungarischen Wappen zu sehen*) (Figure 36).[110]

With workshop assistance Maulbertsch also painted similar sorts of motifs in the reception room of the palace of the bishop of Szombathely (Steinamanger), a newly created episcopal seat. National saints and allusions to local history appear in the frescoes here; they suggest the continuity of Christian with pagan history—Szombathely is on the site of ancient Savaria. Scenes are shown that are related to the local past, with depictions of the emperors Tiberius, Septimius Severus, Constantinus Chlorus, and Attila the Hun (Figure 37).[111] Similarly, Saints Martin and Quirinus, who were both associated with Savaria, are depicted in the ceiling (Plate 16). The theme of the ceiling is similar to that of Louka (Figure 21), and indeed some of the individual personifications are also similar: history is seen to progress through divine foresight or wisdom. In the ceiling fresco at Szombathely, however, stress is placed more on allegorical personifications and representatives of faith.[112]

Maulbertsch's last fresco, a painting on the ceiling of the library of the Premonstratensian abbey at Strahov near the Prague Hradčany also reworks the program of Louka (Plate 17; see also Figure 17).[113] Abbot Mayer of Strahov had bought the bookcases from the library of the recently suppressed convent of his Premonstratensian brothers at Louka, and he had Maulbertsch closely adapt its

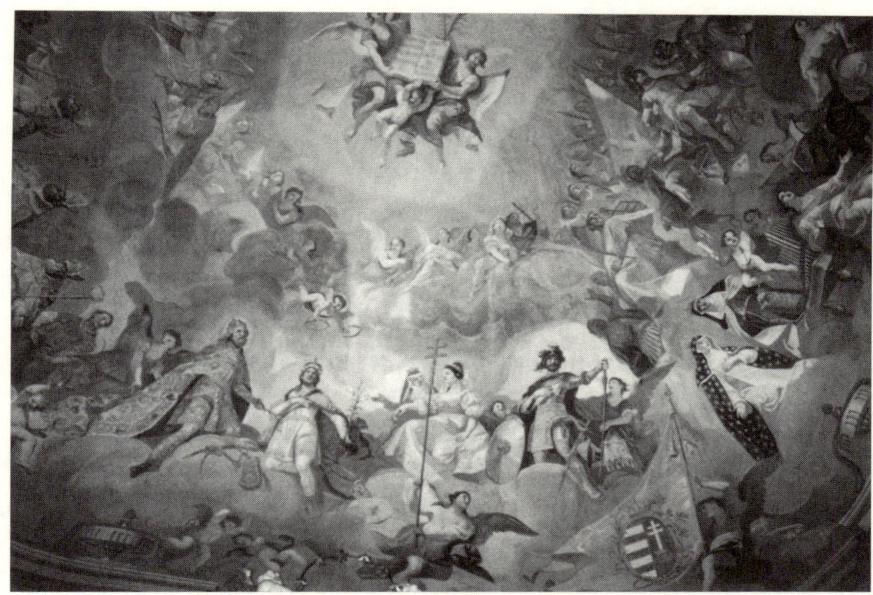

FIGURE 36. F. A. Maulbertsch, *Glorification of All the Saints*, detail of Hungarian saints with flag, ceiling of former chapel, 1793, Lyceum, Eger, Hungary (Photograph: Author)

painted program. Hence at Strahov Maulbertsch again represented the theme of man's progress to Divine Wisdom.

However, the differences between the details of the programs for Louka and Strahov are striking, and they are spelled out in the distinctions made in print by the extensive description for Louka versus that probably written by the historian G. J. Dlabacz for the program designed by Abbot Mayer for Strahov. Opposition to Habsburg policies had also developed to some extent in the 1790s in Bohemia.[114] Just as local Hungarian saints became prominent in the frescoes of the 1780s at Bratislava, Győr, Szombathely, and Eger, the fresco at Strahov has added Bohemian saints to the scheme of Louka. As in the Hungarian examples, they sound a patriotic note that emphasizes the national presence, in response, it might seem, to the imperial claims to embody a supernational state. Moreover, no longer as at Louka does a personification of Reason lead Will to Eternal Light, despite the blandishments of pleasure; instead, it is the Genius of Religion who leads a youth. The economic benefits of learning are no longer shown at Strahov; in contrast all kinds of evil, symbolized by arrows, ghouls, and cups of poison, appear. Finally, in place of the harmonious message of Louka, a combative note is struck at Strahov, as angels drive down those who misprise religion, including

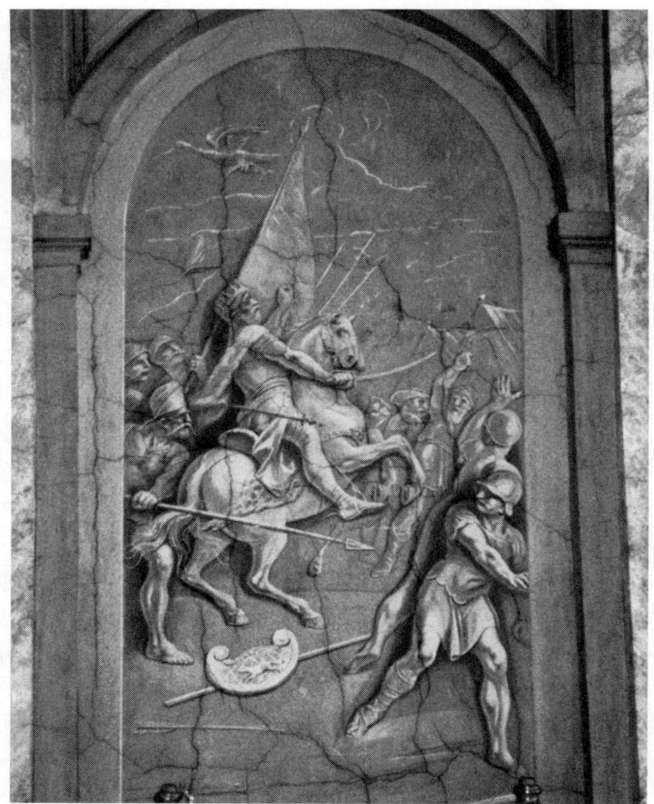

FIGURE 37. F. A. Maulbertsch, Scene of ancient history of Savaria (Attila chases the Romans from Savaria), detail of wall in *Prunksaal*, 1783, Bishop's Palace, Szombathely, Hungary (Photograph: Author)

figures probably identifiable as philosophes. It may well be that at the time of the French Revolution the steadfastness of the church and new emperor (Franz succeeded Leopold II [1790–92], who came after Joseph II) represent a reaction against philosophical radicalism, but reaction nonetheless it is. It seems as if the Counter-Enlightenment triumphs at the end of Maulbertsch's career.

Problems of Pictorial Communication

Several conclusions can be drawn. First, different and often contradictory demands were placed on Maulbertsch by his patrons and publics, who often expressed varying interests. Maulbertsch's relationships to the secular interests of his world and to the spiritual were complicated, and at times contradictory, as were those of many other artists of the time, including notably Jacques-Louis David. Like David, Maulbertsch journeyed on a "spiritual itinerary as a painter of religious themes who negotiated the realms of the sacred and the profane."[115] But how could this be done?

One problem was to find a pictorial vehicle that would be both appropriate to and adequate for the expression of the message that it was to convey. At first Maulbertsch used the traditional language of allegory and emblem common to picture-making in seventeenth- and eighteenth-century Europe. Paintings by Maulbertsch show how this sort of imagery could be adapted to depict new ideas, but they also suggest how labile and problematic such uses might be. Although earlier such symbolic images might have been acceptable for ceiling paintings, allegorical imagery, and especially its use of often obscure personifications, is not always completely decipherable, not to mention that details on a ceiling are often hard simply to apprehend, much less comprehend, from a distance below. One way of dealing with the problem of presentation of allegory was to publish programs; these publications obviously also expanded the possible public for Maulbertsch's work. Several descriptions of Maulbertsch's fresco programs were published—for Schwechat, Innsbruck, Louka, and Strahov—and a manuscript exists for Dyje. A complicated key to explain all the figures was also added to Maulbertsch's own allegory on the Edict of Toleration.

Bruno Bushart has spoken of Maulbertsch's inexhaustible search for means to express new pictorial ideas.[116] Maulbertsch's allegories were also undoubtedly inventive. However, since the early eighteenth century, when Abbé Du Bos had criticized it in his *Réflexions*, the use of allegory in the visual arts had been under attack. Allegorical language was criticized by German contemporaries of Maulbertsch such as Lessing, who decried *Allegoristerei*. Allegory was also criticized in the Habsburg lands by Sonnenfels; Sonnenfels specifically denounced the use of "iconologies," meaning handbooks of images that he says could readily, if odoriferously, be sacrificed.[117]

Like other artists, Maulbertsch tried to negotiate this problem by heeding the call for the creation of a new sort of allegory made by writers including Johann Joachim Winckelmann, whose works, as we shall see, were quite familiar in Vienna. A new sort of allegorical art would display naturalness, truth and likeness to nature, in clear and rational images, and might employ actual scenes from history. Effects of his approach may be represented by the subsidiary scenes Maulbertsch illustrated in vignettes of Tyrolean life that adorned his ceiling at Innsbruck, and in his allegory on Joseph II at Slavikovice.

It has been argued that Maulbertsch's allegory on Joseph II is an appropriate expression of the new image of the monarch, one formulated with the tools of an obsolescent art, much as physiocratic tracts sought to legitimate the traditional institution of monarchy with new representations of its purposeful and functional role in society.[118] But it is open to question how effective even Maulbertsch's newer allegories may have been. In any event, his sketch of 1777 does not seem to have led to a larger commission; after that date he received little patronage from the Habsburgs or the institutions bound to their court. This may also have been a result of Joseph II's known aversion to splendor, his desire for simplicity in artistic expression, and the rationalist aspirations that this aesthetic may represent.[119]

Taste in this matter as in others was changing, and the newer taste in art was not for this kind of image, as Füßli's critique of ceiling paintings indicates. In addition to decrying ceiling paintings as unnatural, Füßli faulted in particular the "mystical and incomprehensible symbolic representations" (*mystische und rätselhafte symbolische Vorstellungen*) of Maulbertsch and his ilk.[120] The production of programs has been described as a product of Enlightenment scholarship, and its attention to concepts of history and art,[121] and it is true that the programs associated with Maulbertsch's paintings were different from earlier ones, and thus more consonant with Enlightenment aims. But, as suggested, it is also true that even such programs continue a tradition that harks back to an earlier period,[122] and that by the later eighteenth century literary explications were not the most up-to-date forms of discussion of art. Newer discourses of art criticism, historiography, and aesthetics were already coming into being.

A retreat from rhetorical embellishment, of the sort represented by allegory and its explications, was also in process. Naturalness, clarity, and simplicity were now demanded.[123] These qualities spoke more to the broader public that had developed for art in the later eighteenth century.[124] A consequence was the rethinking of an aesthetics of effect, meaning the way a work has an effect on, or is received by, the beholder. Here allegory was not necessarily the best vehicle for expression.[125]

Maulbertsch's relation to the Enlightenment thus highlights a crisis of imagery that in turn illuminates a more general crisis of representation. Coming at the end of the ancien régime, this crisis may be related to a crisis of legitimation of the authority that lay behind its forms of representation. This crisis came to a head in the many revolutions of the late eighteenth century, and resembles that found in other periods as well.[126] In the later eighteenth century not only representation and legitimation of authority were challenged, as many sweeping changes came into play: among them was the transformation of the public sphere for art, with consequences for forms and means of artistic expression.

Several issues are at stake. How, in general, can art be used to communicate or emphasize ideas? How, more particularly, can a sensuous visual medium represent often complicated intellectual notions and spiritual ideals in an appropriate manner? Does the demand for rational and clear communication run counter to the way that ideas are to be expressed by the forms available to an artist? What would be the province of art itself in this process of communication? Maulbertsch's painting at Halbturn may have given one answer, but, as we have seen, there has not been a consensus in the interpretation of that answer. The relation of the Enlightenment to the formal or stylistic aspects of Maulbertsch's art clearly calls for further consideration.

THREE

From Fantasy to *Verstand*

Soon after the completion of the ceiling at Halbturn, Maulbertsch's painting starts to change noticeably.[1] Comparison of works executed somewhat earlier and substantially later than the ceiling at Halbturn—paintings of 1757–58 in the parish church at Sümeg (Figure 2; Plates 19, 20, 21), with those of 1782–83 in the parish church at Pápa (Plate 18)—brings into clearer focus the transformation of his art.[2] These churches are located in western Hungary, as was Halbturn, but their frescoes were both commissioned by bishops: at Sümeg by the bishop of Veszprem, Márton Biró; at Pápa by the bishop of Eger, Károly Eszterházy. While the churches are of different dimensions, Pápa being much larger than Sümeg, each contains extensive expanses of paintings, which, although completed with workshop assistance, particularly for the architectural details at Pápa,[3] unquestionably result from Maulbertsch's invention and composition; they reveal striking contrasts.[4]

Frescoes in the naves and choirs of both churches comprise coherent series. (In each, additional paintings are located in other spaces, including sacristies, organ lofts, chapels, and oratories.) Pápa presents the life of St. Stephen the proto-martyr with stories of his companions and followers. The program for Sümeg is much more complicated: among other subjects, it depicts scenes relating to the lives of the Virgin and of Christ, with the Ascension of Christ painted prominently on the altar wall of the choir, as he is received into heaven above. The paintings on the ceiling of the nave at Sümeg alone represent numerous scenes from both the Old and the New Testaments: Moses with the Ten Commandments, the mission of the Archangel Gabriel to Mary, the Annunciation, the Star of Bethlehem, the Journey of the Magi, the Carrying of the Cross (or Way to

Calvary; Plate 20), the Pentecost, and Christ with Angels. A complex theological program, which was probably also devised by Bishop Biró, seems to interweave stories from the Nativity (Plate 19) with those of the Passion and the Mission of the Apostles, along with an image of probable typological significance (Moses).[5]

At Sümeg Maulbertsch employs an elaborate scheme of decoration that extends to the side walls, where the altarpieces are actually frescoes, not easel paintings; their frames and other carved parts are also simulated in paint (Figure 2; Plates 2, 19). The painted scenes on the side walls, rendered as if they were set in frames, treat their individual pictorial spaces independently; these fictive spaces are unrelated either to the conception of space suggested by the complicated compositions on the ceiling, nor to that created by the illusion of the painting in the apse. On the ceiling of the nave, a different system of illusion is in operation: the pictures are shown as if they were placed in their own fictive spaces on top of and behind fictive architecture (Plate 20). Subsidiary scenes on the ceiling are painted in polychrome, and remain largely visually independent of the main scenes. The apse fresco, which is set in the place of the high altar, also does not simulate an altarpiece, but employs another illusionistic device: it represents the Ascension of Christ as if it were a real event occurring before the beholder. The apse wall of the church seems to open up, as observers lean out of the picture or peek around pilasters to catch a glimpse of Christ (Plate 21).

Maulbertsch's participation in the decoration of Pápa is restricted to areas of the ceiling. Although he also painted a study for the high altar that is probably reflected in a sketch of the stoning of St. Stephen,[6] this and the other altarpieces at Pápa were painted by other artists (Hubert Maurer among them). The paintings in the domical vaults (known as Bohemian *Kappengewölbe*) at Pápa give the illusion that the scenes shown are themselves occurring in structures with domes (Plate 22). Subsidiary paintings are executed in grisaille to simulate sculpted reliefs; they complement the central depictions, at the same time that they are subordinated to the fictive architectural ornament of the ceiling.

Illusionistic devices are also employed in different manners within the compositions of the frescoes in the two churches. For instance, the elements of fictive architecture in the ceiling of the nave at Sümeg recall proscenium arches behind which the stories take place (Plate 20). But these scenes are set on separate pieces of ground, seen from an angle from below. They can be regarded as representations of a truly imaginary world, because the ground planes in these pictures are set in what should be the sky—as indeed is indicated in the ceiling of the apse, where the common connotation that the ceiling is celestial is employed to suggest the reception of Christ by God the Father and the angelic host.

At Pápa the angles of vision are more directly related to the position of the viewer below: the individual scenes are positioned so as to be seen as if they are taking place in an elevated space above him or her. The visitor to the church views them from vantage points that are consistent with some of the figures within the paintings, who are placed around the perimeter of the action. The viewer is supposed to be watching the action in each scene from a space located below a series of steps, or other breaks in architecture. Furthermore, one is led to construe this form of fictive construction as consistent with the space of the church. At Pápa an effort is thus made to have this viewpoint consistent with the path the believer takes upon entering the church. This attempt to accommodate the conventions of illusionism to the demands of rationality is stressed by the reduction of the subsidiary scenes to grisaille, in contrast with the polychrome renderings of secondary scenes on the ceiling of the nave at Sümeg. The use of grisaille suggests that they are a form of sculptural decoration, and relates them further to the ornamental surrounds in which they are set.

The forms of the painted architectural and ornamental settings underscore the contrasts found in the two fresco cycles. Sümeg utilizes an ornamental vocabulary of c- and s-curves, shell-forms, and rocaille, replete with banderoles and ribbon ornament, that are associated with what is thought of as rococo decoration. The fictive constructions of the ceiling possess atectonic traits that correspond to features deemed characteristic of rococo architecture.[7] Epitomizing these characteristics, the sinuous herms shown on the ceiling's fictive structures hardly seem to be able to carry the corbels above them.

Such features are absent from Pápa, where the fictive architecture avoids elements that might be called rococo, but tend rather to regularity. Emphasizing the tectonic, its ornamental surrounds suggest the incipient neoclassical, which in France is called the style Louis XVI, and in German is known as the *Zopfstil*.[8] The decoration at Pápa consists of coffering with gilt rosettes, cornucopias, guilloches, swags, vases, and blind medallions with acanthus frames, flanked by Michelangelesque consoles; while around the central domical pictures, set off by gold frames, are acanthus brackets, courses of egg and dart, moldings, and panels. An architecture with classicizing associations is also noticeable within the painted scenes themselves, where the temple interiors, although adorned with reminiscences resembling medieval, Romanesque buildings, suggest ample structures whose domed forms, supported on composite columns, are dressed with coffering. This painted architecture reflects features of the actual building, a church erected beginning in 1774 under the direction of Jakob Fellner after a design by Franz Anton Pilgram, in which the severe, pared down forms have been

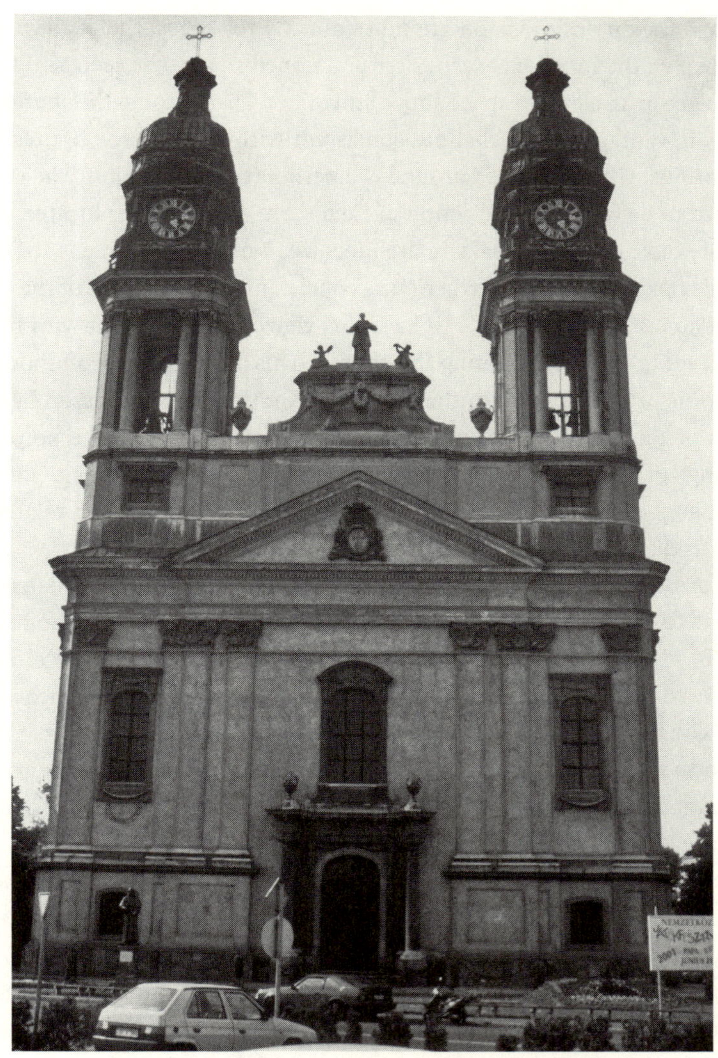

FIGURE 38. Jakob Fellner, after plan by Franz Anton Pilgram, Parish Church, 1774–86, Pápa, Hungary (Photograph: Author)

regarded as forerunners of neoclassicism (Figure 38). Emulating the antique, this style might, however, better be called the Roman style ("römischer Stil"; or one might say *stile alla romana*),[9] to use the terms of the patron of Pápa, Károly Eszterházy. Since neither Pilgram nor Fellner seems to have designed interiors, the opportunity was open for Maulbertsch, and other painters, to decorate the church.[10]

The coloring of the works is also markedly different. In Sümeg pastel pinks, greens, and blues, seen in many works by Maulbertsch of the period, abound; this palette, too, has been associated with rococo architecture. In Pápa, a more subdued tonality tends to grays and greens. (In both, the coloring has changed a bit because of problems in condition.) The change in color is reinforced by the gray fictive architecture, and the appearance of the grisaille paintings, and harmonizes with the revetment and stone decoration, as well as the architectural style, of Pápa.[11]

Distinctive differences are also visible in other features in the "frescoes": the proportions of figures are less elongated at Pápa, the drawing is relatively tighter, and the handling of paint less extravagant. All these characteristics are indications of a major metamorphosis in Maulbertsch's style starting in the later 1760s. The result has often been described as a change from the late baroque, expressive, and subjective visionary manner of the period of the 1750s and 1760s,[12] as exemplified by Sümeg, to an art of greater moderation and calm, whose balanced construction and clearer indications of forms, as seen at Pápa, has been regarded as classicistic.

Regardless of the stylistic terms one uses, the problem is to account for this transformation; for while many art historians have observed that this stylistic change accompanies a change in Maulbertsch's treatment of themes,[13] strong differences of opinion exist about the reasons for these changes. Interpretations of Maulbertsch's stylistic development diverge, as do those of the interpretation of his subjects. Some characteristic ones can be summarized here.[14]

The change in Maulbertsch's style is often interpreted as a decline, or else an abandonment of his authentic position as an artist. For Ivo Krsek, the extreme subjective approach of Maulbertsch's early work allows color to have an almost autonomous role. The artist's retreat from this sort of painting thus signifies an abandonment of the highly personal, nonconformist manner of his best years. It results from the pressures of the changed cultural political relations of the Josephinian epoch.[15]

However, Garas regards Pápa as marking a key stage in Maulbertsch's art, where the patron's interests, shaped by newer views of art, coincided with the artist's own changed attitudes, a situation that pertains to other monuments as well. Although Garas regards the painting at Pápa revealing the existence of a critical situation for fresco painting, she values its accomplishment highly.[16] More generally, she sees a change in style accompanying change in society, but she also explains Maulbertsch's artistic development in personal terms. Here a familiar pattern of biological and psychological development is employed: the aging artist gives up his youthful excesses in favor of greater restfulness. Garas also sees this personal transformation coinciding with a general change in the *Zeitgeist* of the later eighteenth century.[17]

In a sharp critique, Franz Matsche rejects these interpretations. Because of the similarities that exist between Maulbertsch's stylistic development and broader trends in the arts of the Austrian lands, Matsche argues against a "subjective" reading that would emphasize the painter's idiosyncrasies or personal psychology. He also rejects interpreting stylistic change as stemming from a personal reaction to altered socioeconomic conditions. Furthermore, he rejects replacing art historical analysis and explanation for the origins of Maulbertsch's new style with citations "of philosophical and art theoretical postulates, pastoral letters from bishops, and imperial prescriptions."[18] Strikingly, Matsche thus also argues against the simultaneously published essay of Betka Matsche-von Wicht, which relates the changed elements in Maulbertsch's art to what she calls the artistic theories of classicism.[19] Instead, Matsche avers that "the artist and above all the baroque fresco painter is and remains in the first instance a practitioner, and proceeds from possibilities and available models. He always is connected to something, which he changes and forms in his own sense."[20]

While referring to some of the contemporary texts connected with Maulbertsch, Matsche therefore does not interpret these writings, as do most other scholars, as consonant with classicizing art theory, but rather as the result of what he calls an academic reaction to the excesses of Viennese baroque painting.[21] Hence he does not regard Maulbertsch as a classicistic painter. Instead he relates the change in Maulbertsch's art to the impact of Daniel Gran (and Peter Paul Rubens).

No doubt it is important to consider the specific sources of Maulbertsch's style and his possibilities as an artist: a major current in twentieth-century scholarship on Maulbertsch, as enunciated in a key essay by Otto Benesch, has followed this course. While Garas has more recently spoken of Maulbertsch's change of style coming "largely in response to the advance of Neo-classicism,"[22] it is also correct to challenge the simple equation of Maulbertsch's later style with classicism, as we shall see. Nevertheless, if taken in isolation, analysis of intra-artistic factors, however revealing, ignores important data. A conception of art historical interpretation that rejects theoretical and other critical considerations is also exceedingly restrictive. An interpretation that does not take into account the extensive correspondence Maulbertsch carried on with his patrons about the planning of frescoes, and regards his own and their statements merely as an "academic reaction to baroque excesses," also misrepresents a significant source of primary evidence.

Maulbertsch's major commissions all came in fulfillment of contractual obligations. Many of these contracts stipulate numerous, quite elaborate conditions. While the execution of Maulbertsch's frescoes was virtuoso, and seemingly spontaneous, its conceptualization resulted from a process in which there was often continuing give and take with the patron. The existence of numerous oil sketches by Maulbertsch provides evidence for this process. Even though this genre has been regarded as constituting a form of autonomous work of art, for various reasons, as discussed in Chapter 1, this point of view is fundamentally misleading, because Maulbertsch's oil sketches can in many instances be connected with specific projects. Rather, the oil sketches themselves attest to what was frequently a lengthy process of conception, involving considerable correspondence and the submission of designs for approval, even if the final act of execution, like that which went into the making of the oil sketch, may have been rapid.

In any case, a pronounced process of preparation is especially demonstrable for the creation of frescoes that date from the latter part of the painter's later career, the period in which Maulbertsch's stylistic change becomes apparent. Substantial documentation exists for the genesis of the frescoes to be discussed here that were executed in Hungary during the 1780s and 1790s at Eger, Pápa, and Szombathely. The steps in the process of composing paintings remained similar, and were not substantially different from those of many other seventeenth- and eighteenth-century artists.

Some of the choices made in the completion of Maulbertsch's works were thus the fruit of quite deliberate decisions, in which the patron entered into the determination of details of execution or design. For example, like Maria Theresia, Freiherr von Sperges also claimed in a letter that he was specially involved in the Innsbruck frescoes, and said that the side ceilings should have the attributes of the Land (the Tyrol).[23] Besides conceiving the program, Sperges requested that certain changes be made in Maulbertsch's design, probably based on the sketch for the final fresco (likely that in the Getty Museum, Los Angeles, Plate 11): he asked for a change in an element as seemingly insignificant as the appearance of the white horse (Figure 39).

In responding to such demands, Maulbertsch would presumably have acted first as a skilled painter, a profession for which he had been trained from an early age. The erratic spelling that smacks of dialect (even granting the absence of standard orthography during the eighteenth century), inaccurate syntax, and

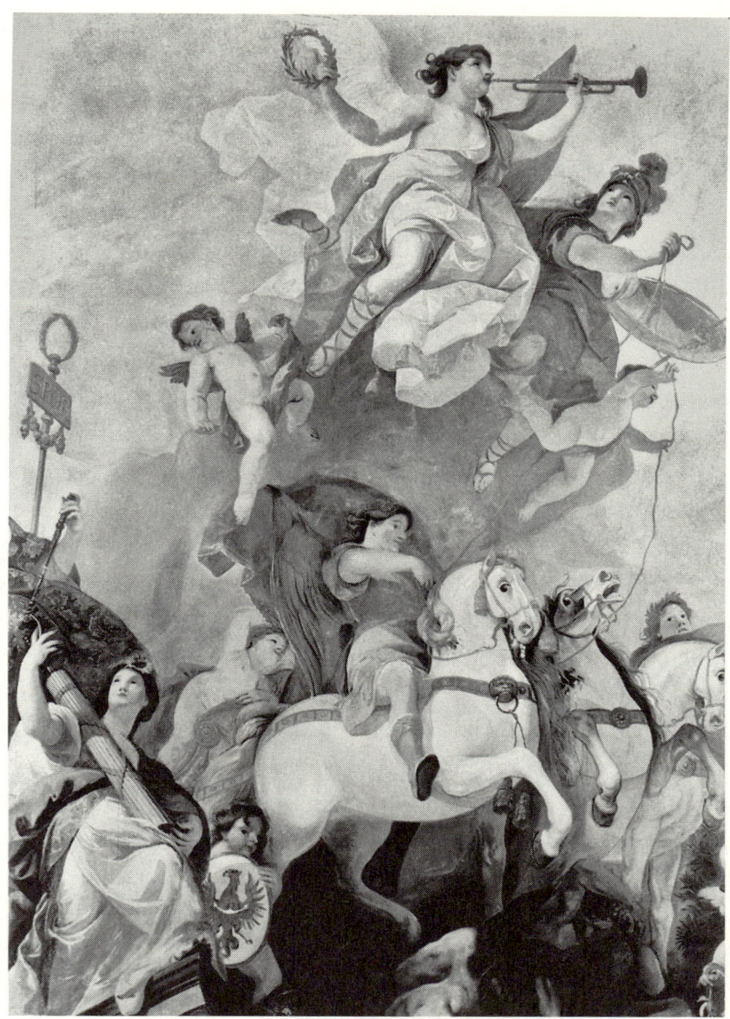

FIGURE 39. F. A. Maulbertsch, *Allegory of the Union of the Houses of Austria and Lorraine*, detail of horse, 1775–76, *Riesensaal*, Hofburg, Innsbruck, Tyrol (Photograph: Bundesdenkmalamt, Vienna)

faulty grammar found in his correspondence do not suggest that he had received much formal education. Nevertheless, the often exceedingly complicated programs that he carried out, as discussed in the preceding chapter, in themselves suggest that his works were the product of considerable cogitation, as well as of bravura execution. The extensive correspondence with his patrons, especially in regard to Pápa and Szombathely, demonstrates that Maulbertsch was much concerned with aesthetic issues that were concretized in the art theory and criticism of the Enlightenment, and that these affected his manner of painting.

Maulbertsch's letters to his patrons indicate that for the painter matters of execution were not exclusive of those concerning conception and content, as well as criticism or theory, but complementary to them. For example, he shows that he was able to keep in mind at the same time both the elements that should go into a particular work of art and the manner in which a text was to be illustrated. A letter of 9 November 1780 written to Bishop Eszterházy while Maulbertsch was preparing the paintings for Pápa states that he was able to follow the bishop's prescriptions, while attending to artistic concerns (*ich habe mich meglichst nach dem Tegst gerichtet, ohne das Kunstmessige fallen zu lassen*).[24]

Because of this web of circumstances, it is not adequate to emphasize internal formal or stylistic considerations related to other works of art alone as being the main determinants in the art of Maulbertsch. Many factors that paralleled or contributed to each other went into the change in Maulbertsch's painting. The previous chapter considered the impact that social, pedagogical, and ethical ideals associated with the Enlightenment had on Maulbertsch. In turn, the present chapter proposes that a review of some of the sources indicates that in a number of important ways Maulbertsch's involvement with Enlightenment art theory and criticism and related circumstances attending the conception and production of art in the later eighteenth century also had major consequences for the transformation of his art. These considerations were directly communicated through the artist's own thinking, as well as being mediated through the ideas of his patrons.

It has been noted that in submitting all aspects of culture and society to critique, Enlightenment thought had an effect on aesthetic considerations, and consequently for the visual arts. Yet seemingly nonartistic concerns of the Enlightenment were inextricably implicated in what might be considered more purely aesthetic issues, by which, conversely, they were informed.

This interrelationship is most apparent in the way rhetorical conceptions were applied to questions of church decoration. According to the application of the rhetorical principle of decorum, the place and public for a work in which a particular content was to be presented needed to be taken into account. In sacred decoration, the highest mode was demanded both for the content of what was to be expressed (the divine), as well as for its location (church), while the public or audience (often uneducated people) would require the lowest form of address. As Enlightenment critiques brought ecclesiastical teachings and institutions into their sights, matters of preaching and church decoration thus also came under fire, as it were. One critique urged simplification and purification of preaching and of church decoration. This movement seems to have provided some important intellectual grounds for the end of the rococo in Bavaria.[25]

Intellectual and aesthetic concerns also formed part of the motivation for the reform of church interiors that was promulgated in Salzburg by Archbishop Colloredo, and then applied more broadly in the Habsburg lands. In his pastoral letter Colloredo said that it was "with the general approval of those of reason" (*mit allgemeinem Beyfall der Vernünftigen*) that "all inappropriate, ambiguous, superstitious, and laughable images, representations, and decorations" (*alle unschickliche, zweydeutige, abergläubige, und lächerliche Bilder, Vorstellungen, und Verzierungen*), which "only heat up the imagination" (or "fantasy"; *nur die Einbildungskraft erhitzt*), were removed from churches in his diocese. For these objects had "offended good taste, and the altars and walls of churches had been more overloaded than ornamented by them" (*was den guten Geschmack beleidiget, und womit die Altäre und Wände mehr überladen, als gezieret*). Such ornament was to be removed from the house of the majestic, solemn divinity, whose most beautiful decoration is noble simplicity lacking in artifice (*aus dem Hause des majestätischen ernsthaften Gottes, dessen schönsten Schmuck edle ungekünstelte Einfalt ist*).[26] Demands of reason and of good taste were thus also at work in this act of purification.

Proponents of the sort of physiocratic theory that subtends the thrust of several works painted by Maulbertsch for the Habsburgs made analogous arguments. They too rejected fantasy, the power of the imagination, in favor of understanding or reason, and the artificial in favor of the natural. For physiocrats such as the marquis de Mirabeau, "true art was not to be found in the realm of fantasy." The "supreme art was agriculture"—whose virtues are of course also sung in Maulbertsch's allegories of the 1770s. The emphasis on agriculture, hence on the cultivation of nature, also implied "an opposition between the natural and the artificial, between a true and useful art and the manifold products of luxury and the *ouvriers de fantaisie*." As Rémy de Saisselin has put it, presenting the image of the monarch at the service of his people, and the people at his service for glory, also implied a rejection of the fantastic and the luxurious—one again thinks of Maulbertsch's image of Joseph II here. On the other hand, the description that Mirabeau uses in criticizing the kind of painting favored in a society dominated by luxury, in which a taste for the fantastic and novelty dominates, could be taken to apply to examples of Maulbertsch's paintings of the 1750s and 1760s, seen at the Piarist church in Vienna, or at Heiligenkreuz-Gutenbrunn, Trenčianské Bohuslavice, and Hradiště (Pöltenberg), where the elements Mirabeau decries appear quite conspicuously. In Mirabeau's words this sort of paint-

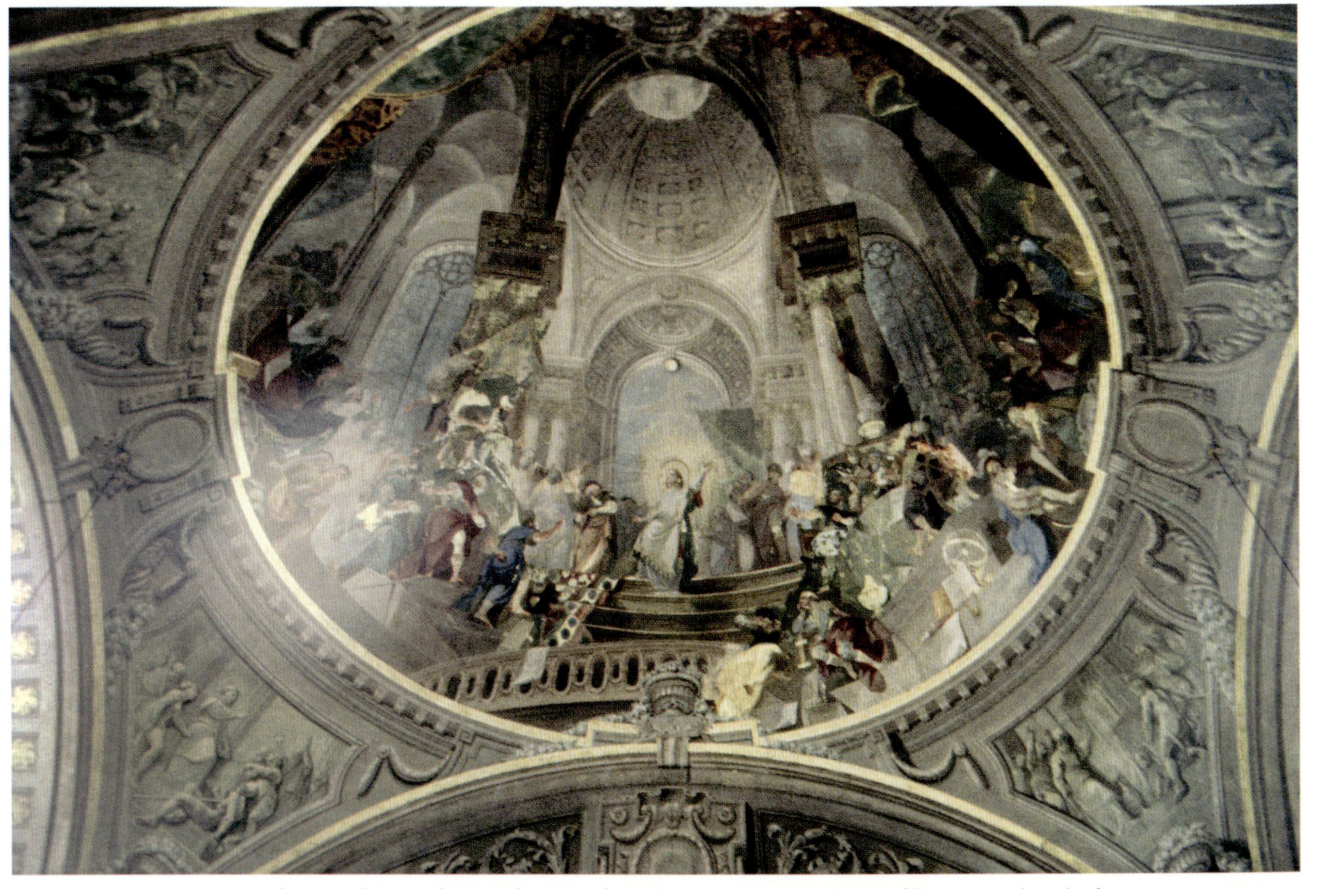

PLATE 18. St. *Stephen Preaching*, with scenes from the lives and martyrdoms of his companions in the pendentives, detail of nave ceiling, 1782–83, Parish Church, Pápa, Hungary (Photograph: Author)

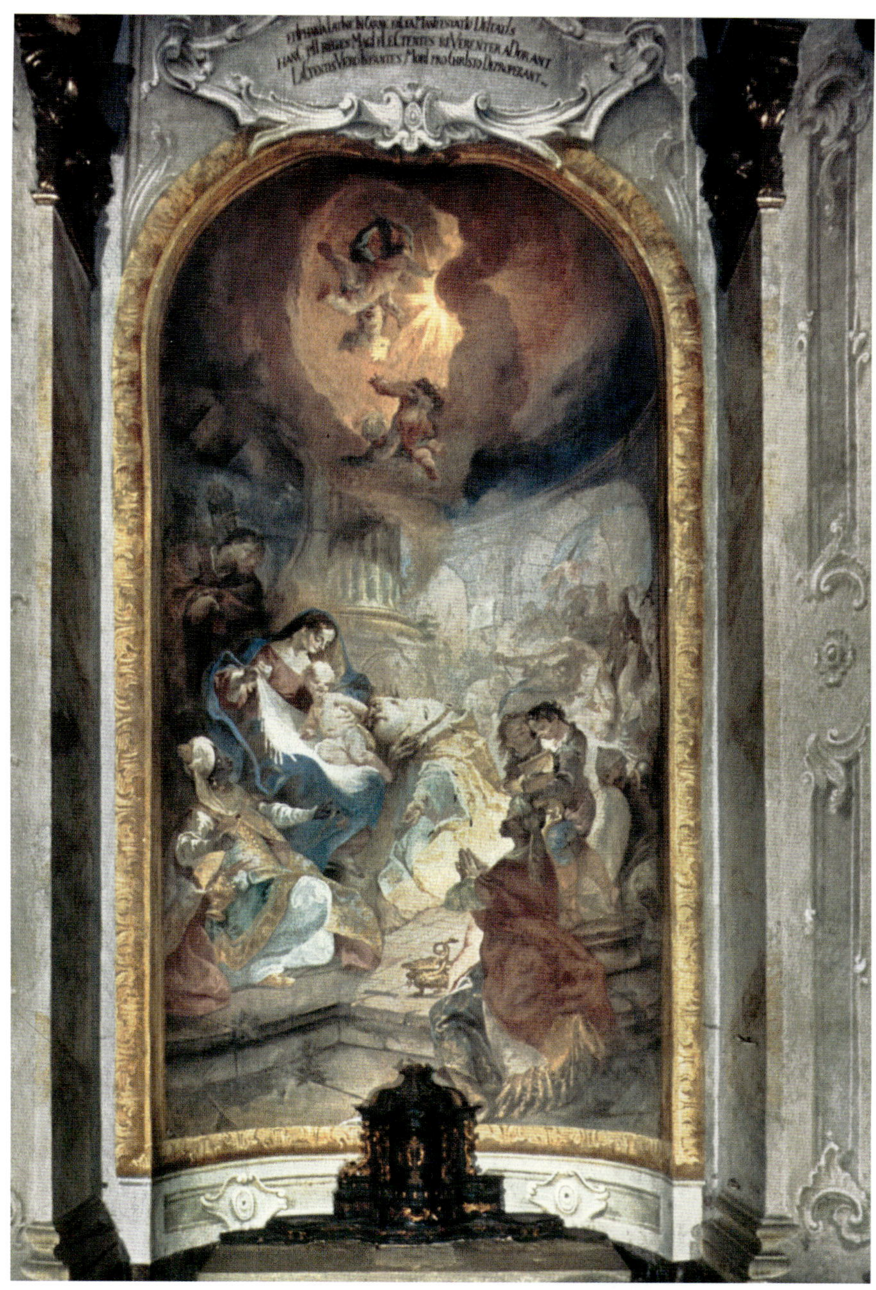

PLATE 19. *Adoration of the Magi*, side altar, 1758, Parish Church, Sümeg, Hungary (Photograph: Károly Szelényi, Magyar Képek / Hungarian Pictures, Budapest)

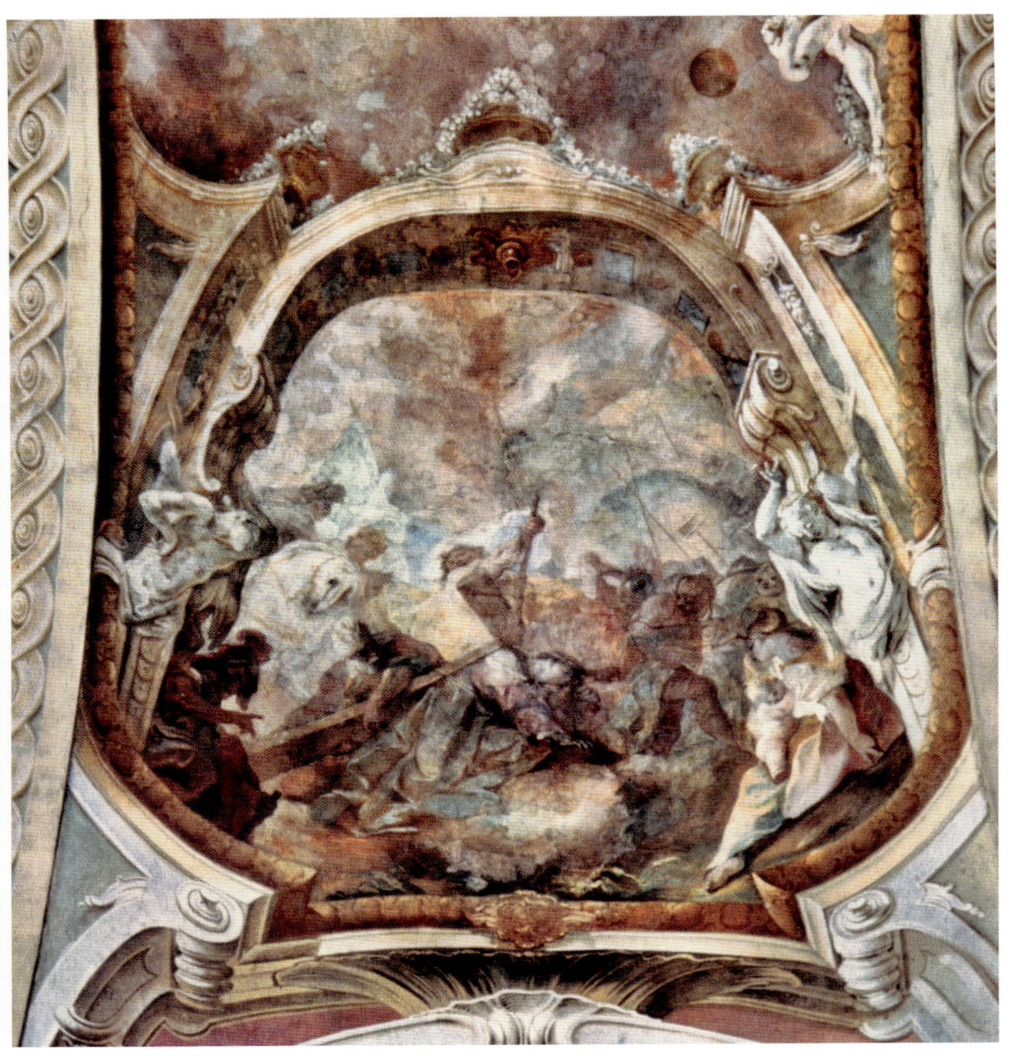

PLATE 20. *Way to Calvary*, ceiling detail, 1758, Parish Church, Sümeg, Hungary (Photograph: Károly Szelényi, Magyar Képek / Hungarian Pictures, Budapest)

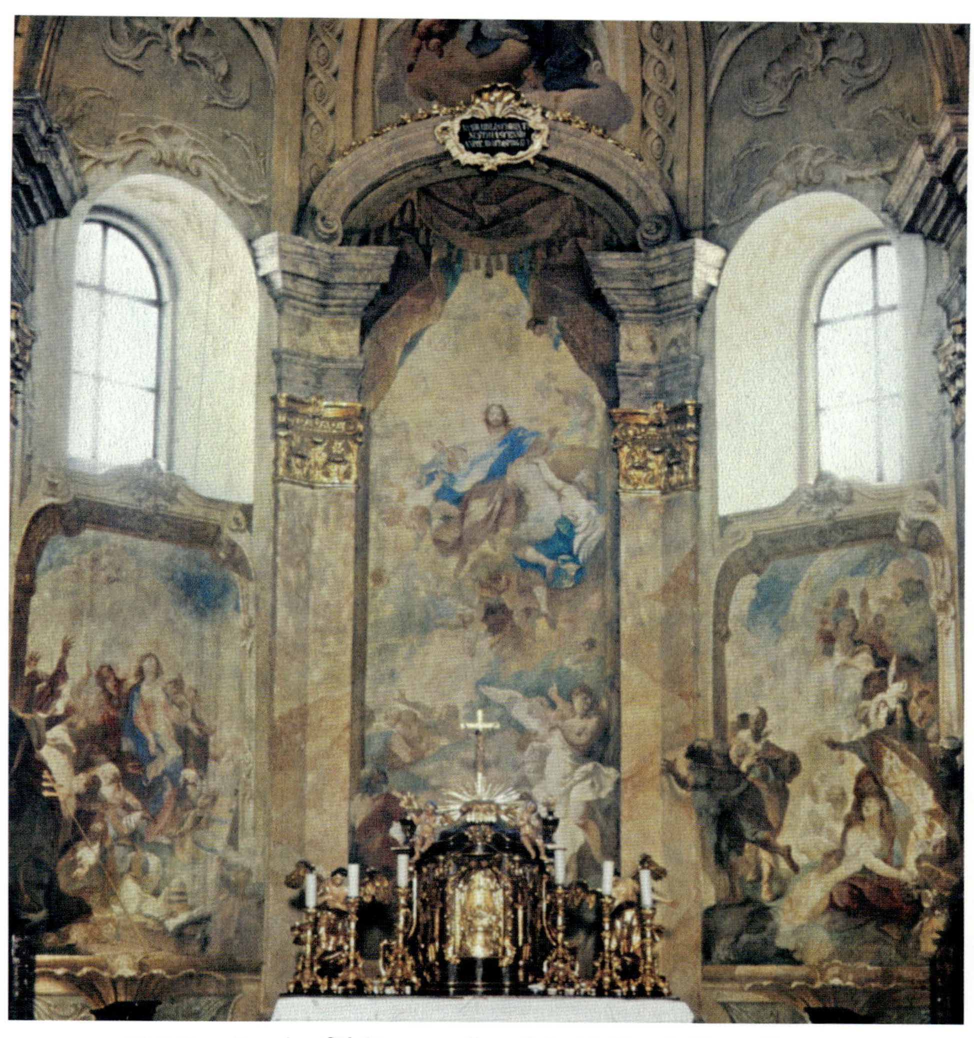

PLATE 21. *Ascension of Christ*, apse wall, 1758, Parish Church, Sümeg, Hungary (Photograph: Károly Szelényi, Magyar Képek / Hungarian Pictures, Budapest)

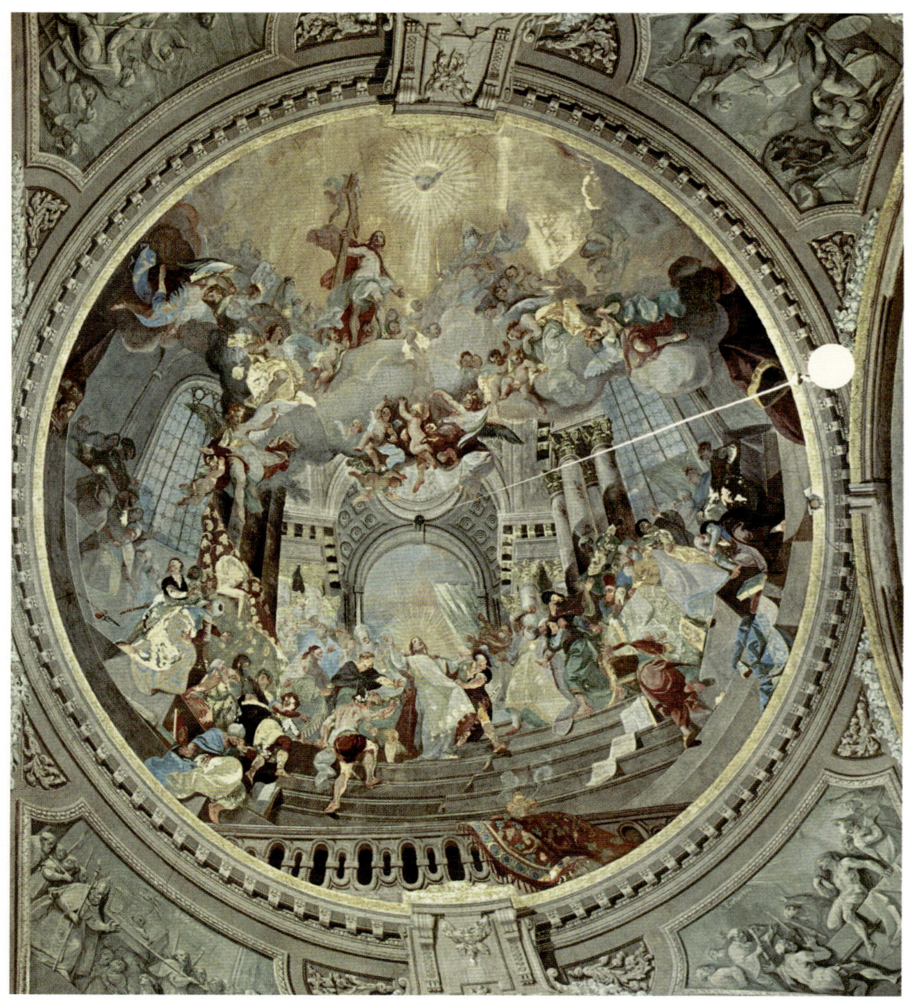

PLATE 22. *Martyrdom of St. Stephen*, detail of choir ceiling, 1782–83, Parish Church, Pápa, Hungary (Photograph: Author)

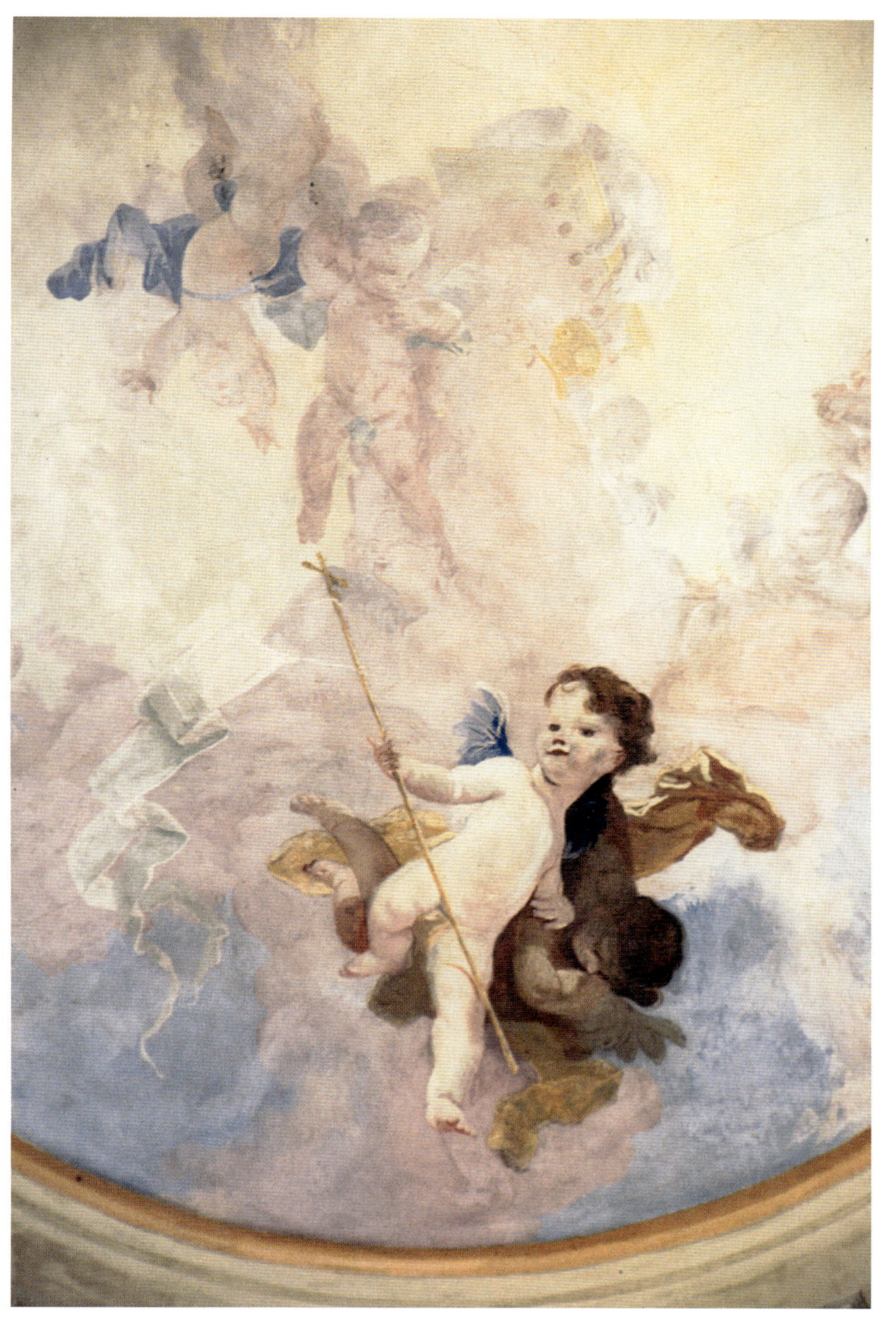

PLATE 23. Angel, choir ceiling, 1768, Priory Church, Hradiště (Pöltenberg), Moravia, Czech Republic (Photograph: Brno University, courtesy Bishopric of Brno)

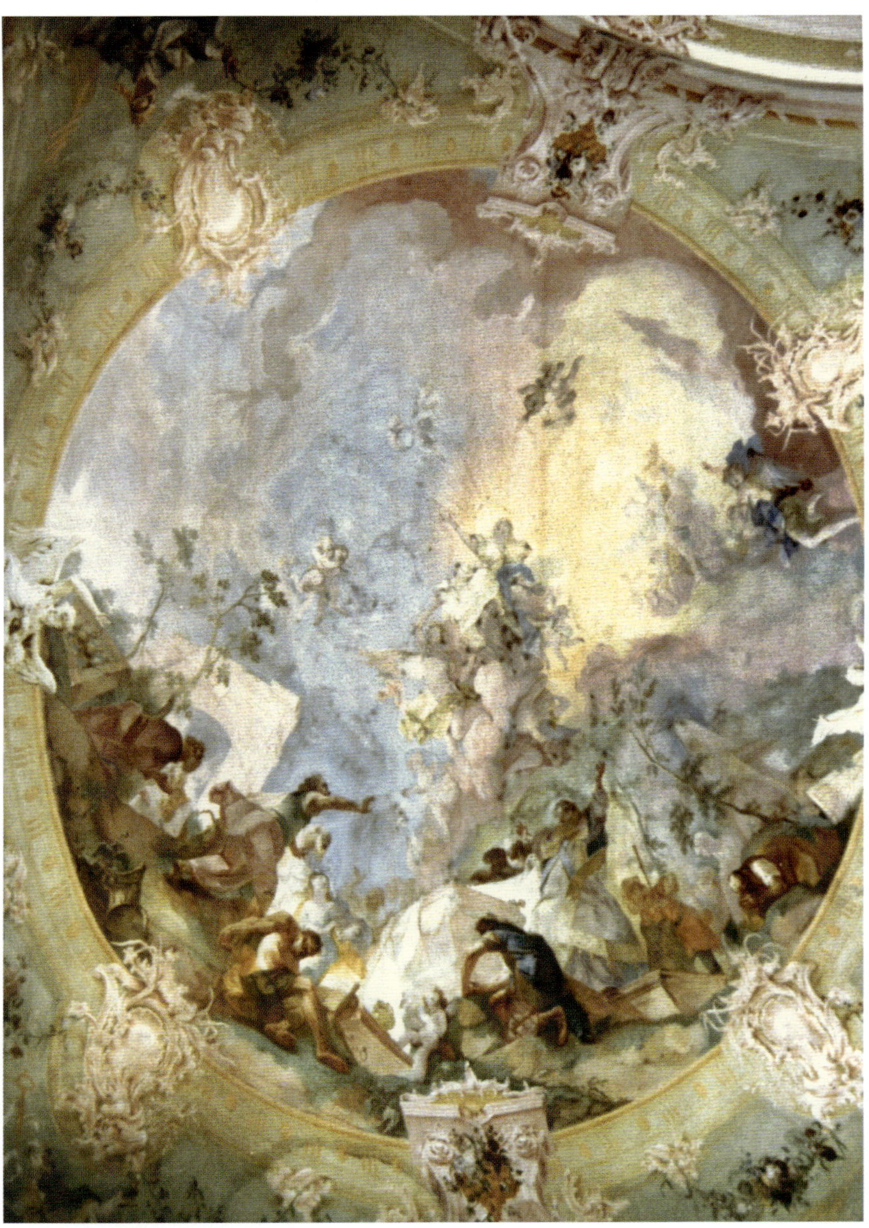

PLATE 24. *Assumption of the Virgin*, nave ceiling, 1763, Chapel, Schloss Erdődy, Trenčianské Bohuslavice, Slovakia (formerly Bogoszló, Upper Hungary) (Photograph: Courtesy of Institute of Art History, Slovak Academy of Sciences [Ustav dejin umenia Slovenská Akadémie Vied])

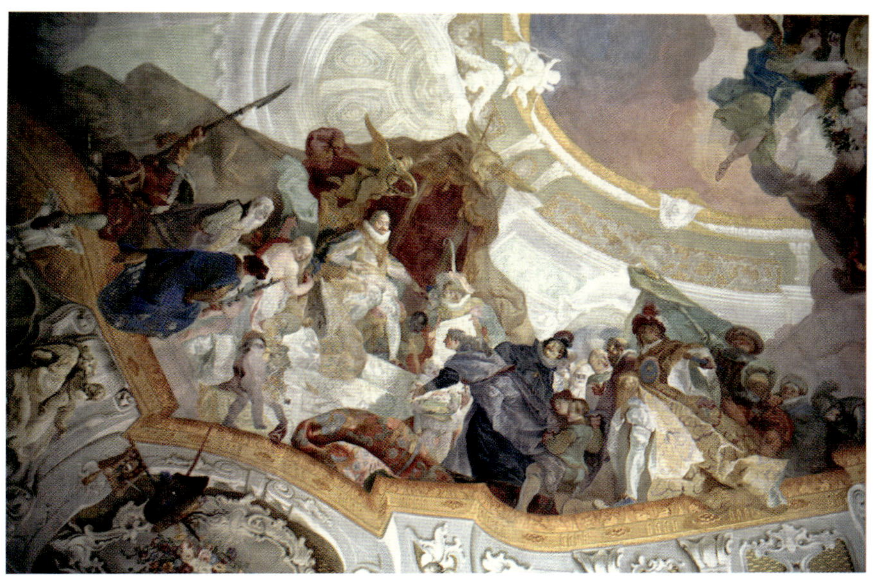

PLATE 25. Detail of ceiling in Feudal Room (*Lehensaal*), 1759, Gift of Ganiovitz to the Cathedral Chapter of Olomouc by Emperor Ferdinand II, Palace of Bishop of Olomouc, Kroměříž (Kremsier), Moravia, Czech Republic (Photograph: Brno University, courtesy Bishopric of Brno)

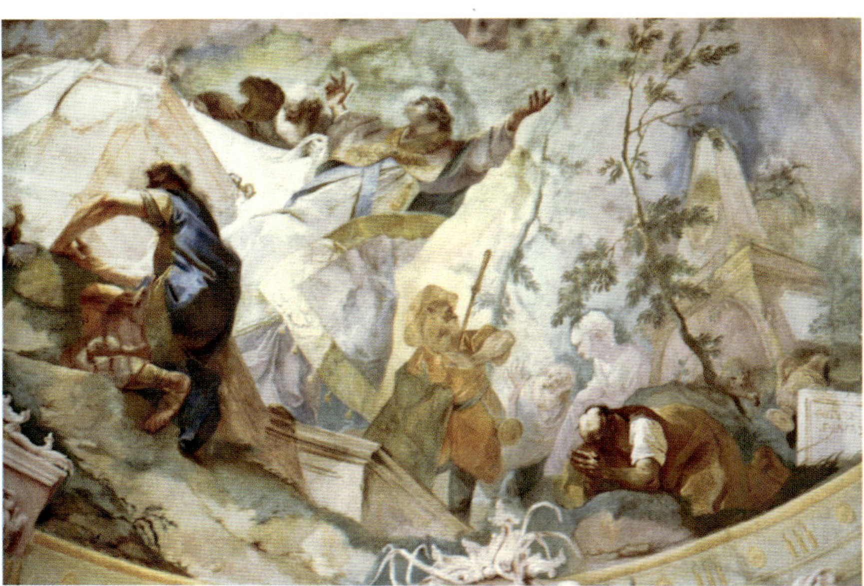

PLATE 26. Detail of nave ceiling, 1763, Chapel, Schloss Erdődy, Trenčianské Bohuslavice, Slovakia (formerly Bogoszló, Upper Hungary) (Photograph: Courtesy of Institute of Art History, Slovak Academy of Sciences [Ustav dejin umenia Slovenská Akadémie Vied])

ing shows "heaven and clouds and nothing more" (*coelum et nubes preteriaque nihil*); all is reduced to white and pink clouds and children (Plate 23).[27]

Taste was a major topic of debate in the eighteenth-century discourse on the arts. It became one of the staples of aesthetic discussion that was carried on in the German-speaking world and elsewhere.[28] While the term "taste," and its concerns, were discussed in various ways by many writers, the sources of the appeal to "good taste" and "noble simplicity" in Colloredo's letter are nevertheless easily recognizable, as several scholars have remarked.[29]

They are to be found in the landmark work of nascent classicizing criticism, Johann Joachim Winckelmann's *Thoughts on the Imitation of Greek Works in Painting and Sculpture* (*Gedanken über die Nachahmung der griechischen Werken in der Malerei und Bildhauerkunst*). Winckelmann began his essay of 1755 with the words "Good taste" (*Der gute Geschmack*), speaking of its origins in Greece. His argument traces the history of good taste from its origins, through the period of its decline, which set in with the Romans, and its continuing history through to the mid-eighteenth century. Good taste was to be restored by the imitation of Greek art. He characterized the ideal in art with the famous words "noble simplicity and quiet grandeur" (*edle Einfalt und stille Grösse*). As in the Bavarian church reforms of 1770 that rejected ornament in favor of simplicity, Colloredo's use of the words *edle ungekünstelte Einfalt* indicates that Winckelmann's ideal lay behind his notions, too.

In his essay Winckelmann's related critique of *Schnörkelwerk*, the ornament and vapid compositions that art historians associate with rococo art, also recalls the terms of the physiocratic critique and its appeal to reason, versus fantasy. Winckelmann charges that in this sort of art "paintings on ceilings and over doors stand there more to fill the empty space and to cover blank spots that mere gilding did not fill up. They do not have any relation to the estate and circumstances of the owner, but in fact even work to his disadvantage. Horror vacui fills the walls, and paintings, empty of thought, are to replace the vacuum."[30] In place of this kind of painting, Winckelmann repeatedly calls in his essay for an art that is informed by the intellect (understanding, *Verstand*).

The concept of good taste—and its role in economic policies—was also in fact a key element in Kaunitz's thinking about the importance of the fine arts and their contribution to society. Kaunitz had said: "Good taste . . . has an effect on manufacture and trades. It can bring into existence sections of the economy; it stimulates industry. A lot of money . . . which previously flowed out of the country remains inside it, and more and more money flows in from outside."[31] This clearly again seems to relate the concept of taste to physiocratic aims.

Winckelmann's essay moreover reveals that already at the time of writing he was familiar with aspects of the artistic scene in Vienna, about which he learned from prints and from Adam Oeser, who had trained at the Vienna academy. Winckelmann speaks well of Daniel Gran, whose ceiling painting that Maulbertsch was later to restore he praises (Figure 30), and also mentions other objects in Vienna. Conversely, the group around Kaunitz, which included several of Maulbertsch's patrons at the imperial court, were not only interested in economic theory and physiocratic doctrine, but also well versed in advanced aspects of Enlightenment thinking on the arts, including Winckelmann's ideas.

Sperges, Maulbertsch's patron at Innsbruck, was an admirer of Winckelmann and tried to have the German historian and theorist become the secretary of the newly founded Kupferstecherakademie, of which he was *Präses* and Kaunitz protector. It was for this reason that Winckelmann was invited to visit Vienna in 1768, when Sperges presented him to Maria Theresia. On this occasion Winckelmann was given some medallions: their theft on his way back to Rome led to his murder in Trieste, then also a city ruled by the Habsburgs. After Winckelmann's death, Sperges oversaw the publication of the second edition of Winckelmann's *Geschichte der Kunst des Altertums*, the first history of art of antiquity to call itself such, and a key work for the foundation of the discipline of art history. This work was being prepared for print in Vienna in the very year, 1776, that Sperges and Maulbertsch were involved with the Innsbruck frescoes.

Sperges had the new edition of *Geschichte der Kunst des Altertums* dedicated to Kaunitz.[32] This dedication was probably well chosen, because Kaunitz was more than protector of the Kupferstecherakademie; his support for the arts was not motivated solely by political reasons. He was a committed amateur, patron of the arts, and collector of paintings, whose collection included perhaps a sketch by Maulbertsch for Kroměříž that is still found in the castle in Slavkov, his residence.[33] Kaunitz had been a student at Leipzig of Johann Friedrich Christ, one of Winckelmann's predecessors in the formulation of a modern history of art, and other evidence, including the sponsorship of the edition of Winckelmann's *Geschichte der Kunst des Altertums*, indicates that Kaunitz was keenly interested in the history of art.[34]

With Winckelmann's departure, Sonnenfels became secretary of the academy. In addition to his official duties and work with Kaunitz, Sonnenfels was also interested in art theory and the importance of arts in society; his comments on allegory have already been quoted.[35] Eventually Anton von Maron, who had been Winckelmann's friend and portrayed him in Rome (Figure 40) became head of the academy, signifying its orientation toward Rome and the study of antiquity.[36]

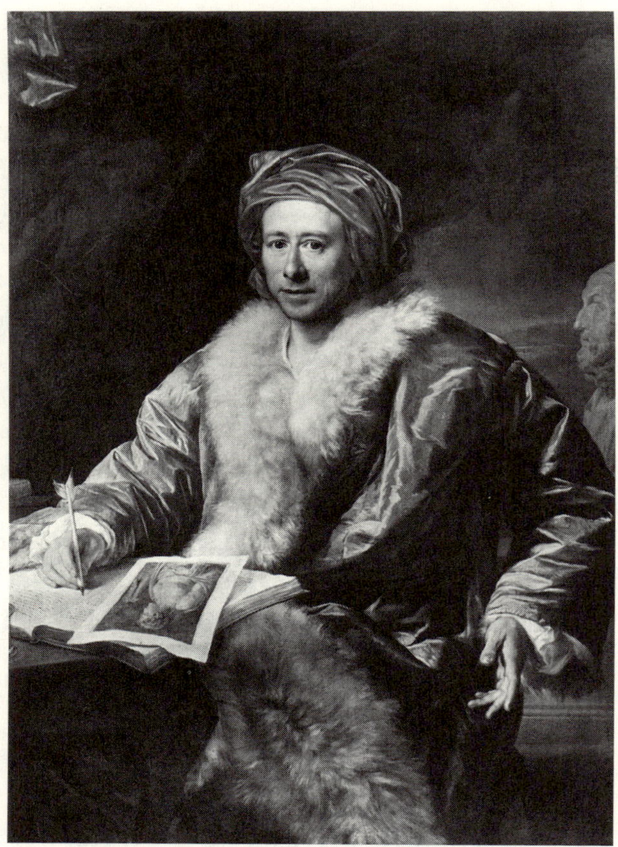

FIGURE 40. Anton von Maron, *Johann Jakob Winckelmann*, Stiftung Kunstsammlungen Weimar (Photograph: Bildarchiv Foto Marburg)

Through his involvement with the academy in Vienna, Maulbertsch no doubt had commerce with Sperges, Sonnenfels, and probably Kaunitz. Indeed, he celebrates them in his allegory on the granting of prizes by the academy (see Figure 28): this was a practice that Sperges had initiated. Through these men, and his connection with the academy he could have become familiar with art theory and criticism, including the thought of Winckelmann.

In Moravia (with which land Kaunitz and Sonnenfels were also associated) Maulbertsch was closely connected with another, lesser-known figure, who, however, also embodied Enlightenment interest in the arts. This is the sculptor Andreas Schweigel, mentioned at the beginning of this book. Schweigel emerged from the workshop of Joseph Winterhalder the Elder in the mid-1760s, just at the time (1764–48) that Winterhalder's like-named nephew was assisting Maulbertsch on projects in Moravia.[37] In 1766–67 Schweigel carved the sculpture on the altarpieces for which Maulbertsch painted the pictures at the Cistercian nunnery at Předklášteří u Tišnova, near Brno (Figure 41). Schweigel also worked at Královo Pole at the same time, 1765–72, that Maulbertsch executed his frescoes there. During the years 1777–79, Schweigel also executed some of the sculpture on the altarpieces in the Paulanerkirche at Vranov near Brno, while Maulbertsch (and his workshop) executed several altar paintings there. He also did the sculpture on the high altar of the parish church at Doubravnik, for which in 1784 Maulbertsch painted the altarpiece.[38] If Schweigel did not facilitate work for Maulbertsch in Moravia, he certainly worked closely with the painter: this is evident at Královo Pole, where the style of his angels closely resembles those of Maulbertsch.[39] Most important, Schweigel was responsible for compiling the first history of art in Moravia: this is one of the first histories of art to conceive of itself as such in Europe as a whole, and has been quoted at the beginning of this book.[40] In his history Schweigel makes important comments about Maulbertsch, to be discussed further in the next chapter.

Maulbertsch could also have become familiar with discussions of art in Saxony. In 1770 Maulbertsch went there to paint the Benno Chapel of the Catholic Hofkirche in Dresden. Dresden had of course been the place where Winckelmann had worked before going to Rome, its collections having inspired in part his essay, *Gedanken über die Nachahmung*, which celebrates them. Dresden remained a major site for Enlightenment discourse on the arts through the 1750s and 1760s. Christian Ludwig von Hagedorn, the author of *Lettre à un amateur de la peinture*[41] of 1755 and the *Betrachtungen über die Mahlerey* of 1762, and C. H. von Heinecken, who published, among other books, his *Nachrichten von Künstlern und Kunstsachen* in Leipzig in 1768, were working in Dresden at the time of Maulbertsch's visit; the thrust of some of their ideas will be discussed further in Chapter 4. It is moot whether or not they were responsible for Maulbertsch's call to Dresden, or if his work already anticipated what they said and was already familiar in Saxony.[42] Maulbertsch could even have had personal contact with these writers.

In any case, writings on art criticism, art theory, and art history are features of the expanding discourse on painting of the eighteenth century. The publication of treatises on these subjects belonged to a flood of writing on the arts. New periodicals on the arts, the so-called *Kunstzeitungen*, appeared at this time. Increasing attention was also given to the figurative arts in newspapers.[43]

The modernizing process of the Danube monarchy also placed importance on the written word; the Habsburgs' reform projects relied heavily on publica-

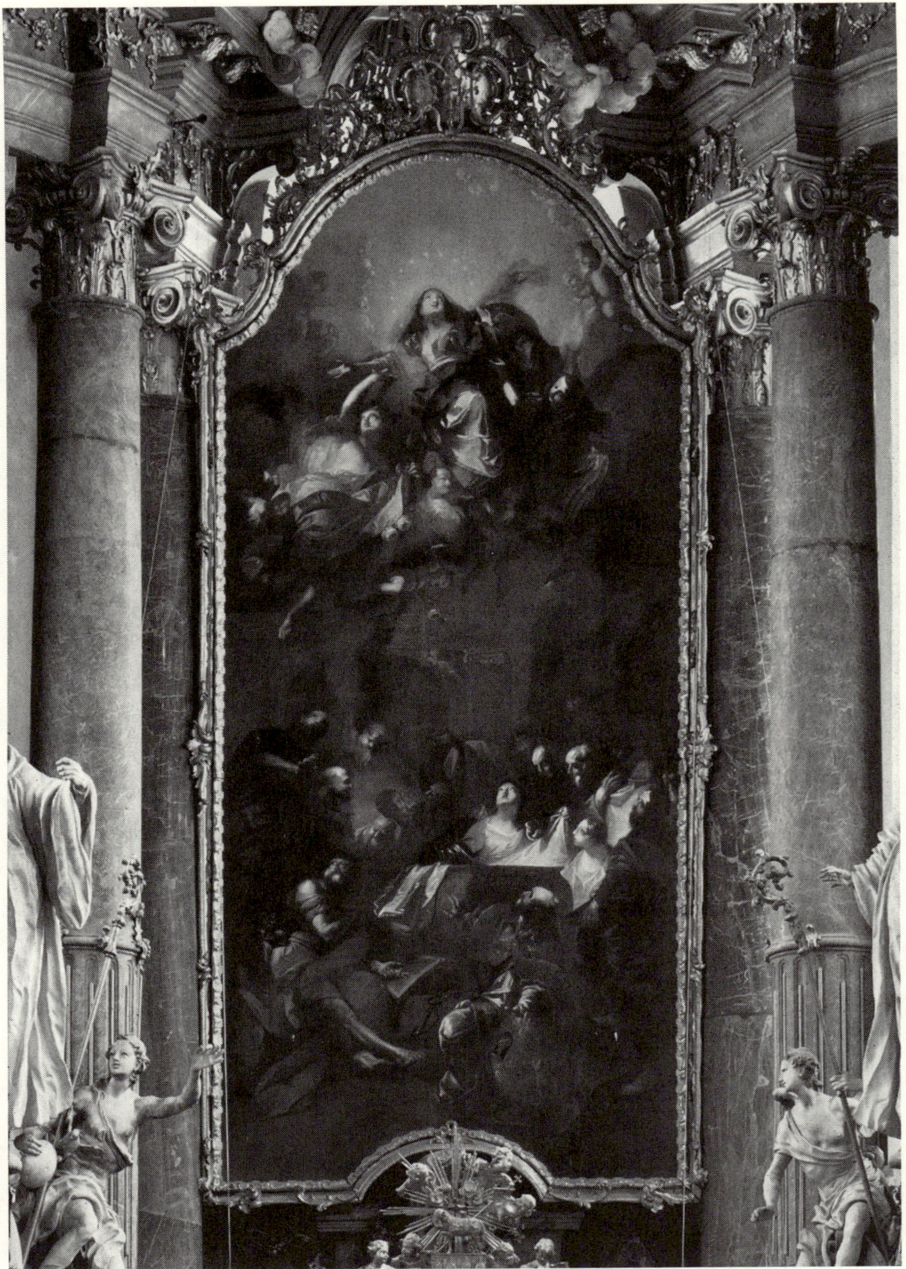

FIGURE 41. F. A. Maulbertsch and Andreas Schweigel, Altarpiece with Assumption of the Virgin, high altar, 1766–67, Cistercian Church, Předklášteří u Tišnova (Photograph: The National Institute for the Protection and Conservation of Monuments and Sites Regional Unit at Brno; courtesy Bishopric of Brno)

tions.[44] Hence while the Enlightenment may in general have arrived late in the Habsburg lands, the production of various genres of *Kunstliteratur* in fact occurred in Vienna more or less simultaneously with the transformation that is notable in Maulbertsch's art, and not much later than such literature on art did elsewhere. Brochures explaining Maulbertsch's frescoes were produced from the 1760s onward, and the first notices of Maulbertsch's art in newspapers and journals also appeared at just about the same time, toward 1770, as the change in his style emerged.

These publications constitute part of the transformation of the public sphere that enlarged the audiences for the visual arts, and the vehicles through which the expanded public, notably the bourgeoisie, could become familiar with it.[45] Two of the classic loci for this change are the coffeehouse, a Viennese institution par excellence, and the salon, including that for art; we may recall that Maulbertsch exhibited his allegory on Joseph II at the salon of 1777. The creation of new institutions also provided a newer environment for the transformation in the public sphere; we may even regard the academy as one of them. The academy housed public exhibitions that evoked critical responses, as was the case with the reaction to a work displayed by Maulbertsch at one such show in 1786. In any event, it has been said that at least by circa 1785 an "active, reasoning, critical public opinion" had already come into existence in Vienna and that it had created its "organs" in "brochures, periodicals, reading cabinets, coffeehouses, salons, and . . . masonic lodges."[46]

While it is possible, it is not necessary to argue that Maulbertsch's art directly reflects or responds to his knowledge of the theory or criticism of the Enlightenment. Such sources may have affected his art in a mediated fashion, through the effect on public opinion, as well as on the changed taste of his patrons. These institutions and ideas provide the social and intellectual context in which Maulbertsch worked, and in which his painting would have been received in any instance.

Some of the first published comments on Maulbertsch do indicate that newer conceptions of art were being applied to his painting just at the time that the first signs of major changes in his style can also be observed. The *Bibliothek der schönen Wissenschaften und der freyen Künste* of 1769 describes Maulbertsch's allegory on Maria Theresia (Figure 31) in the following terms: "The composition is noble and drawn with understanding [or the intellect]" (*Die composition ist edel und mit Verstand gezeichnet*).[47] This echoes the "*edle Einfalt und stille Grösse*" of Winckelmann and that critic's call for *Verstand* in art. It shows that Maulbertsch was already being pulled into the context of a criticism that was formed by Winckelmann, who had just died.

The next printed reactions to Maulbertsch's work comment on the allegory on art that was his *Aufnahmestück* (*morceau de réception*) for admission to the Kupferstecherakademie in 1770 (Figure 27). Among the other critical notions they employ, these provide further evidence that Winckelmann's texts had become broadly known. The *Wienerisches Diarium* speaks of Maulbertsch's poetic and painterly invention and composition (*Erfindung und Anordung*), and says that the poetic composition (*dichterische Zusammensetzung*) of his work is brought about without a garish (*schreyend*) contrast of colors—though this last characteristic, as shall be discussed in Chapter 4, is not necessarily a sign of classicist taste.[48] The *Kunstzeitung* of the Augsburg academy specifically refers to Maulbertsch's poetic fantasy, but couples it with his skill in drawing: these are necessary for allegory. Significantly, the review remarks that Winckelmann's book on allegory is too well known to need to be cited.[49] This also directly attests to the general assimilation of Winckelmann's theory within a very short time after its publication.

Other early critiques of Maulbertsch were generally positive. The earliest survey of the painter's activity, published in the *Allergnädigst privilegierte Anzeigen* of September 1771, praised "his rich source of invention, his ease in execution, his ability to order objects, to render each its due expression, and other techniques with which he knows how to enliven his works, [which] have created for him a mass of jobs."[50] These qualities were also acknowledged in 1775 in a report in the *Frankfurter gelehrte Anzeigen* that provided the basis for several subsequent accounts of Maulbertsch. There it is said that Maulbertsch's thought and composition were great; spirit and fire ruled in his composition; he controlled light and shadow, and gave his works a beautiful coloring.[51]

While Maulbertsch's monochromatic, carefully rendered allegory could be acceptable to criticism informed by Winckelmann, other comments indicate that his art did not in general correspond to that critic's demands. This realization is implicit even in earlier, positive accounts, such as the comment made in the report in the *Frankfurter gelehrte Anzeigen*, where it is noted that "connoisseurs" (*Kenner*) criticized Maulbertsch's "incorrect drawing and diffuse draperies" (*unrichtige Zeichnung und allzuweitschweifige Gewände*)—the latter referring also to draperies that do not cling to and reveal the body.[52] Maulbertsch's draftsmanship was to become a recurring target of criticism.

This critique announces the advent of a newer aesthetic sensibility. Whereas earlier Maulbertsch's artistic fire, his fast-moving brush, might have been in favor, now something more was being demanded. The earlier attitude may be suggested by a remark made in 1768 by Empress Maria Theresia, who complained to the court painter Gregorio Guglielmi that there were not painters around who could work quickly.[53] Instead of this ability, a trait necessary of course for fresco painters, Winckelmann was calling for a more deliberate approach, for a brush that had been "dipped in intellect" (*gedünkt in Verstand*). He also explicitly decried *franchezza*, or what may be defined as the free application of paint, associated with the expression of the painter's fantasy. This quality has also been identified with Maulbertsch's art, and it may be related to what critics described as his fire, or what we have called the fireworks of his art.[54]

The account of a journey to Austria taken in 1776 by the Moravian history painter and architect Ignaz Chambrez shows that the tide was indeed beginning to turn against Maulbertsch. Chambrez described a painting he saw of a St. Florian on the outside of a house in St. Pölten that recalled Don Quixote to him. (See Figure 42 for a related type.) He applied to this description some lines that he tellingly misremembered from Horace: the ability to make things ought to be artful but not immoderate (*Fingendi potestas debet esse artificiosa non etiam immoderata*).[55] This misquotation suggests that by 1776 the power of the imagination, of fantasy, had to be moderated. Henceforth, even though Maulbertsch's work is occasionally mentioned favorably in Viennese publications (for instance, a no longer extant fresco that served for the high altar in the Augustinian Church in Vienna), from the mid-1770s onward Maulbertsch did not frequently receive critical attention.[56] This may be a sign of a decline in the esteem with which he was held, which is also indicated by the fact that after his work for Innsbruck of 1775–76 he rarely received imperial commissions. Although, as suggested in Chapter 2, there may be other reasons why imperial patronage of Maulbertsch dropped off, in any event opportunities for the painter to work in and around Vienna decreased. Instead, he came to be more in demand in provincial Hungary, and the works he did there were only occasionally noticed in Vienna: one journal does describe the frescoes at Pápa as "glorious" (*herrlich*).[57]

Although Maulbertsch did receive some distinctions during his later career, even the positive reactions to his work are not unambiguous. He was admitted to the Berlin academy, and exhibited there, but the Berlin painter (and academician) Daniel Nikolaus Chodowiecki, while speaking of him as a genius, seems to have meant this remark ironically. While Chodowiecki could comment favorably on his invention, composition, and Venetian coloring (a significant detail, as we shall see), he also said that Maulbertsch had absolutely no "finish" (or "execution"; *gar keine Ausführung*).[58]

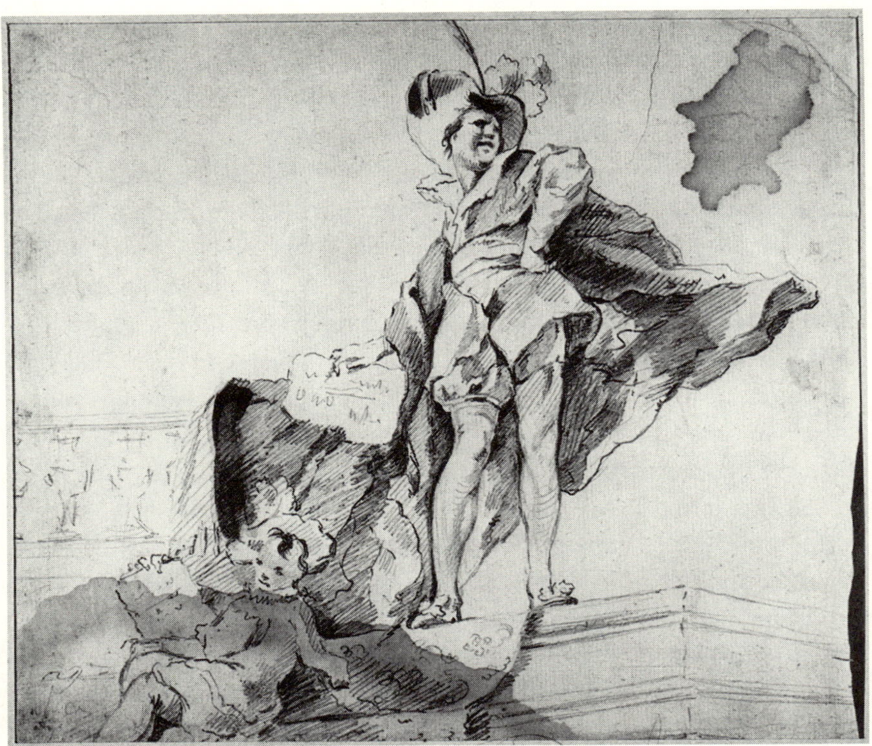

FIGURE 42. F. A. Maulbertsch, *A Cavalier*, black chalk drawing, 1750s, Szépművészeti Múzeum, Budapest (Photograph: Szépművészeti Múzeum, Budapest)

By the later 1780s even Maulbertsch's use of color had come under attack. A commentary on a picture of a satyr and a nymph that Maulbertsch exhibited at the academy in 1786 spoke mockingly of its color. It described the work as a "velvet green" little picture, which, because of its spoiled tones (*des Abstehen halber*), "could be copied on a flea-colored coach."[59]

The way had been prepared for the critique of Füßli, which was published some fifteen years later. While acknowledging some of Maulbertsch's merits, Füßli saw them and those of his contemporaries as having been wasted in merely splendid and decorative works (*Zierwerken*) that aimed at a strong effect for the whole and left the viewer confused with symbolic and mystical allusions. The true connoisseur demanded "more than the pleasure of the eye" (*mehr als optisches Vergnügen*).[60] The tide of criticism had ended in a negative judgment of Maulbertsch: he had become an original strangeling, an artist not appropriate for leadership at the academy, a fresco painter who had not been able to restore history painting.

It is important to consider this critical trend because it helps to situate the attitudes and aspirations of Maulbertsch's patrons, who did concern themselves with questions of taste. Their interest is most evident in their choice of ornament, hence of stylistic details. Contracts for Maulbertsch's frescoes specify the type of ornament that he was to use, and thus they provide a direct reason for the change from earlier sorts of decoration. On the one hand the contract signed on 6 January 1763 for the chapel of the residence of Count Antal (Anton) Erdődy in Trenčianské Bohuslavice (Plate 24) specified that the painter was to depict the architectural elements (the contract uses the curious word *Metopen*, probably referring to cartouches or brackets) *auf die moderne Art*, that is, in the manner then current, what we would call the rococo, that is seen in the paintings as executed.[61] In contrast, the contract for the Innsbruck frescoes drawn up in 1775 stipulated that he was to paint the room with "antique decorations" (*Zierraten*).[62] (See Figures 32 and 35.)

This taste for the antique was shared by the artist's patrons among the clergy. In fact, patrons who commissioned later works specifically called for this type of ornament including, significantly, in the case of Pápa. In a letter to Bishop Eszterházy of 9 March 1782 Maulbertsch says that he is sending a sketch and drawing for the "architectural decoration" (*Architectur Verziehrung*) for the ceiling of the church, indicating that it is being done with *Antic-Verzierung*, antique-style ornament.[63] This would have been what Eszterházy, and Maulbertsch himself, would also have thought of as the "Roman" style. The contract Maulbertsch signed on 25 September 1792 to fresco the chapel of the Lyceum in Eger, Hungary, also specified that the decorations (*Verzierungen*) were to be an antique vase (*Anticc [sic] Wase*), a garland with gold rosettes between the pilasters under the cornice (*Und zwischen der mitt einer Golt Rosen und zirlanten gehänge*), with other garlands with rose fillings, and some "antique-style foliage" (*antic Lauber*) above and below the windows.[64] At Szombathely antique references and ornament also appear in the hall painted in the early 1780s by Maulbertsch in the residence of Bishop János Szily, for whom the architect Melchior Hefele had designed buildings in the new "Roman" style or *Zopfstil*, like those of Fellner. It can be assumed that the paintings, like the buildings, met with the approval of the patron, who had studied in Rome in the time of nascent mania for antiquity.[65]

The choice of the antique also went along with an increased historical or archaeological sense of what was fitting. For example, the references in the episcopal palace at Szombathely were appropriate to the stories connected with the ancient *oppidum* of Savaria, the site of Szombathely, that were represented by the painter. In his correspondence Bishop Szily also offered corrections of historical details in a sketch Maulbertsch sent him for an altarpiece to be placed in the newly constructed cathedral there.[66] The program for the frescoes in Pápa also stipulated that Maulbertsch was to make his frescoes according to sketches and copies taken from objects in Rome, where indeed Bishop Eszterházy had also studied.[67]

Eszterházy added that Maulbertsch was to avoid anything that was shocking or horrible (*schräckend oder schauerlich*). The architecture in the frescoes at Pápa was to be painted not in the traditional manner *di sotto in su*, but in profile. The protagonist of the action (the angelic form of St. Stephen) should stand out. As Andor Pigler first recognized, the tradition of "baroque" illusionism was thus abandoned in favor of a form of representation that would more resemble easel painting.[68] Along with the demands of history, and of taste for the "Roman" or antique style, those of rationality were thus to be heeded in painting.

In addition to the change in public taste, and patrons' demands, Maulbertsch may have had his own reasons for altering his style. A comment made by the historian and lexicographer G. J. Dlabacz, who probably knew Maulbertsch in his last years in Prague, since he probably drew up the description of his frescoes in the library of the Premonstratensian monastery at Strahov, may be so interpreted. Dlabacz states that Maulbertsch admitted that still in advanced age he studied the mistakes he had made in his first frescoes in the Piarist church in Vienna, a landmark of his earliest career (Figure 43). While this passage has been interpreted as meaning that the painter wanted to improve on the mistakes he had made in technique, there is no reason to believe that his mural technique was particularly deficient, especially in his mature period, or that in any case he would have had cause to study his earlier fresco to learn how to improve his technique.[69] On the other hand, in the changed critical context, when classicizing art was increasingly in vogue, especially in the 1790s when Dlabacz could have known him, Maulbertsch may well have had other reasons, chiefly out of a concern with style, for reconsidering what he had painted at an earlier stage in his career.

Other comments Maulbertsch made in correspondence connected with the completion of his painting at Pápa suggest that the transformation seen there from the style represented by the works of his earlier years resulted at least in part from the artist's own adoption of newer aesthetic ideals. In a letter of 24 July 1782 to Eszterházy, Maulbertsch wrote not only that he had followed the prelate's prescriptions as far as possible, but also that he had taken what was useful from Roman drawings. The bishop had previously ordered copies of paintings in the Roman church of Santo Stefano Rotondo as a guide, and presumably there were also available other drawings of Roman exempla that could be sent to the

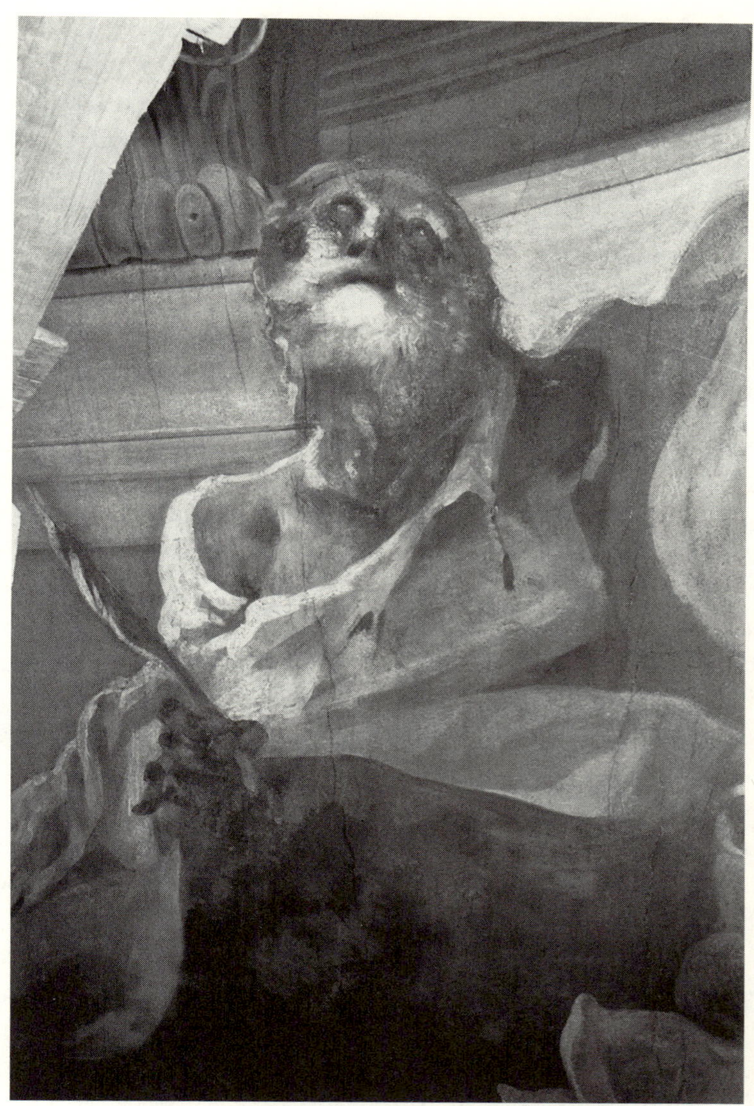

FIGURE 43. F. A. Maulbertsch, St. *Mark*, presbytery ceiling detail, 1752, Piarist Church of Maria Treu, Vienna (Photograph: Eduard Beranek)

painter to serve him as guides.[70] Maulbertsch's letter confirms that he conformed to the desire for historical accuracy. He says he has preserved the sanctity, the quiet order, the characteristic clothing, and the effective meaning of the history (*ich habe nach aller meglichkeit deren Hl. Vorschriften gefolget, auch das Daugliche aus der Remischen Zeichnung bei behalten die heilligkeit, die stille ordnung, das Kenliche in der*

Kleidung, und Wirckhsame Bedeittung der Historie). Another key phrase is apparent here: the reference to *stille ordnung*. It has long been recognized that this echoes Winckelmannian language. Similarly, in a letter of 12 April 1783 Maulbertsch reports that he has made the composition of the painting for the sanctuary at Pápa according to historical accuracy and Roman taste (*Die Composicion ist der Historie gemes, Und nach Remischen gue eingerichtet . . .*).[71]

Like the comments of his patrons, the evidence of contracts, and their echoes in contemporary critiques, Maulbertsch's reference to his adaptation of Roman taste certainly seems to support the thesis that the transformation in his style can be situated in relation to the eighteenth-century discourse on the visual arts. In the end, then, there does seem to be much merit in the arguments of those art historians who have tried to relate Maulbertsch's style to the changes in eighteenth-century aesthetics associated with the dominant personality of Winckelmann and thus with the growing taste for the antique. The features seen at Pápa can in many ways be associated with these changes.

However, Maulbertsch's notion of Roman taste, or the taste for the antique, did not fully realize the possibilities for a new art inspired by the classical, even as far as it could be envisioned in the eighteenth century. Maulbertsch's painting lacks directly classical sources for its forms, among other things. Matsche is thus correct when he says that Maulbertsch cannot be considered a fully classicist painter.

An important distinction exists between the style of Maulbertsch's later works, even those with classical references, and what is considered the neoclassicism of a German contemporary like Anton Raphael Mengs, not to mention the work of other artists such as Jacques-Louis David that was already being produced during the last years of Maulbertsch's life. More specifically, the later work of Maulbertsch is only loosely comparable to the painting of the younger generation of Viennese academicians active during the late eighteenth century, yet these are the artists who have been considered in the most recent scholarship as exemplary of Viennese classicism circa 1800. Unlike artists such as Anton von Maron (Figure 40), Heinrich Friedrich Füger (Figure 44), or Hubert Maurer, another artist active at Pápa but whose application to study with Maulbertsch had earlier been rejected, Maulbertsch did not study in Rome with the support of a fellowship of the sort that had been recently established by the Viennese academy. He did not respond to the example of Poussin or other similar painters, nor did he incorporate elements of classical art into his work, even when his subjects were explicitly antique.[72] Unlike Anton Raphael Mengs, Maulbertsch also did not compose any aesthetic or theoretical treatises.

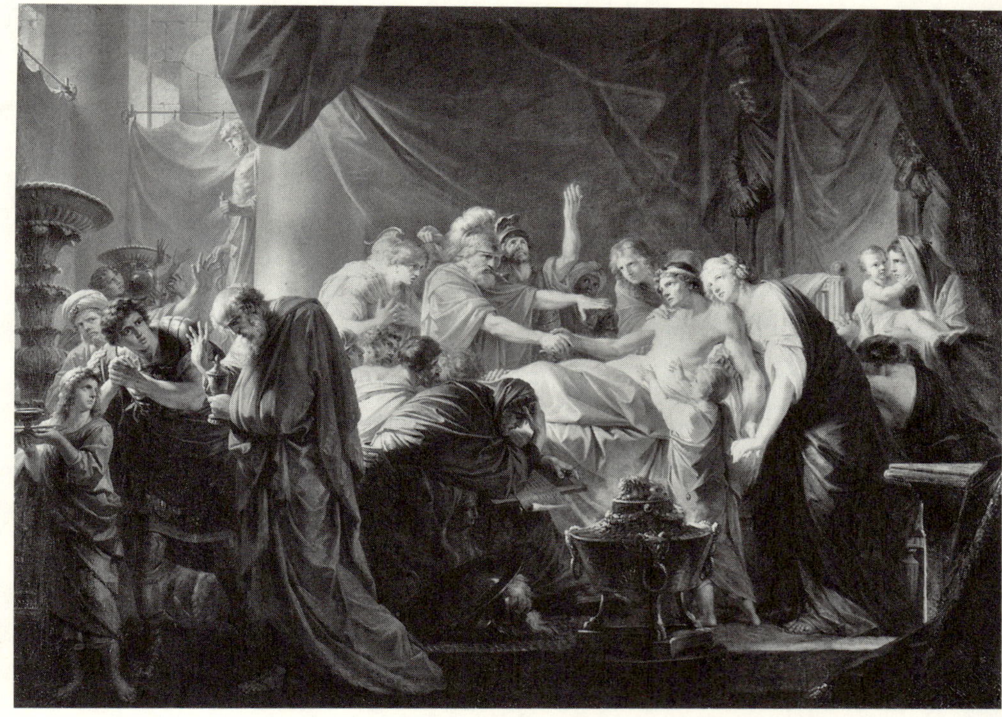

FIGURE 44. Heinrich Friedrich Füger, *Death of Germanicus*, oil on canvas, 1795, Akademie der bildenden Künste, Vienna (Photograph: Gemäldegalerie der Akademie der bildenden Künste, Vienna)

Other artistic problems remain unresolved in his later paintings. Much as Maulbertsch's allegories do not represent a completely successful solution to the problems of communication aired by Enlightenment critiques, in terms of their failure to resolve completely often incompatible political, religious, or pedagogical concepts, so does the perspective of his frescoes at Pápa represent an awkward compromise between the conventions of ceiling painting as they had evolved since the seventeenth century and those of easel painting. His work at Pápa remains hard to read, as has been observed.[73] His efforts to depict narrative in a convincing fashion thus were not entirely successfully negotiated.

These problems do not, however, exhaust the possibilities for associating Maulbertsch's painting with aspects of Enlightenment thought on the arts. Winckelmann has loomed large in this chapter, but it is wrong to associate the Enlightenment exclusively with neoclassicism (or the antique or Roman style) and with Winckelmann.[74] Stylistic plurality reigned in the eighteenth century, and Enlightenment ideals could be communicated in many different styles. It is moreover arguable that any single style was created in the eighteenth century, including that of Mengs, that completely expressed Winckelmann's ideals.

It should not be forgotten that Enlightenment thinkers promoted, and debated, many other aesthetic concepts and ideals in addition to those Winckelmann championed. These notions often run counter to the precepts of line, order, quiet, and the antique that are associated with Winckelmann. Like many other Enlightenment notions, including Winckelmann's own demands, these ideals may not have been completely realized in art during the course of the eighteenth century. Yet they can be directly associated with other significant features of Maulbertsch's art, those moreover that many critics since his time have emphasized: his coloring and handling.

In this regard, it should also be recalled that much as he had spoken out against freedom of handling, Winckelmann had argued that "color . . . should have but little share in our consideration of beauty, because the essence of beauty consists, not in color, but in shape, and on this point enlightened minds will at once agree . . . beauty is also different from pleasingness or loveliness."[75]

Yet, in enunciating this argument, Winckelmann seems here to be countering another point of view that will be discussed presently. In this respect too, his was not the only voice in the Enlightenment discourse on the arts: both handling and coloring also had their advocates. They spoke for another conception of art, for the province of painterly Enlightenment.

FOUR

On the Margins of Modernism

Maulbertsch's coloring has long been a major theme in discussion of his art. Among Central European artists who might seem notable for their treatment of color, Maulbertsch has gained recognition for this specific quality. The most sustained modern commentary on the question of *Colorit* in eighteenth-century Austrian painting has been offered in reference to Maulbertsch by Ivo Krsek. Krsek has observed radical changes of hue appearing within concentrated areas in the fresco Maulbertsch painted in 1759 on the ceiling of the *Lehensaal* in the residence of the bishop of Olomouc at Kroměříž (Plate 25 and Figure 45). Here Maulbertsch displays a predilection for varieties of shot fabrics, *couleur changeant* modeling, and broken areas of color in fabrics or fields of paint. For Krsek such qualities demonstrate an "abstract play of colors." Though subordinated to "the organic breath of light," they reveal Maulbertsch's joy in color for its own sake.[1] Although Krsek's is but one reading of a complex series of phenomena, many other art historians have shared the opinion that Maulbertsch's painting is expressive and subjective, since in his work color and the free application of paint seem to take precedence over accurate draftsmanship. Hence Maulbertsch's painting has frequently been compared to later artistic styles.[2]

However, this sort of treatment of Maulbertsch's coloring (and handling) does not situate the painter in his own time, nor does it correspond to the way that these issues were understood by the artist's contemporaries, not to mention the artist himself. What has been said in regard to a similar problem of dealing with "the purposive use of color" in Tiepolo also applies to Maulbertsch: "It is prudent to check that one is covering with one's own concepts the categorization normal

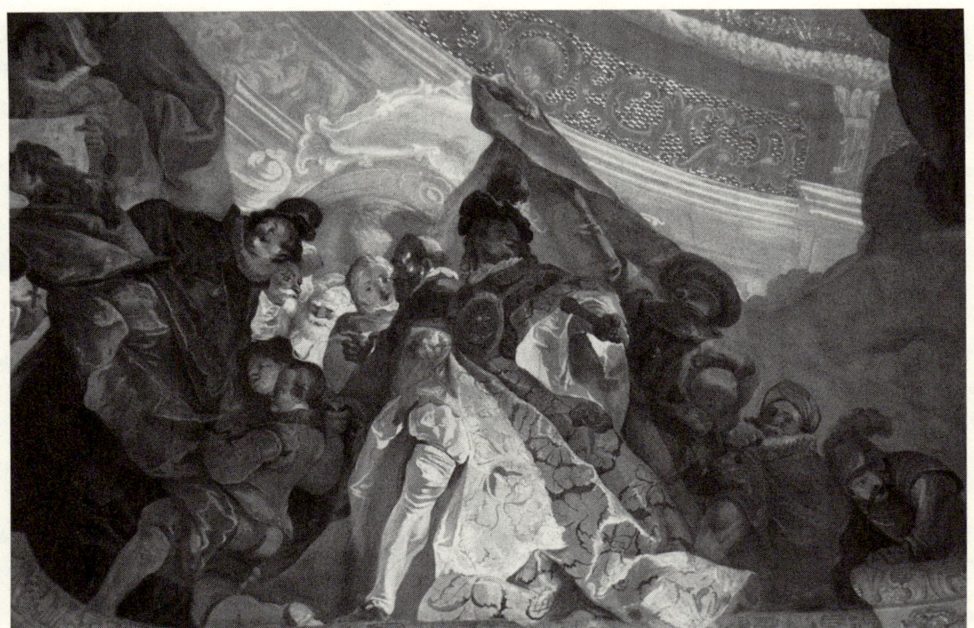

FIGURE 45. F. A. Maulbertsch, detail in Feudal Room (*Lehensaal*), 1759, Palace of Bishop of Olomouc, Kroměříž (Kremsier), Moravia, Czech Republic (Photograph: Brno University, courtesy Bishopric of Brno)

to his pictorial culture."[3] An interpretation of Maulbertsch's coloring can only be given a historical foundation, and the particular or supposedly personal qualities of his art can only be accurately judged, in reference to eighteenth-century practice and theory.

This chapter will therefore examine facets of coloring in Maulbertsch's paintings in regard to texts that express the demands of his patrons, the artist's own opinions, and the critical response to his work. These reveal several hitherto largely unexamined points of view that lead to different sorts of observations concerning Maulbertsch's paintings. Other categorizations result, relating his work to some central issues in eighteenth-century theory and practice, in which coloring was a central theme, and moreover resonate in artistic concerns that have continued to the present.

First of all, details of execution, ornament, and most notably color were clearly important to Maulbertsch's patrons. Such details are frequently stipulated in contracts: for example, that signed by Maulbertsch with Count Anton Erdődy on 6 January 1763 to paint frescoes in the chapel of the count's summer residence at Trenčianské Bohuslavice (Bohuszlavicz, Hungarian Bogoszló, now in Slovakia; Plates 24, 26–28). Like many other contracts of the early modern era, this agreement lays out a number of conditions, several of which determine the subjects that are to be painted. What is significant, however, is that four of the seven terms of the contract do not deal with subject matter, but with elements of ornament and coloring. The first condition, already cited in the previous chapter, prescribes painting the socles and all the fascias (*Gürteln*) in fresco with architectonic forms (called *Metopen*) with gold highlights *auf die moderne Art*: as the paintings reveal, this means using what can be described as rococo forms of decoration (c- and s-curves, cartouches, and the like). The second, referring to the fields that surround the subjects listed, says that they are to be decorated with ornament, with their flowers painted after nature (*nach der Natur*), and that especially the back wall above the oratory is to be decorated most beautifully. The sixth term states that the two smallest cupolas in the chapel are to be painted with architectural surrounds heightened with gold, while inside these frames two tasteful groups of putti are to be shown with their tender flesh painted as if touched by lilies and roses. Finally, "a lovely [*lieblich*] and bright [*hell*] little color" is to be laid onto the walls in the whole church, in the spaces located between the fictive architectural elements, in order to make them distinct.[4]

The combination of interest in ornament and in color is noteworthy. So too is the idea that Maulbertsch was to paint something that was regarded as done according to nature. The phrase *nach der Natur* used in the contract may be related to a long history of discussion of painting after nature, or life (*nach dem Leben*).[5] This is a significant requirement because the demand that Maulbertsch copy nature contradicts the thesis that he could simply express his own fantasy in the execution of details in his art. The reference to flowers being done raises the issue of their color, not solely because it is easy to speculate that accurate rendering of color would have contributed to making them appear natural. An important argument in eighteenth-century literature on the arts held, as we shall see, that it was the quality of color that made things look natural. Maulbertsch wittily realized how the fantastic could be turned into the natural, how an interest in ornament conjoins here with one in color: the rococo ornament with c- and s-curves around his central fresco of the Assumption of the Virgin frequently metamorphose into plantlike forms, like reeds, that are then merged into the ground on which the apostles are standing (Plate 26).

The term *lieblich* in reference to color also reappears elsewhere in documents related to Maulbertsch. The contract for the Eger Lyceum drawn up in 1792 states that everything is to be done *lieblichs Colirt*, to be given a most lovely coloring

(Plate 15). The use of these two terms in tandem suggests that coloring could, however, be considered independent of those other elements of form and ornament that are also indicated in the contract for the Eger Lyceum. As suggested in Chapter 3, discussion of the frescoes called for "antique" ornament. The forms of the figures in the painting may also be considered to be more constrained, in keeping with the "classicist style" of the last years of the artist's career. However, the treatment of coloring was conceived of in the same way as was that of Trenčianské Bohuslavice. Although the individual colors in the two works are not close—pastel, bright tones in the one, cooler tones at Eger—the terms used in the contracts are nevertheless the same. In order to understand how the term *colirt* (or *colorirt*) can make sense in these two seemingly disparate instances, it must be construed as meaning that coloring is not understood as being the same as the individual colors selected. Indeed, seventeenth- and eighteenth-century discussions of the subject stated as much: coloring is to be handled separately from the discussion of individual colors. For Maulbertsch and his patrons, as for other contemporary authorities on the subject, the choice of pigments on a palette was not the equivalent of the way the various elements of the palette were to be painted together.

The references to *lieblich* and *hell*, lovely and bright, may be taken rather as referring to qualities of hue and tone. Observation of the surviving frescoes at Trenčianske Bohuslavice with these terms in mind suggests that they are to be read in this manner. Gilding sets off the bands delimiting the areas in which figures have been painted, and also the separate fields delineated by the architectural articulation of the church. Flowers are painted in a naturalistic manner, and they are reminiscent of roses or lilies. The putti do have pink and white tones recalling these flowers in their flesh (Plate 27). They and the other scenes with figures, such as the *Assumption of the Virgin* in the central field of the chapel ceiling, are placed in relief by the presence of surrounding areas of color on the walls, which is done in what can indeed be called bright coloring. The walls and ceiling are painted a bright, light green that could merit being called *lieblich*. The paint is dragged down the sides and back of the church, conjoining all the surfaces with similar pigmentation. The coloration of the fields on the walls and ceiling in yellow-green tones do make them distinct from the areas of color with pinks and yellows that predominate elsewhere, as the contract demanded (Plate 28).

The coloring of many works by Maulbertsch may be characterized similarly. Throughout his career the painter seems to have given each set of frescoes a distinctive color scheme. Hence the term "coloring" applies better to the overall effect, rather than to the impression made by the effect of individual colors within a work. This quality is especially evident in places where Maulbertsch, even when he may have had workshop assistance, painted all of the available surfaces of an interior, which one finds to be conspicuously the case at Sümeg. (See Figure 2 and Plates 19–21.) Maulbertsch painted the entire church, including the fictive altarpieces, in 1757–58: grayish pink and green tones may be discerned throughout the entire ensemble.

This sort of color effect is particularly apparent in works painted at the beginning of Maulbertsch's independent career as a mural painter, for instance in the Piarist church in Vienna in 1752–53. Even though a specialist in architectural painting may also have been involved in frescoing the church, one overall scheme of decoration seems to be in operation: documentation suggests that this was due to Maulbertsch's conception, since his work on the ceiling of the presbytery was approved, while that of the architectural specialist was in fact rejected (Plate 29).[6] In any event, not only the ceilings, on which Maulbertsch is documented to have worked, but also the walls are done in a similar color scheme. While individual figures stand out in the scenes of the Assumption and glorification of the Virgin on the central cupola, in that of the evangelists and the Virgin in the presbytery, and in the scenes in the side chapels, the background architectural ornament of the whole is given a light gray effect, that sets off the ocher, pink, and blue tones found in the figural depictions.

Though less well known than Sümeg or the Piarist church in Vienna, perhaps because of its location and because of the ruinous state of the Schloss itself, the well-preserved chapel of Schloss Suttner at Ebenfurth was also completely frescoed by Maulbertsch in 1754. It was probably painted largely by the artist himself, to judge from the free-hand incisions, pentimenti, and impasto found even in areas of ornament. Although only the ceiling of the Ebenfurth chapel is usually mentioned in the literature on the artist, not just it but also the walls have been painted in similar hues and tones. The walls are adorned with fictive sculpture, vases, and busts (Figure 46). The color scheme found in the ceiling is the same used throughout the chapel. Framed panels are given shades of rose pink, lavender, and soft green, with bluish casts in the ornament. The fictive sculptures, both that shown as if in the round and that shown as if in relief, are painted in tones of green heightened with white. The scheme of lighting shown in the fresco is keyed to the windows: while the busts and statues are done in greenish tones, the shadows cast by them are mauve (Plate 30). The same set of greenish, mauve, pink, lavender, and soft green tones is seen in the clouds, sky, and figures in the depiction of the glorification of St. Leopold painted on the ceiling (Figure 10).

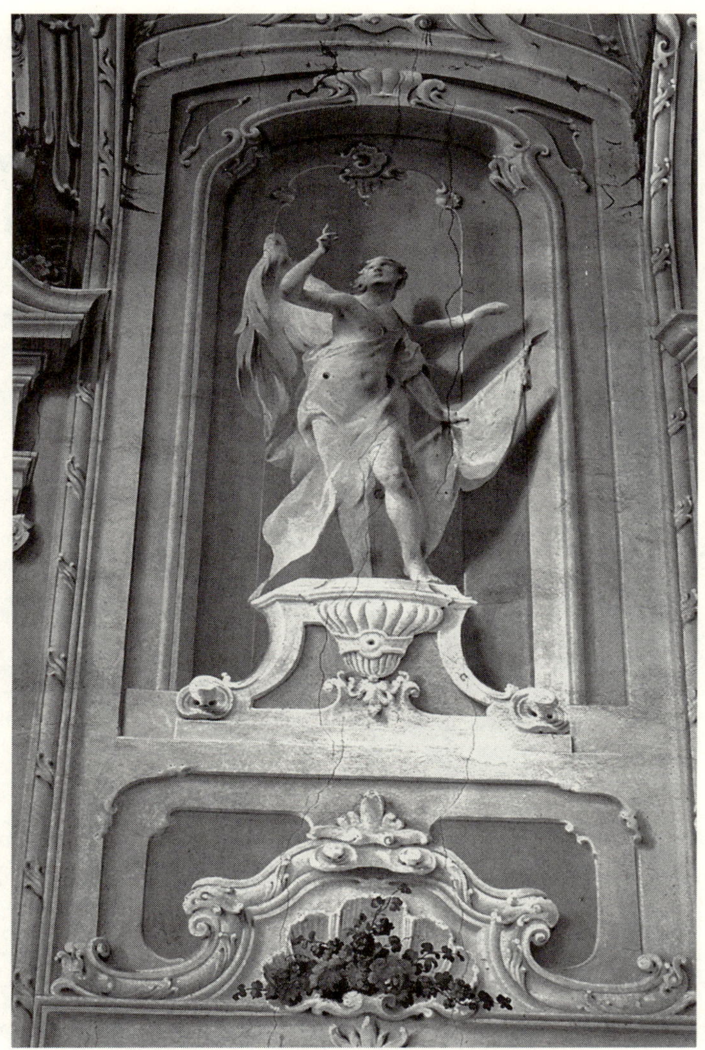

FIGURE 46. F. A. Maulbertsch, detail on chapel wall, 1754, Schloss Suttner, Ebenfurth (Photograph: Eduard Beranek)

Similar color schemes are found in Maulbertsch's painting of the later 1750s and 1760s. In 1757 the pilgrimage church at Heiligenkreuz-Gutenbrunn received an apple-green and lavender coloration (Plate 31). The gold highlights on the architectural ornament are like those stipulated for Trenčianské Bohuslavice. This detail is also specified in other contracts with Maulbertsch, such as that for Kroměříž, signed in 1759, which determined that he was to paint highlights in gold

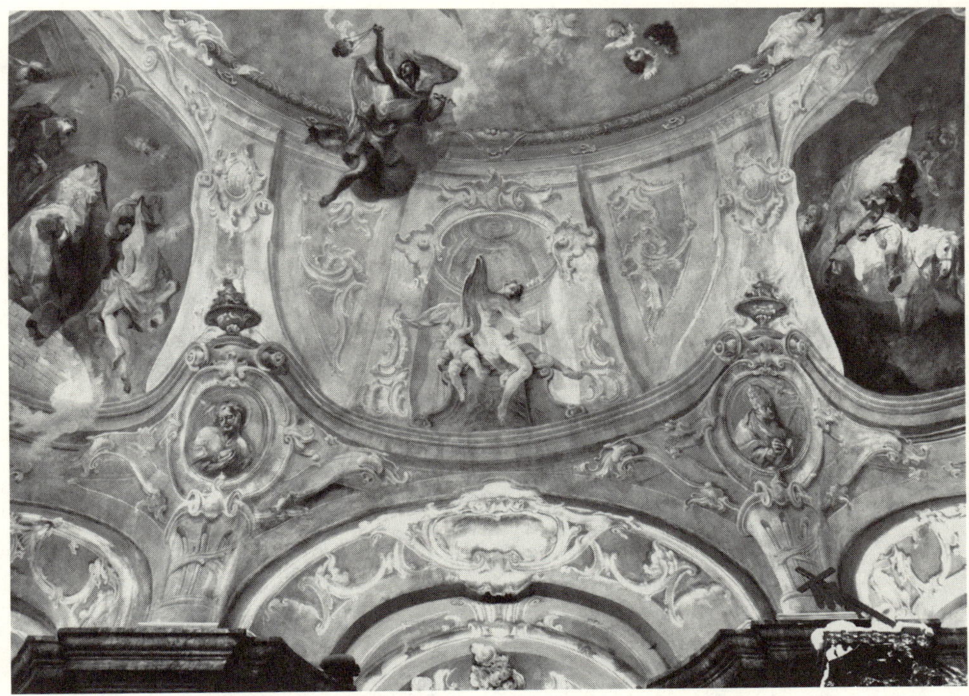

FIGURE 47. F. A. Maulbertsch, detail of ceiling paintings, 1759, former Piarist Church, Mikulov, Czech Republic (Photograph: Brno University, courtesy Bishopric of Brno)

(most likely *a secco*).[7] The contract for the Innsbruck ceiling states further that good gold is to be used.[8] Where I have observed such details from scaffolding (as at Dyje), the artist does seem to have used gold leaf.

In addition, as at Trenčianské Bohuslavice (Plate 32), Heiligenkreuz-Gutenbrunn, the Piarist church in Vienna, and elsewhere, throughout his career in those churches for which Maulbertsch also supplied actual altarpieces in places where he had frescoed the walls and ceilings, the pictures over the altars are related to the overall color scheme. The altars stand out because they possess a darker coloration. They contrast with the more brightly colored walls and ceilings. The altarpieces reverse the tonality of the frescoes, since they are essentially dark, with light figures within them; in contrast, figures with more saturated color are set against brighter backgrounds in the frescoes.

Although its altarpieces are easel paintings set in carved frames, at the Piarist church at Mikulov (Nikolsburg) in 1759 (Figure 47), Maulbertsch treated the building as a whole, including both walls and ceiling, as he did Sümeg. While he no doubt received some help from assistants, including an artist named Angst and Felix Ivo Leicher, the latter of whom painted altarpieces[9]—Maulbertsch probably conceived the scheme for the whole church nevertheless. It possesses an overall grayish tonality.

Other ceilings of the mid-1760s are executed in variants of a greenish tonality like that found at Trenčianské Bohuslavice. This is seen in the blue-green-gray tonality of the Probsteikirche at Hradiště (Pöltenberg) in southern Moravia (Plate 33), painted in 1766, although here Maulbertsch probably also had extensive workshop assistance, primarily from Joseph Winterhalder the Younger, whose participation is documented in the latter's own list of his works,[10] and is evident in the evangelists painted in the pendentives of the cupola. The effect of this tonality is surprisingly more noticeable where Maulbertsch has painted a larger space, such as that in the Carmelite church at Székesfehérvár in Hungary, where Maulbertsch worked in the following year, 1767 (Plate 34). In Székesfehérvár the fields of fresco are considerably larger: Maulbertsch has worked both in the choir, painting its pendentives, and in the area over the high altar, as well as in the nave, whose cupola and pendentives he also did. In addition, he painted the side altarpieces in the church. The greenish overall coloring of the walls and ceiling provides a very effective way of providing a contrast with individual scenes, by emphasizing the presence of the figures, who are colored differently, at the same time that it links the whole together, by providing what may be considered a ground tone. It thus helps the eye to elide the otherwise varied architecture and the complicated iconography of the program.

The architectural ornament in these works may be called rococo (the contract at Trenčianské Bohuslavice specifically stipulated *auf die moderne Art*, meaning something contrasting with classically derived ornament, in the antique manner), and it might be argued that the color schemes found in these works from the earlier part of Maulbertsch's career fit this appellation. But the use of similar overall schemes of color, and to a degree even a similar palette, are also to be found in works that date from the time after a supposed stylistic change in Maulbertsch's work had occurred, starting in the 1760s. In this respect the frescoes at Královo Pole, painted in 1769, may represent a transitional phase. At Královo Pole some change in the artist's choice of palette may be noted, but the frescoes still are similar to earlier works in their approach to overall coloring. The chapter room, though in bad condition, and radically restored, possesses very bright pastel colors and a light green overall tonality; the sacristy, executed in a different coloristic mode, displays a gray and purple tonality, in which more saturated colors appear. This differentiation also indicates the painter's sensitivity to the relative light conditions of the two spaces, relatively dark in the sacristy and bright in the chapter room.

In contrast with Maulbertsch's works with rococo ornament, a different style of ornament is to be noticed in the architectural elements of the actual building of the primatial palace in Bratislava, where Maulbertsch worked in 1781 as part of a program of renewal. The palace is marked by the classicizing exterior designed by Melchior Hefele, which is comparable to other works of the *Zopfstil*, or "Roman" taste.[11] Maulbertsch painted the pediment of this building, now lost. In the interior, he still, however, gave the painting in the cupola of the chapel a uniform tonality, like that seen in his earlier works. Moreover, pastel shades of light blue, pink, and purple predominate in the sky (see plate 13).

At Győr the architectural and ornamental elements painted around the frescoes that Maulbertsch executed in the 1770s were probably not done by the artist himself, and a drawing for the walls of the presbytery was made by an assistant.[12] Nevertheless, the overall decorative schemes for Győr must be Maulbertsch's (see Figure 16): the coloring with pastel shades in the central scene painted in the nave in 1781, with its gray surrounds, points toward the employment of coloring seen at Pápa, which was painted at approximately the same time.

Pápa possesses a color scheme that is predominantly a cool gray. (See Plates 18 and 22.) Lavender, rose, and green accents are found in the individual figures within the scenes of the life of St. Stephen. While this coloring is cooler than that found in his earlier works, as mentioned in the previous chapter, Maulbertsch's conception of the function of coloring remains the same: it is treated uniformly throughout. Because problems with the condition of the paintings at Pápa have disclosed details of the technique used, even Maulbertsch's procedures here indicate how much the choice of coloring was very much part of the painterly process. Where the overpaint in secco on the figures has flaked off, a grayish tone has been revealed. Indeed, if the painting in secco had been better preserved, the effect of the whole would have been considerably brighter.

Comments made by Maulbertsch himself elucidate the preceding observations concerning the coloring of his works. In the letter of 5 November 1780, quoted in part in Chapter 3, in which Maulbertsch assures Bishop Károly Eszterházy that he is going to paint the frescoes in Pápa according to the text, the artist adds that he will do this in an artful manner (*kunstmessig*).[13] Sending the bishop sketches for Pápa on 9 March 1782, in another letter, that has also been cited, he repeats the notion that they have been done true to both history and the rules of art (*getreu der Historie und Kunstmässigen Regeln der Schilderung bestens darinnen beo-*

bachtet).[14] Some of the meaning of this coupling of terms has been explicated in Chapter 3, but there is more to it: the word *kunstmessig* (i.e., *kunstmässig*) appears in other contracts (for example, that for Eger), where the artist is promising that everything will be *lieblichs colorirt*.[15] For Maulbertsch doing things according to art, *kunstmässig*, evidently involves coloring, as he makes explicit when he says that he will paint the frescoes in Eger "*in Erhabenen lichteren vnd schatten guet in gedeilten grobien Colorit und haltung*" (well in highlights and shadows, with coloring and color balanced in divided groups).[16]

Evidently for Maulbertsch *Colorit* means among other things attending to the distribution of light and shade, the division of areas of color, and in general the color harmony, or balance of light and color in a painting, what was called *Haltung* in German. The concept of *Haltung* has a long history of discussion in German and in Dutch, where it is called *houding*.[17] Maulbertsch's treatment of areas of color and light thus appears to have been a matter of conscious intention related to overall effects of balance and harmony, not just the treatment of individual colors.

The achievement of balanced as well as harmonious coloring may be seen both in the overall color schemes used for the mural and ceiling paintings and the interiors of churches and in the distribution of color accents within individual frescoes from every phase of Maulbertsch's career. For example, at Heiligenkreuz-Gutenbrunn, in frescoes dated 1757–58, a burst of bright yellow is placed in the center of the composition; this is reinforced by intense yellow accents in the garments of angels seen directly overhead, and to the left, in the position of nine o'clock on a watch, with the Virgin and cross regarded as being at six o'clock. These accents in turn are picked up by a vessel located at approximately one o'clock, in garments of a figure at three o'clock, and in the vestments of the Virgin and in St. Veronica at six o'clock (Plate 31). Similarly, pink tones that harmonize with the yellows are distributed not only throughout the clouds but also in matching places in the composition. In some areas bright green tones accompany these tones. (See Plate 31.) A later example, the central ceiling fresco completed 1783 in the bishop's palace in Szombathely, distributes pale mauve garments through the quadrants of the composition; they set off the gold garment worn by the central female figure, whose bright color is picked up by the trumpeting angel below, and by the burst of yellow-gold light around the figure of wisdom above. As the placement of the most intense lights in relation to darker lights around them suggests in both these frescoes, similar observations could be made about the distribution and balance of light effects. (See Plate 16.)

In fact, Maulbertsch does directly indicate that he thinks of the choice of individual colors in relation to the overall idea of composition and of the effect of individual portions of the composition in relation to the whole. In the letter of 9 March 1782 where Maulbertsch deals with antique ornament for Pápa, he says that he has conceived of coloring in two ways (*auf zweiyerley Art colorirt*) the four bas-reliefs with four miracles around the central scenes. In order to vary the colors, he states that one could employ yellow highlights in the middle ceiling (*könnte wegen Abwechselung der Farben im mittleren Plavon das Gelb liechte beybehalten werden*). Thus the highlights would achieve a different effect.[18] (See Plates 18 and 22.)

Maulbertsch's treatment of variety in coloring is thus also an expression of his concern for the whole color scheme of a work. The consideration of whether or not one applies more or less color in frescoes in relation to the way that the eye takes in the whole design accordingly provides a key topic in a letter the artist sent to Bishop János Szily on 11 March 1794. Discussing a question concerning the frescoes that were to be painted in the cathedral at Szombathely, Maulbertsch proposes leaving the area above the high altar without anything colored (*nichts farbiges hinein zu mahlen*). Maulbertsch says that leaving the area uncolored would give the eye a chance to rest, so that it would not be overburdened. As a result, the most splendid aspects of the design can be perceived without being diminished (*. . . damit das Auge allzeit eine abwechselnte Ruehe haben kan, um nicht mit al zu viller iber häuffung, das grose herliche verringert wirde*).[19] This again gives the sense that the painter was treating the use of color in the composition in order to achieve an overall aesthetic effect.

Contemporary criticism further indicates what the conception of coloring may mean in Maulbertsch's art. Maulbertsch's coloring and the term *Colorit* are encountered repeatedly in discussions of his work, and they are consonant with Maulbertsch's own usage. The first published critical account of his work, the description of his 1770 *Aufnahmestück* for the academy (already discussed in part in Chapter 3), is especially telling: "The lights and shadows are without harsh contrast, and combined in a comprehensible union (*in einer verständigen Vereinigung*) that charms the eye, but at the same time provides us the necessary change, and points to the needed resting places that make for the magical work of chiaroscuro. The figures are noble and given character, the whole picture done with three colors, but with notable freedom of the brush."[20] It is striking how much this text resembles what Maulbertsch himself said about allowing for a change in lights and providing resting places for the eye. Moreover, the critique speaks of the contrast of light and shadow, defined as chiaroscuro (*Helldunkel*), and describes it as producing a unifying result. This achieves a pleasant alteration for the eye, but also creates its own effect, by allowing the eye to rest.

The generally favorable report on Maulbertsch published in the *Frankfurter gelehrte Anzeigen* in 1775 praised the artist's spirit and fire ("*Geist und Feuer*"), as previously remarked. Maulbertsch's accomplishment is here also defined as the result of his *Colorit*. Maulbertsch is described in the following words: "He knows how to distribute light and shadow and to give them a charming coloring that, although it is motley, remains pleasant itself on the plaster, surprises connoisseurs, and bedazzles the ignorant."[21] Hence, although Maulbertsch's colors are bright (the explication of his destroyed frescoes in Schwechat in 1765 calls them "*hoch getrieben*," too),[22] the overall effect is charming, the colors are pleasant, and light and shadow well distributed; as the description of Schwechat also says, the painter is justifiably highly regarded by every connoisseur (*Kenner*). This description not only is consistent with the definition of coloring we have seen so far, but confirms the sorts of observations that have been made here of his work.

A report dated 20 September 1776 by Count Heister to Maria Theresia about the frescoes painted in Innsbruck significantly also uses a vocabulary familiar from Maulbertsch's contracts. It describes them as having a "pure and lovely coloring" (*reine und liebe Colorite*).[23] This recalls other passages on Maulbertsch's "lovely" coloring. Even the somewhat ironical response made by Chodowiecki praises his "Venetian *Colorit*," about which more presently.[24]

In his descriptions of Maulbertsch's art in Moravia, Andreas Schweigel, who, as noted, knew Maulbertsch well, singles out his *Colorit* as the master's major merit. The *Lehensaal* at Kroměříž (Plates 3, 6, 25) is done in *frischem färbigem Collerit* [*sic*] (he says that although it has some exaggerated expressions: it is freshly colored). In the description of other paintings in the bishop's residence at Kroměříž, Schweigel provides a definition of coloring that again does not tally with Krsek's description of the same work: he relates *Colloriet* [*sic*] to *schöne Harmonie*.[25] For him coloring brings about beautiful harmony. Reading this comment together with the critique in the Frankfurt journal provides a better way of regarding the frescoes at Kroměříž: one should concentrate on the overall effect that is also comprised by the ceiling, rather than on the individual color accents that are used to set off the figures—although this effect is somewhat difficult to apprehend, since the ceiling is relatively low. (See Plate 3.)

Schweigel also describes Maulbertsch's paintings in the charterhouse at Královo Pole as being executed with all graces, good order, and a beautiful, pleasant, melting coloring.[26] This indicates that Maulbertsch's coloring was pleasant because it blended together tones. Schweigel's statement thus provides more evidence that for Maulbertsch's associates *Collerit* (*Colorit*) does not refer so much to the choice of individual colors as it does to how they are painted together to achieve a harmonious effect.

In Schweigel's marginal notes on the same page where Královo Pole is described, in the same passage that describes Maulbertsch as a true original, he also says that the artist possesses a *frisches angenehmes Collerit*, a fresh, pleasant coloring (in his painting), that is said to draw all eyes to him. Moreover, Maulbertsch's grace is such that his treatment of colors means that even his incorrect exaggerated drawing (*sogar die unrichtige übertribene Zeihung [sic]*) is reduced to something that pleases. He remains a model of coloring (*ein Modell von Collerit*) to all students of the time.[27]

All these statements concerning coloring in Maulbertsch's painting evoke the terms of debate found in a well-known discourse in the literature of art, the discourse on coloring. This is most familiar from arguments about *colorito* in Italian, or *coloris* in French, but discussion of these issues also occurred in German. Roger de Piles (1635–1708), although he was only one participant in a debate over *coloris*, penned the most important treatises of his day on the subject, the *Discours sur le coloris*, first published in 1673, republished in numerous editions, and then expanded in his *Cours de peinture par principes* of 1708.[28] De Piles enunciated a series of principles that are apropos of this discourse as it continued to be carried on into the eighteenth century, and they pertain both to contemporaneous discussions of Maulbertsch's paintings and to visual observations of them.

Resounding in the discussions of Maulbertsch, many aspects of the language of the debate over *coloris* help situate observations of his work in reference to categories of its own time. For instance, according to de Piles coloring, *coloris*, is different from color. While color makes things visible, *coloris* involves the distribution of colors for the maximum effect of deceiving the eye. Coloring is what makes things seem natural. It comprises the knowledge of particular colors, the sympathy and antipathy found among them, the manner of employing them, and the understanding of chiaroscuro.[29] Variation and draining of hue (one recalls here Maulbertsch's *nichts farbiges*) are necessary for the rest (*repos*) of the eye. Notably, the variety of colors in materials helps create the harmony of the picture, to characterize objects, and to practice chiaroscuro.[30] However—and this again supports observations made here—"the beauty of coloring does not consist in a medley of different colors, but in their just distribution, so that objects have their natural color" and that the ensemble produces an "agreeable union."[31]

De Piles's arguments were echoed in German texts of the later eighteenth century; they suggest that the debate over *coloris* had been continued in the German-speaking lands as well as in France. In fact, a number of treatises by de Piles were made directly accessible in German in the eighteenth century, including a translation of the *Cours de peinture par principes* that was published in 1760.[32] While the French texts could also be used by Germans—Christian Ludwig von Hagedorn cites the French edition—Hagedorn's *Betrachtungen über die Mahlerey* of 1762 also indicates that the German translation was being used soon after its publication, since he cites it as well, recommending it to German painters.[33]

Hagedorn follows many of the arguments of de Piles about *coloris*, which he translates as *Farbengebung*.[34] He adopts notions such as the necessity for resting places for the eye, which he calls *Ruhestellen* (one thinks here of Maulbertsch's use of the word *Rueplätze* [*sic*]), the need to have sympathy (*Freundschaft*) between neighboring colors, the importance of *clair obscur* (which he calls *Verständnis des Hellen und Dunkeln*), and the harmony of the whole. His theory of *coloris* (*Farbengebung*) emphasizes the presence of a certain tone that unites broken colors into a harmonious whole.[35]

Another handbook of Maulbertsch's time, the *Handlexikon der bildenden Künste*, which was in fact a translation of a work by Antoine-Joseph Pernety (1716–1801) on painting, also directly cites de Piles.[36] Pernety repeats much of what de Piles and Hagedorn say, but the vocabulary in the German edition of 1764 is even closer to that used around Maulbertsch. Here *coloris* is translated as *Colorit*.[37] Pernety defines *Colorit* as one of the essential parts of painting, which involves imitating the true colors of objects as exactly a possible, taking into account their distance and the effects of light on them. Coloring involves understanding local colors and *chiaroscuro* (*Helldunkel*). This concerns the entire composition of a painting and demands familiarity with the nature of colors, that is, their antipathy and sympathy; *chiaroscuro* determines the divisions of light and shadows.[38] Very few masters of the past three hundred years—notably Titian and Rubens—have mastered coloring, which necessitates altering local coloring according to the subject matter depicted, the time of the day and action, the place, the mood, and the relation of each point in a painting to every other. The painter is like a musician who can tune his instrument as he will, but he is more bound to rules determined by the external conditions of what he wishes to represent. Furthermore, the tones of a painting must agree with the action, and with the chief color of the most prominent figure, but for a good effect a variety of colors is necessary.[39] Pernety also argues that the beauty of the coloring of the whole of a painting consists even less in the presence of many different colors, but in a correct division of them, informed by familiarity with their accords. Thus beauty is dependent on the mixture and breaking of pigments on the palette, so that they can all be combined together into a pleasant unity and a seductive harmony.[40]

This argument suggests that the contrasting colors that are seen in close proximity in Maulbertsch's painting, as at Kroměříž (Plates 6, 25), should be seen rather as complementary. This sort of practice is also especially noticeable in his earlier works, for example in use the complementary colors in shadows, seen at Ebenfurth (Figures 10, 46; Plate 30). Thinking in such terms was current in Maulbertsch's milieu. The conception of complementary color is the product of Newtonian and post-Newtonian color theory, and it was a Viennese contemporary of Maulbertsch, Ignaz Schiffermüller, who wrote one of the most comprehensive applications of Newton's color theory. Schiffermüller's extensive theory of pigments, published in 1771, has been described as epitomizing the eighteenth-century project of cataloging the whole of the natural world, thereby characterizing the method of Enlightenment taxonomies. In it complementary colors are laid out on a wheel.[41]

Hence treating Maulbertsch as a colorist in terms related to the early modern debate over *coloris* not only validates observations made from looking at his works, as here proposed, but also opens up discussion of his painting in several more ways. Not the least of these is that it provides an alternative to the discourse on beauty of Winckelmann, who tried to relate beauty to reason. Coloring does not submit to Winckelmann's constrictions; it reveals other sorts of beauty.

The discourse on the beautiful was neither the only discourse on art carried on in the eighteenth century nor the only discourse to which Maulbertsch was related. While some discussions of art had moved with Winckelmann from the pole of fantasy to that of *Verstand*, during the course of the century the discourse on the sublime had also been developed. And the discussion of *coloris* is also linked to concepts of the sublime.[42]

By the 1750s the sublime had become an alternative to the beautiful in aesthetic thought. Its importance as an alternative concept is demonstrated by its being paired with the beautiful in Edmund Burke's *Philosophical Enquiry into the Origin of Our Ideas of the Sublime and Beautiful* of 1757 and Immanuel Kant's *Observations on the Feeling of the Beautiful and Sublime* of 1763. Kant's and Burke's notions of the sublime are not to be closely associated with Maulbertsch, however, and it is important to remember that the discourse on the sublime originated considerably before their discussion of the term at around 1760, and certainly long before the treatment of the sublime in Kant's *Critique of Judgment* (*Kritik der Urteilskraft*) of 1790.

The modern discussion of the sublime started in France, at the time of Boileau (Nicolas Despréauz) in the late seventeenth century: Boileau translated the ancient treatise on the sublime traditionally attributed to Longinus. Discussion of the sublime spread quickly to England and to Germany. By the time Maulbertsch had arrived on the scene, the sublime could be posed as an alternative to the beautiful in considerations of the visual arts, as well as of other forms of aesthetic experience, and the experience of nature. According to the general tenor of arguments about the sublime, especially those voiced in discussions of the 1760s, the sublime was understood to be something that was not to be controlled by order and reason. Beautiful disorder exceeds reason; it is related to an expression of grace beyond the reach of art, to a "*je ne sais quoi.*" Hence servile following of the rules can never produce sublime art.[43] This is the province of the genius, who goes beyond the rules of art.

Though more familiar from the discussions that took place in France and England, the discourse on the sublime was also conducted in the German-speaking world, where Burke's text attracted lively interest.[44] There is good reason why it did, because discussion of the sublime had been carried on in German writings since the 1730s. In the 1730s both Immanuel Pyra and Carl Heinrich von Heinecken translated and intended to comment on the ancient text attributed to Longinus. The concern with the sublime was also picked up in the literary debates that centered on Johann Christoph Gottsched; Gottsched was an associate of the *societas incognitorum* in Olomouc, and was clearly known in intellectual circles throughout Central Europe. In a debate with Gottsched the Swiss authors Johann Jakob Bodmer and Johann Jakob Breitinger were concerned to validate the power of imagination, *dichterische Phantasie*. The sublime was for them an expression of this power, and in their critique of Gottsched they joined Pyra's earlier critique of that author.[45]

In putting some of their discussion into the mouths of painters in their writings known as *Discourse der Mahlern*, Bodmer and Breitinger brought their discussion close to painting. So did Heinecken, in his own person: Heinecken was a counselor of the Saxon court who was charged with the organization of the Dresden *Kupferstichkabinett*, and in general with the reorganization of the Saxon collections. As noted in Chapter 3, he was working in Dresden, as was Hagedorn, at the time Maulbertsch went there to paint. Furthermore, Hagedorn also quotes Bodmer and Breitinger, and also cites Gottsched; he does this moreover exactly in those passages where he discusses harmonious paintings (*harmonische Gemählde*) in relation to the use of colors.[46] Hagedorn also cites Gottsched in another passage where he is relating the harmony of the whole of a painting to its overall tone, or *tonos*.[47] Thus the debate about the sublime can clearly be brought into proximity with the discussion of *coloris* in the German-speaking world.

By 1750 the *grand gusto*, or grand style in painting, had also come to be related to the sublime in painting and to arguments over color stemming ultimately from de Piles.[48] A statement published in a Venetian journal in 1762 records that Tiepolo himself said that "the mind of the painter should always tend to the sublime, to the heroic, to perfection."[49] Whether or not the sublime (*das Erhabene*) was fully articulated in similar terms in German discussions of painting, the word surely shared a common charge, and it was related to painting in the later eighteenth century. In German discussions it also clearly formed a pole opposed to that of the rational, complementing that of the beautiful. The sublime was an expression of original genius, original because it demonstrated depth of feeling and emotion.

The relevance of these considerations to the present argument is that Maulbertsch's art was brought directly into the discussion of such notions of the sublime. It has already been noted how the concepts of poetic fantasy, genius, and original were all deployed in the criticism of Maulbertsch's work. So were ideas of grace. Most important, the term "sublime" (*erhaben*) was also specifically applied to Maulbertsch. Furthermore, this connection of Maulbertsch with the "sublime" was enunciated in a number of texts where it is linked with his poetic inventions, color, and handling.

The 1777 description of the *Trattnerhofkapelle* in Vienna says that its invention is not *nach dem gemeinen Stil*, not according to the common (or popular) style. Along with boldness in his brushwork, the sublimity in his thoughts (*Erhabenheit in Gedanken*) raises Maulbertsch above the common. Even more tellingly, Anselm Elwert's lexicon article on Maulbertsch of 1785 embellishes the standard critique of Maulbertsch by stating that the features that are usually attributed to him amount to the sublime: Maulbertsch is said to have painted "histories in a sublime style on wet plaster, with figures full of spirit and fire (*Geist und Feuer*), and a beautiful coloring (*Kolorit*)."[50] In other writers this notion of fire also connotes a quality of the sublime.[51]

Finally, the discussion of *coloris* helps situate Maulbertsch in a longer historical context. De Piles explicitly praised Rubens and Venetian painting, who, as Pernety's text indicates, continued to be regarded as paragons of coloring. De Piles represented the side of the Rubensistes in the *querelle* with the Poussinistes. The importance of Rubens for the art of Maulbertsch has often been discussed.[52] The Austrian painter took motifs from his illustrious predecessor and from Van Dyck. He owned prints after Rubens.[53] Furthermore, he could have seen numerous paintings by Rubens in the Liechtenstein, imperial, and other collections in Vienna. By 1780 the imperial collections had been made publicly accessible in the Belvedere palace,[54] and Maulbertsch, as a painter in court employ and mem-

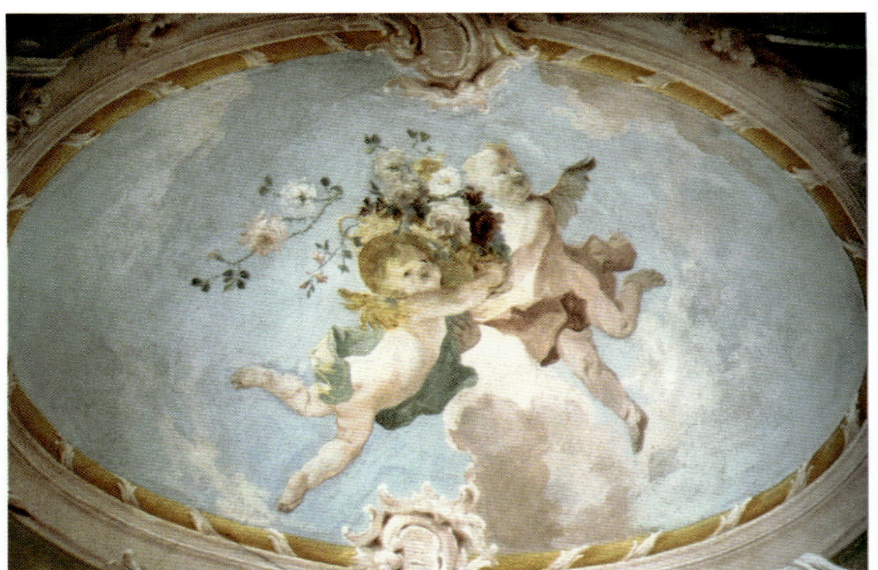

PLATE 27. *Putti with Flowers*, detail of choir ceiling, 1763, Chapel, Schloss Erdődy, Trenčianské Bohuslavice, Slovakia (formerly Bogoszló, Upper Hungary) (Photograph: Courtesy of Institute of Art History, Slovak Academy of Sciences [Ustav dejin umenia Slovenská Akadémie Vied])

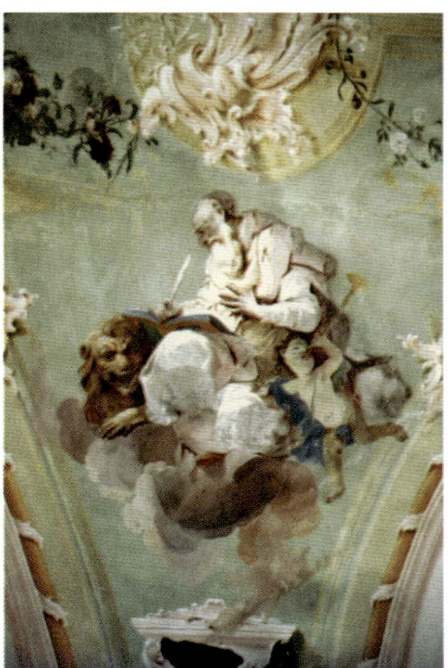

PLATE 28. *St. Jerome*, pendentive of nave ceiling, detail, 1763, Chapel, Schloss Erdődy, Trenčianské Bohuslavice, Slovakia (formerly Bogoszló, Upper Hungary) (Photograph: Courtesy of Institute of Art History, Slovak Academy of Sciences [Ustav dejin umenia Slovenská Akadémie Vied])

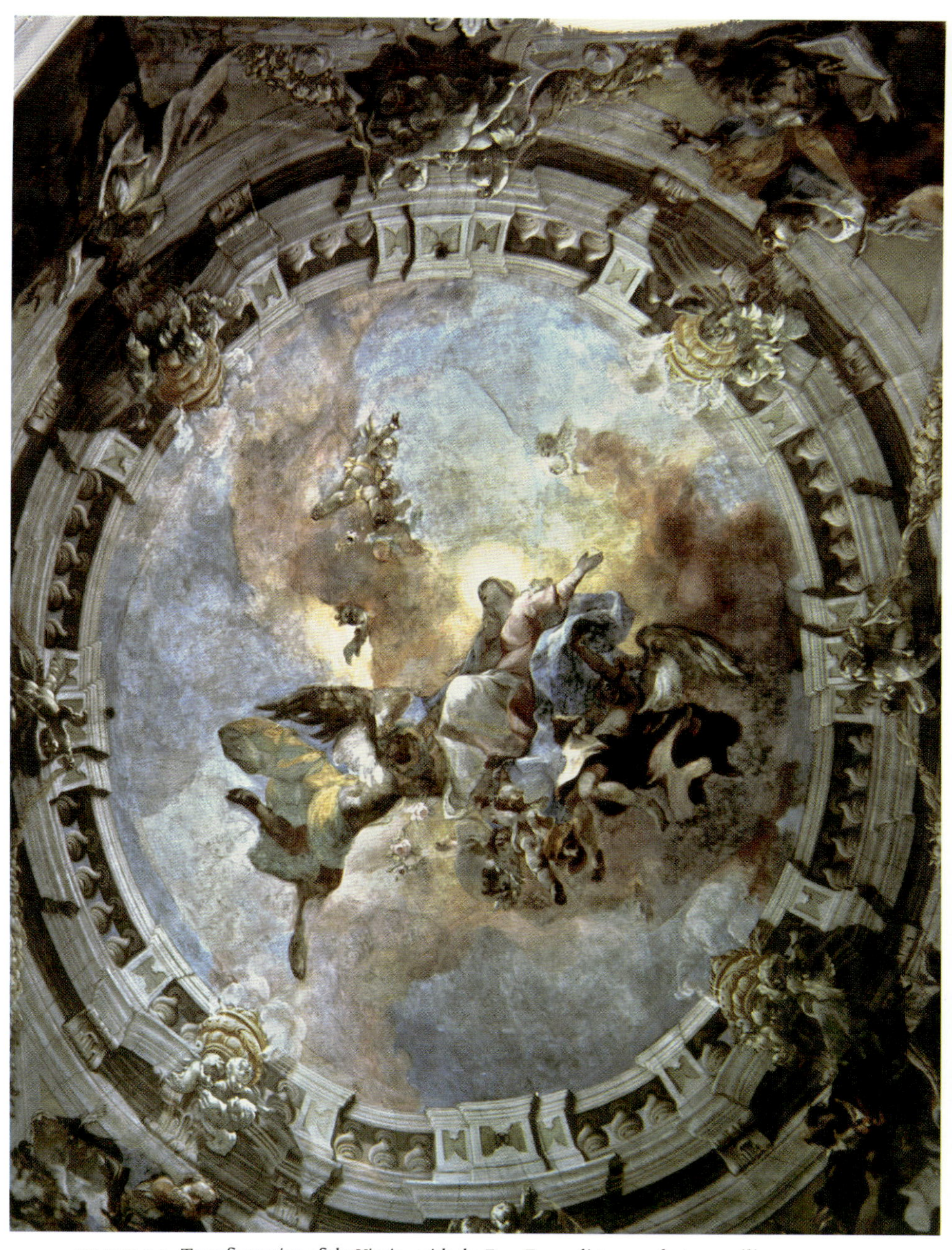

PLATE 29. *Transfiguration of the Virgin, with the Four Evangelists*, presbytery ceiling, 1752–53, Piarist Church of Maria Treu, Vienna (Photograph: Eduard Beranek)

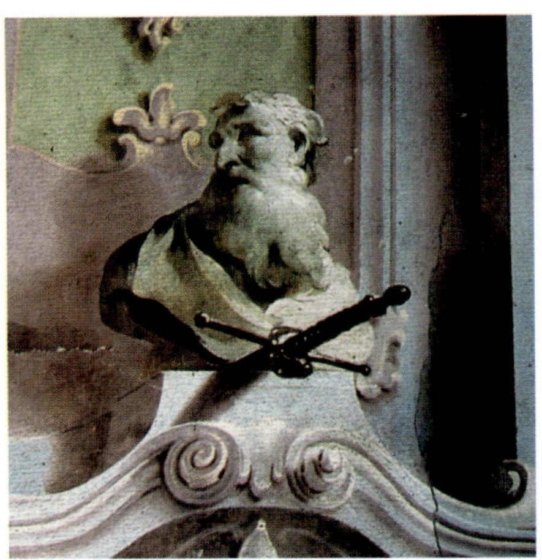

PLATE 30. *Bust of St. Paul*, detail of apse wall, 1754, Schloss Suttner, Ebenfurth, Lower Austria (Photograph: Eduard Beranek)

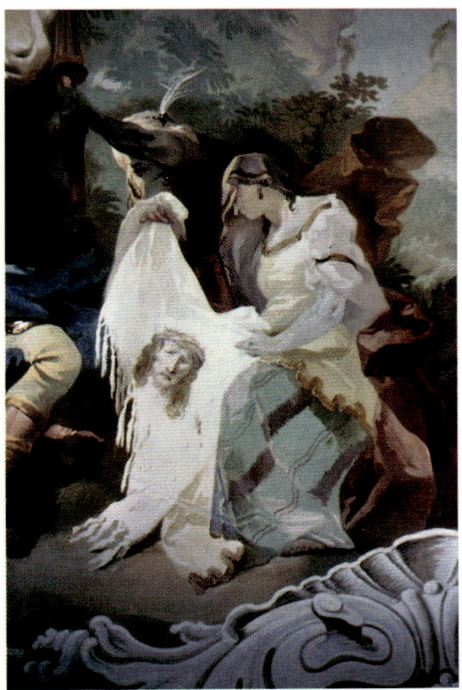

PLATE 31. *Glorification and Invention of the True Cross*, detail of nave ceiling showing St. Veronica, 1757–58, Parish and Pilgrimage Church, Heiligenkreuz-Gutenbrunn, Lower Austria (Photograph: Bundesdenkmalamt, Vienna)

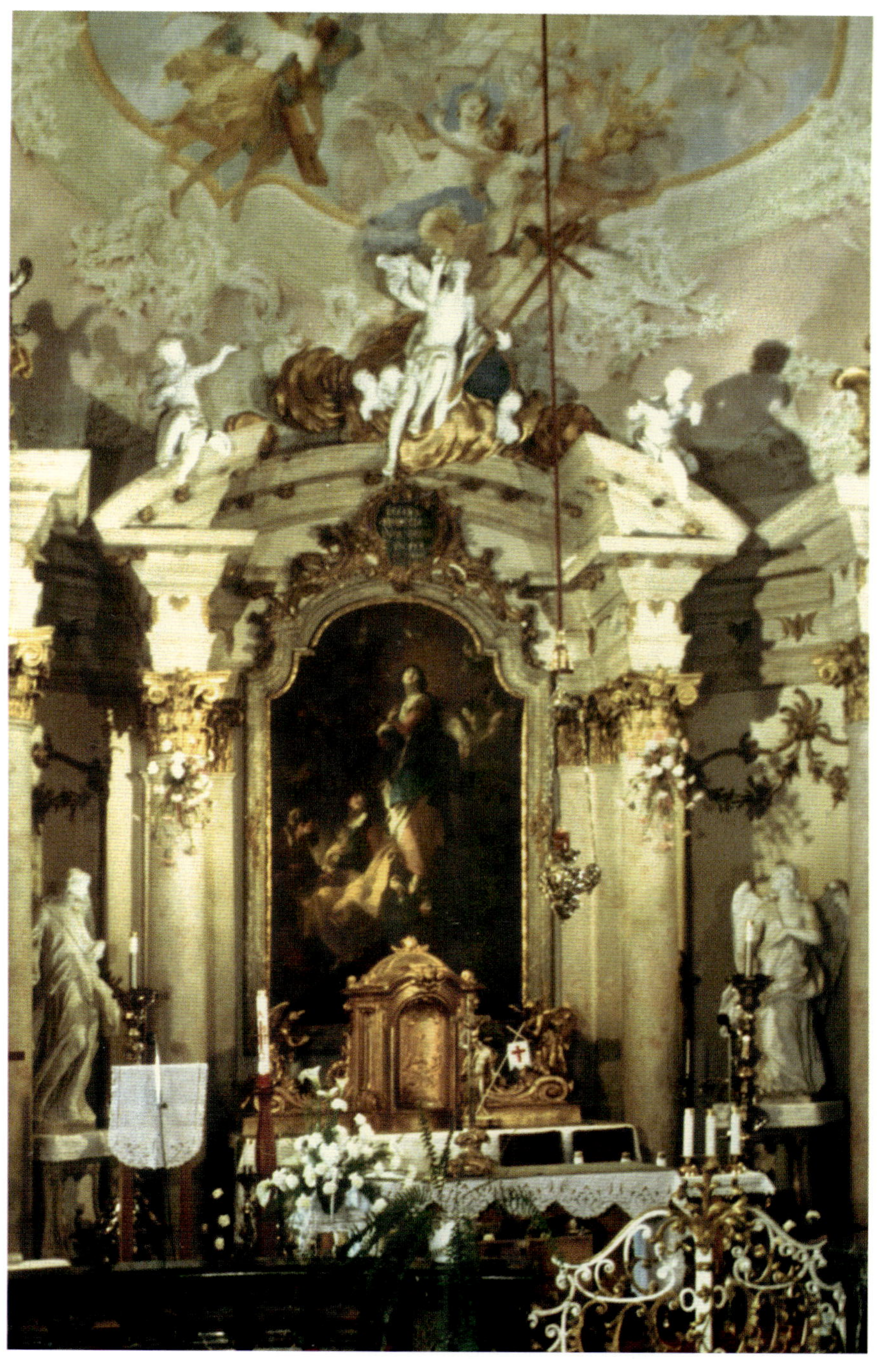

PLATE 32. *The Virgin Immaculate with Saints Joachim and Anna*, high altarpiece, 1763, Chapel, Schloss Erdődy, Trenčianské Bohuslavice, Slovakia (formerly Bogoszló, Upper Hungary) (Photograph: Courtesy of Institute of Art History, Slovak Academy of Sciences [Ustav dejin umenia Slovenská Akadémie Vied])

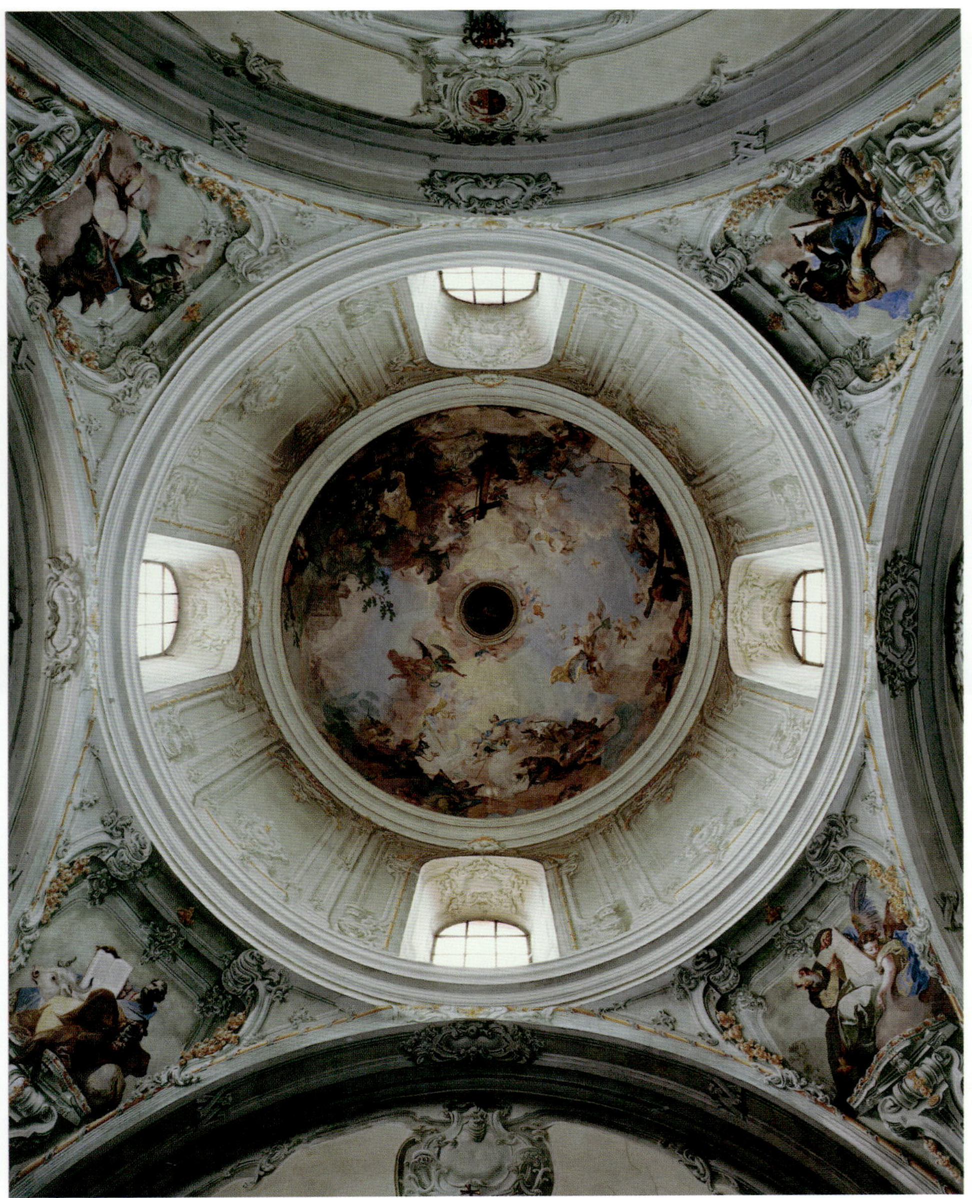

PLATE 33. *Invention of the True Cross* (evangelists in pendentives by Winterhalder), nave ceiling, 1768, Priory Church, Hradiště (Pöltenberg), Moravia, Czech Republic (Photograph: Brno University, courtesy Bishopric of Brno)

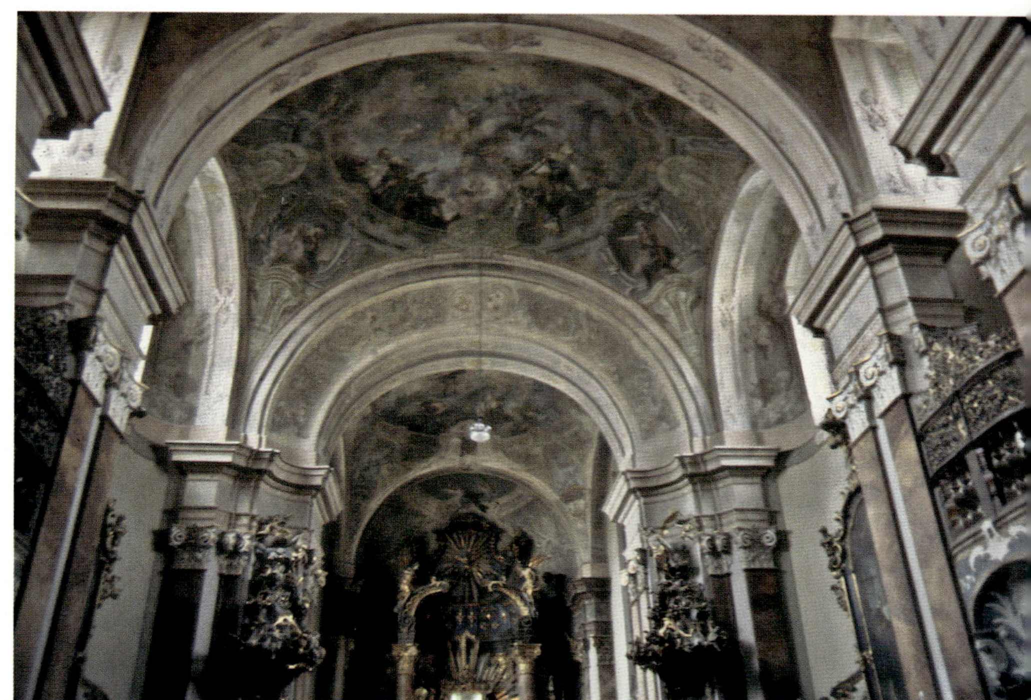

PLATE 34. Ceiling paintings, Carmelite Church, 1767, Székesfehérvár, Hungary (Photograph: Author)

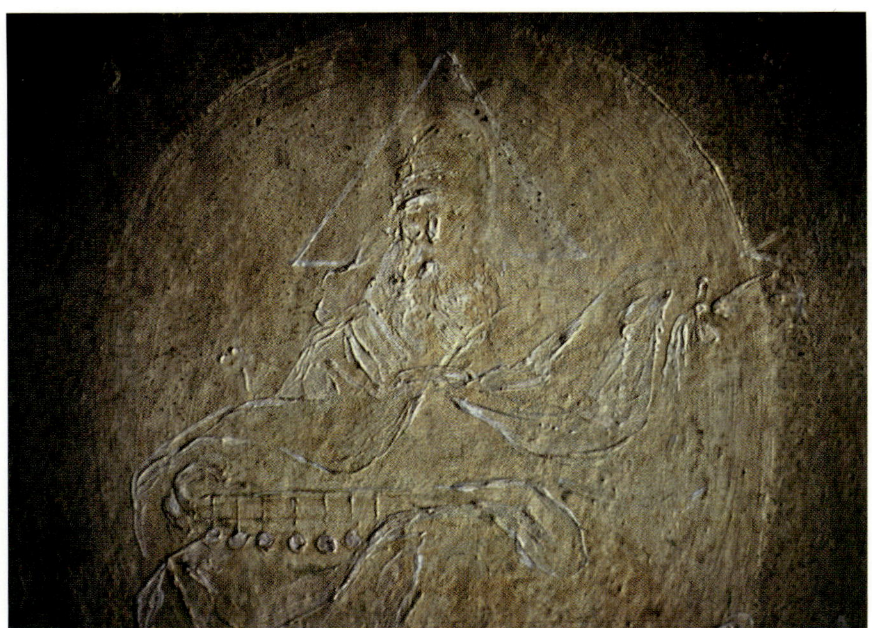

PLATE 35. *Vision of St. John on Patmos*, detail of God the Father, mural in sacristy, 1769, former Carthusian Church, Královo Pole (Brno; Königsfeld/Brünn) (Photograph: Author)

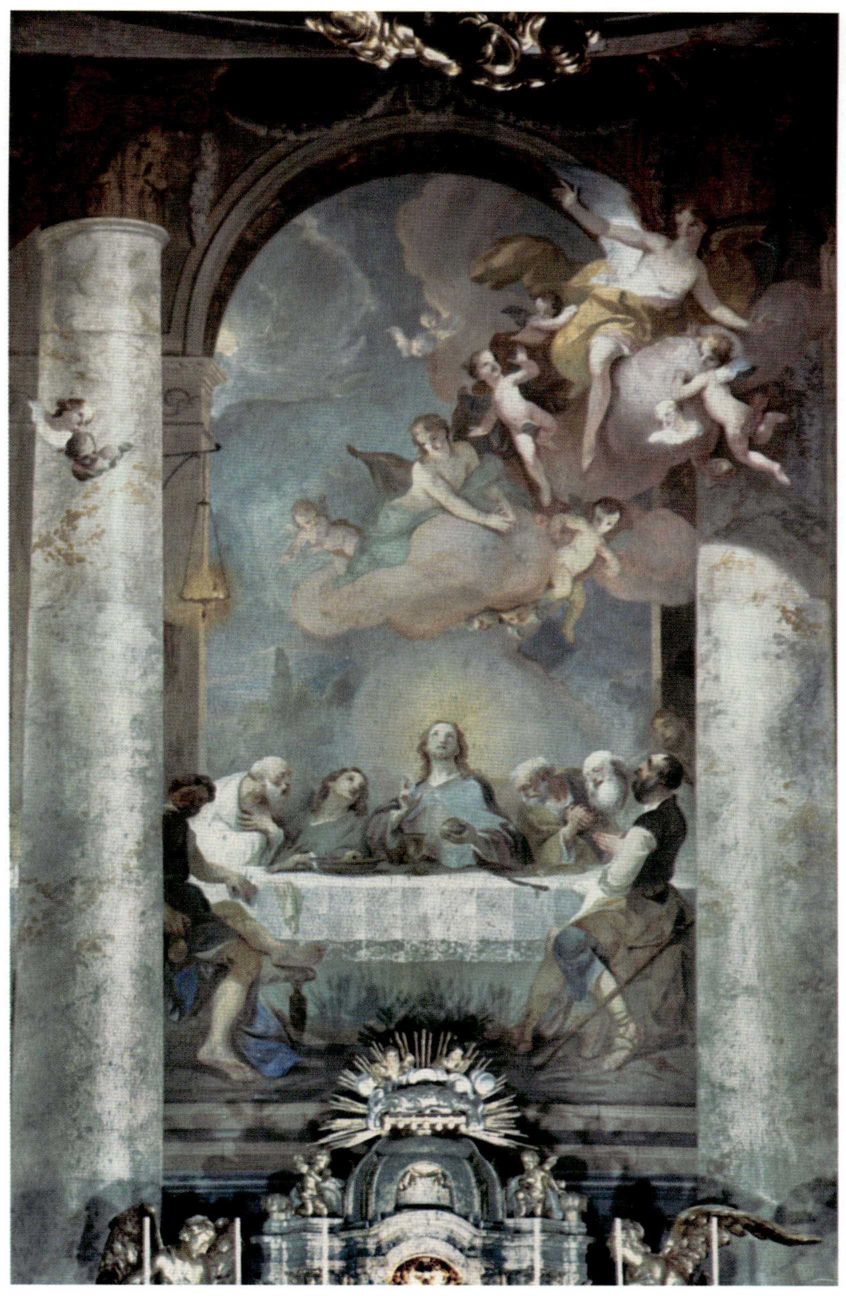

PLATE 36. *The Last Supper*, high altar mural, 1773, Augustinian Church, Korneuburg, Lower Austria (Photograph: Author's Archive)

ber of the academy from the later 1760s, probably had access to them before that date. Yet aside from his general concern with coloring, it is unclear how Rubens's art is in this respect to be related to the coloring of Maulbertsch.[55]

There are firmer reasons for stressing Maulbertsch's relation to coloring in Venetian art. Since Benesch's pioneering study on the sources of Maulbertsch's style,[56] the impact of Venetian art on Maulbertsch has been noted: nevertheless, the question of *colorito* can be reexamined further. For, as remarked, a knowledgeable contemporary, the Berlin painter Chodowiecki, pithily described Venetian *Colorit* as one of the outstanding features in Maulbertsch's art.

Since Chodowiecki most likely was familiar with easel paintings by Maulbertsch, it is probably in this realm that the issue of the relationship of coloring in Maulbertsch and Venetian painting should be considered first. In easel painting the use of grounds, the basic paint layers, and of overall tones applied over the ground, called dead painting by the Dutch, were essential for giving a unified color effect. The evolution in the use of grounds in Tiepolo and Maulbertsch progressed in a similar direction. Tiepolo originally used dark red earth grounds to prime his canvases. But from the 1730s he started adding a second, overlying, layer of ground, usually a pale yellowish gray, mixed from ocher, lead white, and a little charcoal black.[57] Recent investigations of Maulbertsch's painting technique have revealed that he similarly first used a standard sort of Roman or Bolognese technique, which employed a ruddy ground often painted with bole. In his later works, however, he began to employ a second ground in light gray that was placed over the initial ground in red.[58]

Observations about a similar approach to grounds may also be extended to their mural paintings.[59] Although Tiepolo's fresco technique has not been so thoroughly studied, he seems to have blocked out areas in earth colors.[60] As noted in regard to Pápa, a general tone seems to have been applied as a sort of ground in Maulbertsch's painting. Where I have been able to observe this from a scaffolding, as at Královo Pole, this tone seems to have been ocher; Maulbertsch painted his other colors over such a ground, using it as a middle or background tone in many instances. (See Plate 35.)

Color is of course applied by the brush: Maulbertsch's coloring is also closely related to his handling, and in this too he may be compared to the Venetians. Documents relating to his color connect it with his manner of execution: a 1771 account of his production praises it for his "lightness of execution" (*Leichtigkeit der Ausführung*), for example.[61] A description of a lost altarpiece painted in the Trattnerhof chapel in Vienna in 1777 mentions "boldness in brushwork" (*Kühnheit im Pinsel*) as a sign of Maulbertsch's mastery.[62] Later, in the same passage where Schweigel sings of his coloring, he lauds his "charming brush" (*reizendes Pinsel*).[63] At Maulbertsch's death his father-in-law, Jakob Schmutzer, who was then also director of the Vienna academy, when called on to find a replacement for the recently deceased master to complete the paintings in the cathedral at Szombathely said that any artist would have to be a great master who could execute them in his spirit (*für sich schon ein Grosser Künstler sein muss, um Maulpertschs Geist tättig ausführen zu können*). Specifically, Schmutzer says he did not know of anyone who could carry out such a work who had the qualities of both coloring and handling of the brush that Maulbertsch did.[64] Even a more negative critic such as Füßli recognized the ability of Maulbertsch and other contemporary history painters to make a quick and lively impression on the eye, which was due among other things to their "harmonic mixture of colors, idealized draperies in great masses, capricious application of light and shadow, along with a marked and bold application of the brush."[65]

In this regard Maulbertsch is also related to Venetian art: in addition to their coloring, the Venetians' handling of the brush, most obvious in Tiepolo's oil sketches, has long been recognized as one of their special attributes. The notably fluid execution of a painter like Tiepolo, whom Maulbertsch again resembles in this regard, was, to repeat, above all necessary in working on wet plaster. The capacity to cover large areas was something that was desired from all accomplished fresco painters. But this capacity was possessed to an exceptional degree by Tiepolo and Maulbertsch. Tiepolo painted the Palazzo Labia at the rate of five square meters a day,[66] and Maulbertsch seems to have worked at a similar speed; the side chapels of the Piarist Church, which are relatively intricate in terms of their design and numbers of figures, were painted in ten days.

Just this quickness and ease of execution was what Winckelmann deplored, and it is what he means by *franchezza*. Speed may have been a sign of the outpouring of genius and fantasy, but for Winckelmann it did not signal the deliberate application of reason or the intellect to painting. As discussed in Chapter 3, speed did not evince a "brush dipped in *Verstand*," in understanding or judgment. Winckelmann emphasized this point in a memorable passage in which he refers to Tiepolo. In a well-known statement in his 1763 essay on the beautiful in art, Winckelmann says that "Tiepolo did more in a day than Mengs in a week, but the former is seen and forgotten; the latter remains forever."[67] This critique is also especially noteworthy when read in its context because Winckelmann's next point is to discuss the application of color and the speed with which color is painted.

Although they are related to the art of Tiepolo and his other Venetian contemporaries, the qualities of Maulbertsch's work are, however, also distinct from and even more extreme than theirs, as indeed they are from the qualities of other Austrian contemporaries who otherwise employed a similar technique. In his fundamental essay on the sources of Maulbertsch's style, Benesch stressed the basic historical, stylistic, and spiritual differences between Maulbertsch and Tiepolo, stating that their art is the culmination of two different traditions.[68] Since Tiepolo remains the contemporary artist who comes most readily to mind in most reactions to Maulbertsch, especially for those not familiar with painting in Central Europe, in order to point out Maulbertsch's singular qualities it is useful to consider what some of the distinctions between him and Tiepolo may be, especially as they are seen in the treatment of light and color in drawing and painting.

While Tiepolo was a prolific draftsmen, strikingly the mass of paintings by Maulbertsch, strikingly fewer drawings by him seem to have survived. The continuation of a workshop may facilitate the preservation of such shop material, and one reason for the continuing existence of many drawings by Giovanni Battista Tiepolo may be that his sons were also important artists, with shops of their own, who could well have used and preserved his drawings in their ateliers. Maulbertsch, on the other hand, seems to have had no direct heir as a painter: while he may have collaborated with a number of good painters,[69] his most distinguished assistant, Winterhalder, who had worked with Maulbertsch during the mid-1760s and then at Dyje in the mid-1770s, and who executed Maulbertsch's designs for the cathedral in Szombathely after his death, did not inherit his workshop. In fact, in his autobiographical notes Winterhalder indicates that he had broken with Maulbertsch while he was working for him, long before.[70] In Maulbertsch's latest period, no artist seems to have continued to work with him regularly. After the death of Maulbertsch the contents of his house, including what seem to have been objects pertaining to a workshop, were sold in 1797: although drawings by Troger and Palko were in his possession, no works in the medium by Maulbertsch himself are mentioned.[71] From the evidence that does survive, it appears that Maulbertsch may have worked even more than Tiepolo in color, through oil sketches, or directly with paint on the wall or canvas.

Moreover Maulbertsch's authentic surviving drawings disclose further differences from the Venetian master. In Tiepolo, light is treated as an external feature that reveals forms: shadows take shape as they relate to light; shading and shadows are cast by an external source whose existence can be assumed (Figure 48). In Maulbertsch's drawings, however, shading often remains an integral part of

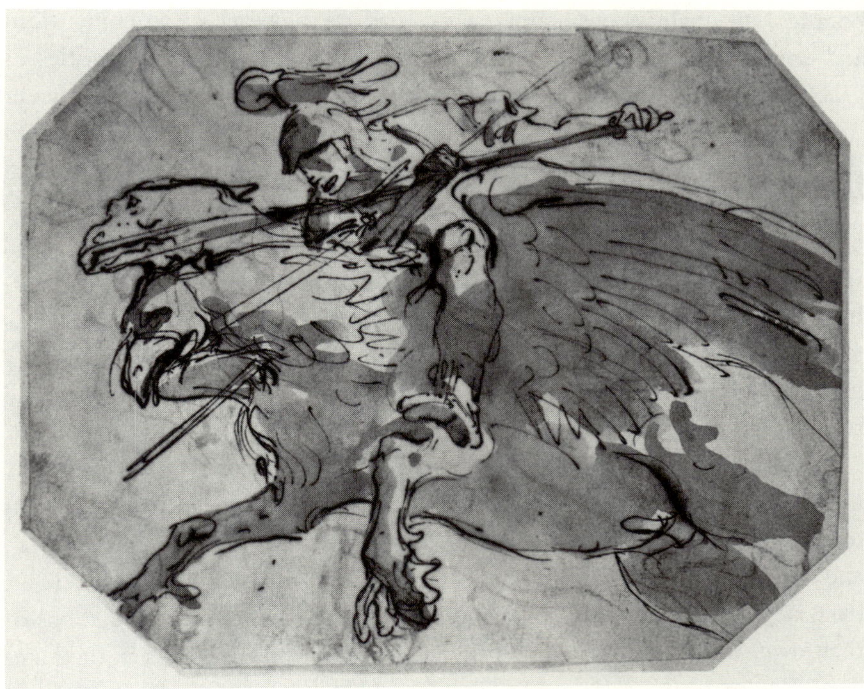

FIGURE 48. Giovanni Battista Tiepolo, *Ruggero on the Hippogriff*, pen and ink and wash drawing, 1757, Princeton University Art Museum (Photograph: Princeton University Art Museum. © 2003 Trustees of Princeton University)

the form, and neither attached shadows, nor cast shadows, may give an adequate clue as to the external source of lighting (Figure 49). While light sources are suggested more clearly in Maulbertsch's executed paintings, his conception of drawing thus suggests that the form itself, hence ultimately the color, in his works emerges from the light. This point is important to keep in mind when considering Maulbertsch's coloring in comparison with Tiepolo's.

Where Tiepolo paints what are effectively colorless cast shadows, which appear like a dark film over his figures, in his earlier paintings Maulbertsch gives his shadows a color that is distinctly different from the forms that cast them; his shadows take up elements of complementary hues from the materials they cover. This approach appears even in later frescoes, where shadows seem more closely to approximate the effects of Tiepolo's: in Maulbertsch's work at Innsbruck, for example, the hues of shadows are still tinted with complementary colors. While the coloring of Maulbertsch's figures is keyed to light, at Ebenfurth, Halbturn,

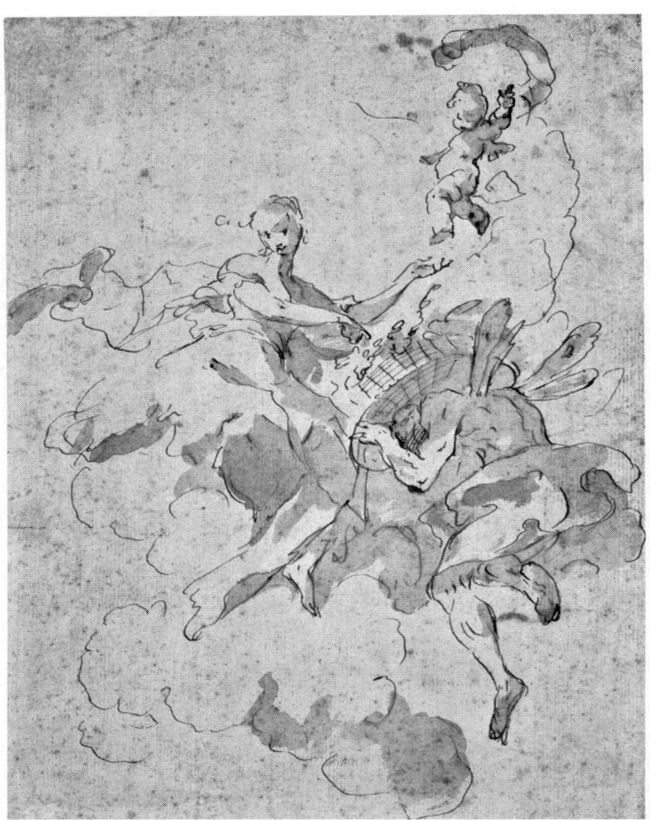

FIGURE 49. F. A. Maulbertsch, *Flora*, pen and ink and wash drawing, c. 1754, Fogg Art Museum, Cambridge, Massachusetts (Photograph: Courtesy of the Fogg Art Museum, Harvard University Art Museums, Friends of the Fogg Art Museum Fund)

and in the Piarist church in Vienna, Maulbertsch's treatment of the effect again indicates an approach to coloring in which not light, as in Tiepolo, but color itself is a primary element.

Color in Maulbertsch is used to impart more than form. In a painting like his fresco at Korneuburg, it also imparts meaning (Figure 50, Plate 36). Through the use of illusionistic architecture, Maulbertsch extends the space of the Augustinian church at Korneuburg, where the interior had been redesigned by J. F. Hetzendorf von Hohenberg. The institution of the Eucharist is shown occurring behind the altar, where believers would experience its reenactment in the Mass. Maulbertsch here employs iridescent coloring in pastel shades around the fig-

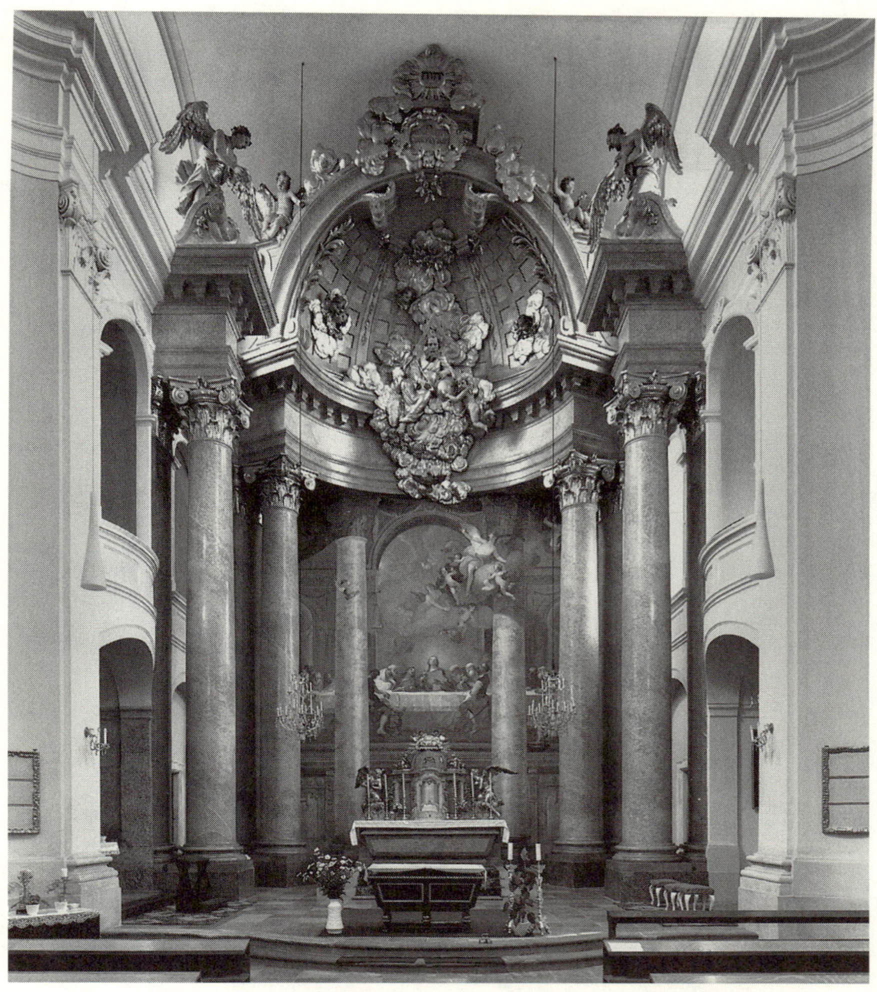

FIGURE 50. J. F. Hetzendorf von Hohenberg, with high altar mural painting by Maulbertsch of Last Supper, 1773, Augustinian Church, Korneuburg, Lower Austria (Photograph: Bundesdenkmalamt, Vienna)

ures of Christ and the apostles to suggest the numen of Jesus and the divine transubstantiation of his being. Similar use of color (instead of allegory) to suggest a mystery of the faith has been observed at Dyje (Figure 51).[72]

Maulbertsch carried tendencies of coloring and handling in mural painting even further than did his contemporaries in Central Europe. Like most mural painters of the seventeenth and eighteenth century in his region, Maulbertsch does not work in a true fresco technique, strictly speaking. Instead of taking up

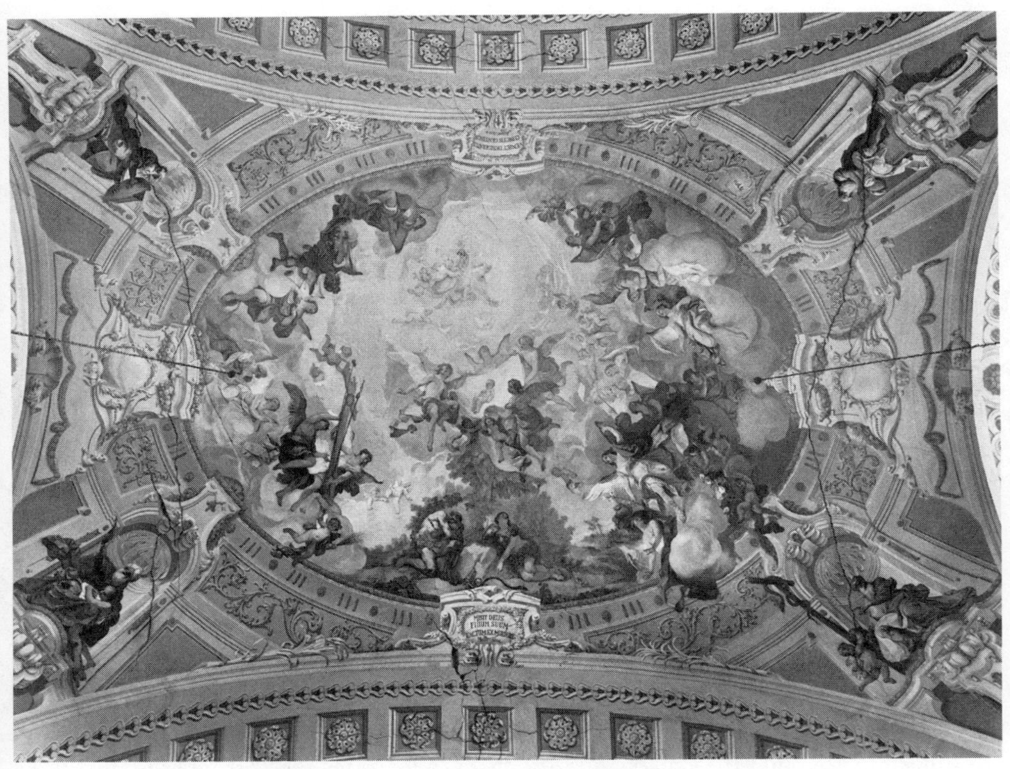

FIGURE 51. F. A. Maulbertsch, *Allegory of Salvation*, nave ceiling, 1776–77, Parish Church, Dyje (Mühlfraun), Moravia, Czech Republic (Photograph: Brno University, courtesy Bishopric of Brno)

the classic Italian method of working in true fresco ("*buon fresco*"), Central European artists used a technique that has been called *Kalkmalerei*. They worked with water and lime-based pigments on an already dried plaster surface slaked with sand. This surface may have been gone over a number of times. They may have applied paint on the dry wall in secco (*a secco*) with a variety of binding materials. Secco details are added for more saturated hues, or where the tones must be applied with pigments that are not soluble in water.

Although Maulbertsch was not concerned with the kinds of fictive architecture and perspective discussed in Andrea Pozzo's treatise, and also used assistants for the painting of fictive architecture, Pozzo, whose book was widely known and available in German translation, provides instructive information for the technique of fresco painting used by artists of Maulbertsch's time.[73] Pozzo had recommended working with a loaded brush and using impasto (*caricare et impastare*).

Over a neutral ground, Maulbertsch applies the paint, often in layers wet in wet; he builds up surfaces with impasto, especially in the highlights. This combination of layers of paint and impasto allows for the creation of luminous coloristic effects similar to those seen in oil painting.

In this sense as well Maulbertsch may be regarded as the "finest flower of a universal painterly culture," as Hempel put it. Similarly Füßli linked Maulbertsch with other Central European artists, expressly naming Gran, Troger, Palko, Unterberger, and other contemporary history painters. But Füßli also recognized Maulbertsch's singular qualities. He indicated as much when he singled Maulbertsch out as an original strangeling—as did Schweigel when he called him a true original—for the painterly effects in mural paintings observable in other Central European artists of Maulbertsch's time (most noticeably in those of Johann Lucas Kracker [1719–79], as at Jasov [Jaszó] or Nová Říše, for example)[74] seem even more pronounced in his oeuvre. Here, as in many other respects, he epitomizes and transcends his colleagues.

This is observable in Maulbertsch's working procedures as well. Lines inscribed into the walls are conventionally interpreted as the results of the use of cartoons. So, for example, the outlines of painted figures in frescoes by Tiepolo (as visible for instance in detached frescoes from the Palazzo Valle now in the Metropolitan Museum of Art, New York) correspond closely to the lines that have been incised into the wall, suggesting that the incisions result from the transfer of designs from cartoons to the wall. Similar details are observable in the architectural elements of walls painted by Maulbertsch and his crew, as for example at Dyje, where it is known that he received assistance, and thus likely that these areas were so outlined to allow for execution by the workshop. In contrast, where marks are inscribed in the surface of the figural compositions of the ceiling at Dyje, they suggest that he was using the incisions in wet plaster as a kind of preliminary design. The presence of such deviating lines in ornamental areas in Maulbertsch's earlier works, in smaller spaces where he could have executed the whole design, as, for example, at Ebenfurth, suggest his hand and composition (Figure 52). Similarly, on the ceiling at Dyje, many pentimenti, changes in design, are visible in the painting of figures. While sgraffito indentations in the interior of figures are also found in the work of other Austrian artists, interpreting them together with such pentimenti suggests that he may have worked freely on the wall. This inference also seems consistent with what the observation that with Maulbertsch invention is synonymous with execution—as it is with a later painter who was much concerned with color harmony and balance, Paul Cézanne.[75]

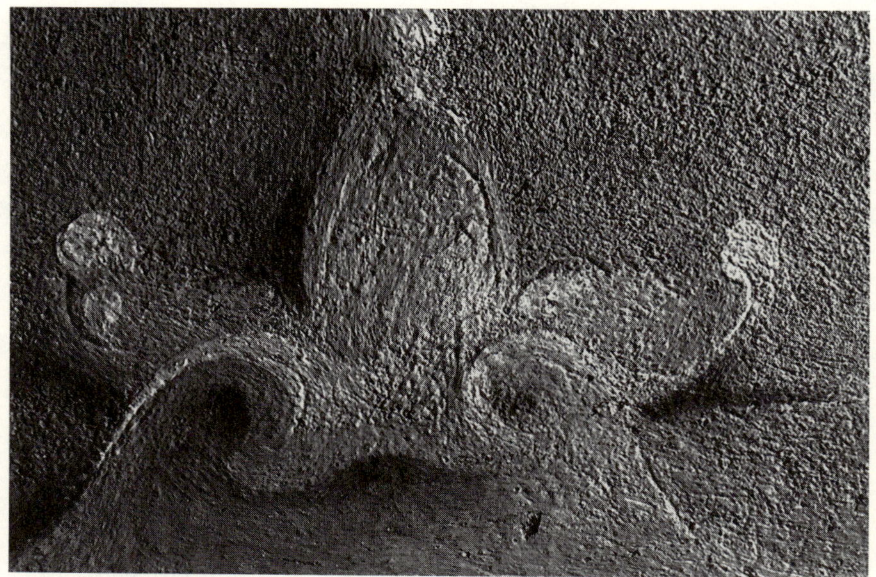

FIGURE 52. F. A. Maulbertsch, detail on chapel wall, 1754, Schloss Suttner, Ebenfurth (Photograph: Eduard Beranek)

Maulbertsch moreover seems to have pushed the possibilities of his media to their limits. In some cases, such as the representation of God the Father in his mural of the Vision of St. John in the sacristy of the (former) Carthusian church at Královo Pole (Plate 35), he models a figure using just the ground and plaster or white lime-colored paint itself for highlights, with the incisions scratched into the surface for outlines. This technique represents an extreme stage in the development of the painterly tendencies of the epoch. Hence, while Maulbertsch may be compared to contemporary muralists in Central Europe and elsewhere, he may also be seen to take things further. His coloring and handling take the practices of his day to a such a degree that more general reflection is provoked.

De Piles and those who represented what he stood for in the debate over coloring contradicted implicitly the theories of vision advanced by Locke, Newton, and others who had maintained that color was a secondary quality. De Piles considered color to be of primary importance. Color was essential to effect the unity of a painting, since this unity was perceived through the action of coloring on an observer's perception of the composition.[76]

Pictorial unity was accordingly no longer to be found in the subject matter of a painting, but in the elements of painting themselves, that is, in its visual qualities. Above all color constituted these visual qualities. Since it can thus be argued that *coloris* was what pertained to the visible in a picture, de Piles attributed to *coloris* the specifically visual attainments of painting.[77] Since color is what is imparted by paint, and coloring and handling are paramount in painting, de Piles's thesis may moreover be interpreted as representing a preliminary statement of the "autonomy thesis in visual aesthetics, that is, the idea that the work of art reaches its maximum degree of authenticity to the extent that it dramatizes the material possibilities and limitations of its unique medium."[78]

This thesis was reinforced by other currents of eighteenth-century thought that also diverge from the line of Winckelmann. The signal text here is Lessing's *Laokoon*, where Lessing takes issue with Winckelmann's ideas of noble simplicity and quiet grandeur ("*edle Einfalt und stille Grösse*") as expressed in his analysis of the ancient sculpture. As is well known, in this critique Lessing severed the connection between poetry and painting that had been the foundation stone for basing artistic theory on poetics or rhetoric. Lessing argued that painting and poetry work according to their own principles and processes.

Lessing published this work in 1766, at a crucial time of change in Maulbertsch's style, and he certainly had connections with the Habsburg lands. In the early 1770s Lessing was in contact with Kaunitz, and thus with circles with whom Maulbertsch was also involved. Lessing sought to get a position at the academy in Vienna, with which the painter was associated; in 1775 he was received at court.[79] Thus not only the arguments over coloring but literary theories as well may be taken into account for establishing some of the critical parameters for an understanding of Maulbertsch's work.

As Thomas Crow has suggested, the autonomy thesis of the arts advanced for the first time in the eighteenth century is a concept central to twentieth-century accounts of and arguments for pictorial modernism.[80] "Towards a New Laocoon" is the manifesto of one of its most important advocates, Clement Greenberg. Its central argument is that the arts have their own autonomous principles, which are related to their specific media.[81] In pushing painting of the ancien régime to the limits of the possibilities of the painterly aspects of art, those in which the elements of painting themselves express both the form and the meaning of the work, Maulbertsch may be regarded as having moved to the margins of modernism.

Just as he was not a neoclassicist, Maulbertsch was to be sure neither a romantic nor an impressionist; nor was he an expressionist. Nevertheless, echoes of the painterly aspects of his art are present in later times. The approach to color that he represented, including the use of broken color, and color harmonies, are topics of importance in the writings (and art) of Eugène Delacroix, Stendhal, and Charles Baudelaire.[82] De Piles's idea that *coloris* demands a certain distance for its effects to be taken in[83]—relevant to Maulbertsch, as is clear from the problem of apprehension in Kroměříž—resonates in much color theory of the nineteenth century and in impressionist practice. One does not have to argue that Maulbertsch is a forerunner of the romantics or the impressionists, as some art historians have done, to see how these concerns, and much of the discussion of coloring in relation to Maulbertsch, have had a continuing history that Maulbertsch anticipates.[84]

Moreover, the "sublime" aspects of Maulbertsch's art revealed in his use of color and handling—that is, the use of materials of painting itself to convey the spiritual, as seen at Korneuburg—also resonate. These were just the elements of his art that appealed to Oskar Kokoschka. Even if Kokoschka's observation about Maulbertsch and the light-filled spiritual is idiosyncratic and anachronistic, there is an important kernel of truth in his recognition that there was still something more to Maulbertsch's coloring, that it may have had a spiritual quality. It also does not seem unjustified to suggest links between Maulbertsch's use of color and observations on the spiritual impact of color made by later artists like Kandinsky.[85] One also does not need to speak, as does Krsek, of the "*nordico*" in Maulbertsch's art, or to evoke a "northern tradition,"[86] to compare the sublime effects of Maulbertsch to those of a painter like Mark Rothko. Rothko also spoke of the transcendent effects of color, and these effects may be regarded as meaningful.[87] Finally we may recall that Rothko painted wall-sized paintings, as well a chapel in which he tried to express spiritual values through the medium of color. Rothko moreover found this solution in an age when, as in Maulbertsch's time, painting had difficulty expressing such values with conviction and persuasive power.[88]

Maulbertsch is clearly not a modernist painter. He obviously cannot be closely compared to Kokoschka, Kandinsky, or Rothko. Despite some elements that have been seen in details of his pictures, his art was never abstract, and his coloring always served a distinctive purpose. Moreover, while it has been said that it was possible to argue for the autonomy of painting only by drawing on interests and values hostile to those of a tutelary and disciplinary rationalism,[89] it was precisely these values that were being expressed in a critique of art to which Maulbertsch himself was subjected. His painting, a creation of his time, had only limited followers, such as Winterhalder, who could work in mural media. Beautiful and extraordinary as it is, Maulbertsch's art therefore epitomizes painterly Enlightenment, with all the contradictions and paradoxes in this concept. In the end, while Maulbertsch's painting possesses elements and expresses interests comparable to those of later artists, he must be regarded as having remained on the margins of modernism.

This book has tried to introduce and to explicate some aspects of the seemingly paradoxical notion of painterly Enlightenment. Maulbertsch was an outstanding painter in a traditional medium, who worked in established genres at a time of change and crisis for the arts and social institutions. He tried to negotiate between contradictory tendencies and demands. But the paradoxes and contradictions that Maulbertsch faced are not restricted to the issues of his own time. Maulbertsch may be seen first of all as an outstanding painter of the ancien régime, but his work is not only of antiquarian interest. Maulbertsch introduces some of the major problems involved in making art in the modern era.

Notes

CHAPTER ONE

1. For this notion, see Carol M. Armstrong, *"Odd Man Out": Readings of the Work and Reputation of Edgar Degas* (Chicago and London, 1991). Maulbertsch is much more left out of the trajectory of art history and its canon than is Degas.

Maulbertsch is so spelled in this book, although in Austrian and South German pronunciation the name is often pronounced Maulpertsch, and is occasionally so written.

2. See Otto Benesch, "Maulbertsch: Zu den Quellen seiner malerischen Stiles," *Städel-Jahrbuch* 3 (1924): 175; Bruno Bushart, "Die Offenbarung der göttlichen Weisheit: Zur Augsburger Bildskizze des Franz Anton Maulbertsch," *Alte und moderne Kunst* 16, no. 115 (1971): 31; Karl M. Swoboda, *Die Kunst des 18. Jahrhunderts* (Vienna and Munich, 1982), 238; Oskar Kokoschka, "Vorwort," in Klára Garas, *Franz Anton Maulbertsch: Leben und Werk* (Salzburg, 1974), 7.

3. I follow the dating of the Schweigel manuscript in Jiří Kroupa, *Alchymie štěstí: Pozdní osvícenství a moravská společnost* (Kroměříž and Brno, 1986), 163 (see passim for more on Schweigel). Cf. Bohumil Samek, "Počátky dějin umění na Moravě," *Umění* 32 (1984), 100, where it is dated to the winter months of 1784/85, with additions having been made later, but before 1809.

Miloš Stehlík, "Andreas Schweigl (1735–1812): sculpteur et 'artiste savant,'" in *La Moravie à l'âge baroque, 1670–1790: Dans le miroir des ombres* [exhibition catalog, Musée des Beaux-Arts de Rennes] (Paris and Brno, 2002), 325–35, supplies an accessible introduction to Schweigel's work.

4. C. Hálová-Jahodová, "Andreas Schweigel, Bildende Künste in Mähren," *Umění* 20 (1972): 184. More of Schweigel's comments will be considered in greater detail in chapter 4.

5. For the evolution of this conception, see David Quint, *Origin and Originality in Renaissance Literature: Versions of the Source* (New Haven and London, 1983), and for its eighteenth-century transformation, 217–20.

6. "Maulbertsch aber, ein origineller Sonderling, der damahls den Ton im großen historischen Fache zu geben anfing, würde, ungeachtet seiner schätzbaren Kunsteigenschaften, den jungen Akademikern mehr schädlich als nützlich gewesen seyn, wenn er die Leitung über sich genommen hätte; weil es noch weit bedenklicher ist, angehende Künstler ganz aus dem Kreise der Fundamentalregeln treten zu lassen, als sie mit einer gar zu

großen Menge Regeln zu beschweren." Hans Rudolf Füßli, *Annalen der bildenden Künste für die österreichischen Staaten* (Vienna, 1801), 1:19.

Except where otherwise noted, all translations are my own.

7. Ibid., 1:67–143. For these painters and the movement of "classicism" that they represent, see most comprehensively Ksenija Rozman, *Franc Kavčič/Caucig* [exhibition catalog, Narodna galerija] (Ljubljana, 1978), and more recently Bettina Hagen, *Antike in Wien: Die Akademie und der Klassizismus um 1800* [exhibition catalog, Akademie der bildenden Künste, Vienna] (Mainz, 2002), with further references.

It is noteworthy that Maulbertsch had rejected Maurer as a pupil.

8. See Klára Garas, *Franz Anton Maulbertsch, 1724–1796* (Graz, 1960), 174; this part of the present account (which expands on and differs from Garas) is taken from her treatment, 167–76, of Maulbertsch in the literature of art, in which Garas also sees romanticism as having had an impact on the reception of Maulbertsch.

9. For aspects of the impact of nationalism on the geographical configuration of the historiography of art, see Thomas DaCosta Kaufmann, *Toward a Geography of Art* (Chicago, 2004), 47–61, 70–90.

10. See Elisabeth Springer, "Biographische Skizze zu Albert Ilg (1847–1896)," in *Fischer von Erlach und die Wiener Barocktradition*, ed. Friedrich Polleroß (Vienna, Cologne, and Weimar, 1995), 319–43.

11. Albert Ilg, "Die Rococozeit," in *Kunstgeschichtliche Charakterbilder aus Österreich-Ungarn*, ed. Ilg (Prague, Vienna, and Leipzig, 1893), 323: Maulbertsch was "sehr tüchtig im historischen Fache, am geistreichsten in seinen Skizzen, in der farbigen Ausführung bisweilen allzu süß und zierlich."

12. See Otto Benesch, "Vorwort," in *Franz Anton Maulbertsch und die Kunst des österreichischen Barock im Jahrhundert Mozarts* (Vienna, 1956), 5: "Zugleich wurde aber Maulbertsch durch seine kühne Kunst, die selbst vor Verzerrung dem Ausdruck zuliebe nicht zurückschreckte, zu einem staunenerregenden Vorläufer des Zeitalters des Expressionismus, das ihn nicht umsonst wiederentdeckt hat."

13. Hans Tietze, "Programme und Entwürfe zu den grossen österreichischen Barockfresken," *Jahrbuch der kunsthistorischen Sammlungen des allerhöchsten Kaiserhauses* 30 (1910): 1–28.

14. Max Dvořák, "Über Greco und den Manierismus," in *Kunstgeschichte als Geistesgeschichte* (Munich, 1928), 262–76. Dvořák's view of the "anaturalistic" aspects of El Greco's art should be noted: "Von Michelangelo übernahm Greco den Anaturalismus der Form, von Tintoretto die anaturalistische Farbe und Komposition" (269).

15. Max Dvořák, *Zur Entwicklungsgechichte der barocken Deckenmalerei in Wien* (Augsburg and Vienna, n.d. [1920]), 17–18: "Seine Ausdrucksmittel teilt er mit der gleichzeitigen Kunst tiepolesker Richtung, doch was bei seinen Vorgängern und Zeitgenossen mehr oder weniger eine konventionelle Sprache war, nimmt bei Maulpertsch ein individuelles Gepräge an von unerhörter Kraft und Originalität. Die Bewegungen steigern sich zu einem Orkan, die Farben und Beleuchtungseffekte zu wahren Orgien, die Formen verbinden sich zu ungeahnten Möglichkeiten und die irdisch-himmlischen Kompositionen, durch die Gewalt der individuell lebensvollen Erfindung zu neuen Einheiten verbunden, gehören wohl zu dem Kühnsten, was wir der Malerei des 18. Jahrhunderts zu verdanken haben."

16. See Almut Krapf-Weiler, "Zur Bedeutung des österreichischen Barock für Oskar Kokoschka," *Wiener Jahrbuch für Kunstgeschichte* 40 (1987): 197, 199, 200, from which the quotations by Kokoschka are also taken.

17. Adolf Feulner, *Skulptur und Malerei des 18. Jahrhunderts in Deutschland* (Wildpark-Potsdam, 1929), 230–34. Nikola Michailow, *Österreichische Malerei des 18. Jahrhunderts: Formgestalt und provinzieller Formbetrieb* (Frankfurt a. M., 1935), 24–28, deals with "expression" in Maulbertsch's work, but considers him an exemplar of provincial painting.

18. Benesch, "Maulbertsch," 107–76.

19. Franz Martin Haberditzl, *Franz Anton Maulbertsch* (Vienna, 1977). The Vienna dissertations of Josef Mühlmann, "Die Kunst Anton Maulbertschs" (Vienna, 1913), and Ernst Goldschmidt, "Maulbertschstudien: Zu seinen Altar- und Andachtsbildern" (Vienna, 1930), remained unpublished.

20. Garas, *Maulbertsch, 1724–1796*.

21. Kokoschka, "Vorwort," 5–7.

22. Klára Garas, "Neue Bücher über den Barock," *Acta Historiae Artium Hungarica* 25 (1979): 319.

23. *Franz Anton Maulbertsch: Ausstellung anläßlich seines 250. Geburtstages; Wien Halbturn Heiligenkreuz-Gutenbrunn* (Vienna and Munich, 1974); *Franz Anton Maulbertsch és Kora* (Budapest, 1974). The only previous exhibition featuring Maulbertsch had been organized in the Graphische Sammlung Albertina by Otto Benesch, *Franz Anton Maulbertsch und die Kunst des österreichischen Barock im Jahrhundert Mozarts* (Vienna, 1956).

24. *Franz Anton Maulbertsch und sein Kreis in Ungarn* (Sigmaringen, 1984); *Franz Anton Maulbertsch und der Wiener Akademiestil* (Sigmaringen, 1994); *Franz Anton Maulbertsch und sein schwäbischer Umkreis* (Sigmaringen, 1996).

25. Dimitri Schelest, *Maulpertsch in Lemberg: Ölskizzen und Zeichnungen österreichischer Barockmaler aus dem Legat des k.k. Majors Karl Kühnl (1818–1872) in den Sammlungen der Ukrainischen Akademie der Wissenschaften und aus der Lemberger Gemäldegalerie* (Salzburg, 1990).

26. *Maurer, Kalk und Sand oder der Maler Franz Anton Maulbertsch: Materialien zu Leben und Werk, 1724–1796*, ed. Nora and Gerhard Fischer (Vienna, 1998).

27. I have been able to find only two articles on Maulbertsch in French: Jean Bourdeillette, "Maulbertsch (1724–1796)," *Gazette des Beaux Arts* 6, no. 74 (1932): 105–11, and Boris Lossky, "Une Esquisse de Franz-Anton Maulbertsch au Musée de Tours," *Gazette des Beaux Arts* 55 (1960): 51–6. The Musée du Louvre has also recently acquired two sketches by the artist.

Lubomír Slavíček, "Franz Anton Maulbertsch et son cercle en Moravie," in *La Moravie à l'âge baroque*, 217–31, provides an introduction in the context of an exhibition held in Rennes in 2002 at which some paintings by Maulbertsch and his circle were shown.

28. Heinrich Schwarz, "Franz Anton Maulbertsch in American Museums," *Baltimore Museum of Art News* 23 (1959): 9–15; Klára Garas, "A Genre Painting by F. A. Maulbertsch," *Register of the Museum of Art, The University of Kansas* 2, nos. 9/10 (1963): 2–7; H. S. Francis, "Franz Anton Maulbertsch: The Presentation of Christ in the Temple," *Bulletin of the Cleveland Museum of Art* 51 (1964): 14–18; Edward A. Maser, "Franz Anton Maulbertsch as Portraitist: Some Questions about the Vienna Self-Portrait," *Pantheon* 29 (1971): 292–307; Peter Cannon-Brookes, "The Oil Paintings of Franz Anton Maulbertsch in the Light of the 1974 Exhibitions," *Burlington Magazine* 109 (1976): 19–31.

29. For example, in Eberhard Hempel, *Baroque Art and Architecture in Central Europe* (Harmondsworth, 1965), 296–300; Thomas DaCosta Kaufmann, *Court, Cloister, and City: The Art and Culture of Central Europe, 1450–1800* (Chicago and London, 1995), 425–32, 449–58.

30. See, for example, Julius S. Held and Donald Posner, *17th and 18th Century Art: Baroque Painting, Sculpture, Architecture* (Englewood Cliffs and New York, n.d. [1979]), 406. This book illustrates the frequently reproduced study of St. James for paintings once in Schwechat (Österreichische Galerie, Vienna); another frequently reproduced image is a sketch of an unknown saint (often called St. Narcissus) in the same collection: see the next note.

31. Robert Harbison, *Reflections on Baroque* (Chicago, 2000), 27, 33. Harbison's distinction between Pozzo and Maulbertsch may be acceptable to the extent that the Italian painter's concern with complicated architectural settings and perspective constructions is not shared by Maulbertsch, who seems often to have employed specialists in architectural painting for such elements in his frescoes. Hence although it might seem that Pozzo, who did work in Vienna and Bratislava, would have had an influence on Maulbertsch, this is difficult to discern. Of course, as is discussed below (in chapter 4), his prescriptions for the actual application of paint as commonplaces are applicable to Maulbertsch.

32. Kokoschka, "Vorwort," 5.

33. For these themes, see *Verdrängter Humanismus—verzögerte Aufklärung: Österreichische Philosophie zur Zeit der Revolution und Restauration (1750–1820)*, ed. Michael Benedikt (Vienna, 1992); Ernst Wangermann, *Von Joseph II. zu den Jakobinerprozessen* (Vienna, Frankfurt a. M., Zurich, 1966). The meaning of Enlightenment in this context is discussed in chapter 2.

34. For the general historiographic situation, see Thomas DaCosta Kaufmann, "Central European Drawings, 1680–1800, Introduction," in *Central European Drawings, 1680–1800: A Selection from American Collections* (Princeton, 1989), 3–7, and Kaufmann, in collaboration with Heiner Borggrefe and Thomas Füsenig, "Introduction," in *Art and Architecture in Central Europe, 1550–1620: An Annotated Bibliography* (Marburg, 2003), 14–23.

35. In *Tiepolo and the Pictorial Intelligence* (New Haven and London, 1994), 6–8, Svetlana Alpers and Michael Baxandall also make the point about the location of Tiepolo's paintings and his supposed lack of critical attention.

36. Tiepolo remains the recurrent comparison for Maulbertsch, but Benesch, "Maulbertsch," 108–12, already criticized this association, although he made comparisons with other Venetian painters. Differences between Maulbertsch and Tiepolo will be considered at greater length in chapter 4.

37. Germain Bazin, *Baroque and Rococo Art* (London, 1964), 242, noted that the coloring of Austrian baroque painting was "brighter, more joyful, more voluptuous" than that of contemporary German painting.

38. As by the older criticism of Feulner, *Skulptur und Malerei des 18. Jahrhunderts in Deutschland*, 230–34; Hempel, *Baroque Art and Architecture in Central Europe*, 296–300.

39. See David Batchelor, *Chromophobia* (London, 2000).

40. Jacqueline Lichtenstein, *The Eloquence of Color: Rhetoric and Painting in the French Classical Age*, trans. Emily McVarish (Berkeley, Los Angeles, and Oxford, 1993), 4, 149. In view of the comments on Maulbertsch's painterly "fire," a statement of Lichtenstein's seems apropos: "Fascinated by painting, philosophical thought has always burned itself in the fires of color" (4).

41. As distinct from the question of the treatment of color in art theory, or modern theoretical discussions of the role of color in art, recently there have been some important contributions to the treatment of color in art history: see Paul Hills, *Venetian Colour* (New Haven and London, 1999), and especially the work of John Gage, *Color and Culture: Practice and Meaning from Antiquity to Abstraction* (Berkeley and Los Angeles, 1993), and *Color and Meaning: Art, Science, and Symbolism* (Berkeley and Los Angeles, 1999), both with extensive bibliographies.

42. Günter Brucher, "Deckenfresken," in *Die Kunst des Barock in Österreich*, ed. Brucher (Salzburg and Vienna, 1994), 254: "Nicht nur die Figuren untereinander, sondern auch die Figuren und ihr Hintergrund, seien es Himmel, Wolken oder Architektur, sind oft farblich so angenähert . . . , daß sie aus der Farbe herauszuwachsen oder wieder in sie zu versinken scheinen." (Not only the figures are approximated so closely to each other through color, but so are the figures to their background, whether it be heaven, clouds, or architecture, that they seem to grow up out of it, or else to sink back into their surroundings).

43. The problem presented by the fact that Maulbertsch's greatest paintings are murals or ceilings in out-of-the-way places underscores the difficulty art history has in dealing with this kind of object—and particularly with paintings on ceilings. This presents an acute problem of reproduction, also evident in the present book. However, I disagree with the terms in which this discussion has been put in a recent debate that seemed to have downplayed or misunderstood the importance of illustrations: see the correspondence of Adrian Lewis, James Elkins, and Katerina Duskova in the *Art Bulletin* 84 (2002): 700.

44. Compare plate 1 with plate 32 in Garas, *Maulbertsch: Leben und Werk*.

45. Some technical observations have been made in reference to easel paintings by Maulbertsch that have been restored: see Manfred Koller, "Zum Problem der Übermalung im Werk von Franz Anton Maulbertsch," *Österreichische Zeitschrift für Kunst und Denkmalpflege* 28 (1974): 183–94. Reports have occasionally been published about the restoration of his ceilings: for example, Joseph Zykan, "Die Fresken von Franz Maulbertsch in der Piaristenkirche und ihre Restaurierung," *Österreichische Zeitschrift für Kunst und Denkmalpflege* 2 (1948): 82–98. However, in general it has hitherto been necessary to rely on comments scattered in other articles, notably by Manfred Koller; the publication of technical information regarding the restoration of the frescoes in the Piarist church that occurred after the 1974 exhibition, and was announced as forthcoming in 1989, by Koller, "Neugefundene Gemälde von Franz Anton Maulbertsch," *Acta Historiae Artium* 34 (1989): 218 n. 2, had still not been published at the time this book went to press, nor is this information accessible in the Bundesdenkmalamt in Vienna. The essays in *Barockberichte* 34/35 (2003) contain much of interest on baroque wall and ceiling painting in Austria, but, aside from general summaries, little specifically on Maulbertsch: see Manfred Koller, "Barocke Wand- und Deckenmalerei in Österreich: Technologie und Restaurierung," *Barockberichte* 34/35 (2003), especially 327, and also in general Hubert Paschinger, "Putz- und Farbanalysen zur Wandmalerei des Barock in Österreich," ibid., 332–36.

46. Koller, "Zum Problem der Übermalung," 185, makes this point in regard to the problem of overpainting in Maulbertsch.

47. For Maulbertsch's journeys, entrepreneurial activities, and working methods, see Monika Dachs, ". . . *Mahlergehilfen, Materialien, Kost und Reisespesen* . . . Der Maler Franz Anton Maulbertsch (1724–1796) als künstlerischer Unternehmer," in *Reiselust und Kunst-*

genuss: Barockes Böhmen, Mähren und Österreich, ed. Friedrich Polleroß (Petersberg, 2004), 201–18.

48. Bruno Bushart, "Die deutsche Ölskizze des 18. Jahrhunderts als autonomes Kunstwerk," *Münchener Jahrbuch der bildende Kunst* 15 (1964): 145–276; Bushart, "Die barocke Ölskizze als autonomes Kunstwerk," in *Barock Regional-international*, Kunsthistorisches Jahrbuch Graz, 25 (Graz, 1993), 49–59.

49. See most comprehensively Christiane Lemmens, *Studien zur Bildgenese im Oeuvre des Franz Anton Maulbertsch (1724–1796): Zeichnung—Ölskizze—Ausführung*, Studien zur Kunstgeschichte, 2 (Bonn, 1996).

50. Documents connected with Maulbertsch's estate do not indicate that he possessed a collection of his own drawings; Garas, *Maulbertsch, 1724–1796*, 284, docs. clxv and clxvi.

51. These issues are considered in the *Habilitationsschrift*, still unpublished at time of writing, of Monika Dachs, "Franz Anton Maulbertsch und sein Kreis: Studien zur Wiener Malerei in der zweiten Hälfte des 18. Jahrhunderts," 3 vols. (University of Vienna, 2003).

52. Heinrich Schwarz, who had been curator in the Österreichisches Barockmuseum, and would therefore have been familiar with the largest collection of the artist's oil sketches, recognized this long ago; see Schwarz, "Maulbertsch in American Museums," 9.

53. Koller, "Zum Problem der Übermalung."

54. As raised in arguments by Dachs, "Maulbertsch und sein Kreis."

55. Feulner, *Skulptur und Malerei des 18. Jahrhunderts in Deutschland*, 230.

56. Hempel, *Baroque Art and Architecture*, 297.

57. Heinrich Wölfflin, *Kunstgeschichtliche Grundbegriffe: Das Problem der Stilentwicklung in der neueren Kunst* (Munich, 1915]), 20–79.

58. Hempel, *Baroque Art and Architecture*, 299.

59. Kokoschka, "Vorwort," 5.

60. Most notably by Bushart, "Die Offenbarung der göttlichen Weisheit," especially 30.

61. For detailed consideration of Maulbertsch's relation to the surroundings of his early years, see Hubert Hosch, "Franz Anton Maulbertsch und Süddeutschland: Anmerkungen zu Ein- bzw. Rückwirkungen und zu Fragen der Eigenhändigkeit," *Zeitschrift für Geschichte des Bodensees und seiner Umgebung* 108 (1990): 161–97, and further *Maulbertsch und sein schwäbischer Umkreis*.

62. For this problem, in relation to questions of attribution, see Bruno Bushart, "Der lyrische Maulbertsch," in *Imagination und Imago. (Festschrift für Kurt Rossacher)* (Salzburg, 1983), 25–39; Klára Garas, "Franz Anton Maulbertsch: Neue Zuschreibungen und neue Probleme," in *Kunst und Kultur um den Bodensee: Zehn Jahre Museum Langenargen; Festgabe für Eduard Hindelang*, ed. Ernst Ziegler (Sigmaringen, 1986), 143–60. See further the works cited in the following notes.

63. See Hubert Hosch, "Das wiedergefundene Akademiepreisgemälde von Franz Anton Maulbertsch und sein Umfeld," *Pantheon* 58 (2000): 113–17.

64. Questions concerning Maulbertsch and his contemporaries at the Vienna academy are considered most thoroughly in *Franz Anton Maulbertsch und der Wiener Akademiestil*; see especially Hubert Hosch, "Franz Anton Maulbertsch und die Wiener Akademie," 14–92.

65. Maulbertsch's estate included a collection of prints; see Garas, *Maulbertsch, 1724–1796*, 284, doc. clxvi.

66. For a review of the question of Italian influence in Vienna during Maulbertsch's student years, see Klara Garas, "Der italienische Einfluß und der Wiener Akademiestil zur Zeit von Franz Anton Maulbertsch," in *Franz Anton Maulbertsch und der Wiener Akademiestil*, 93–110.

67. See the useful summary by Christoph Becker, Axel Burkarth, and August Bernhard Rave, "The Habsburg Empire," in "The International Taste for Venetian Art," in *The Glory of Venice: Art in the Eighteenth Century*, ed. Jane Martineau and Andrew Robison [exhibition catalog, Royal Academy, London, and National Gallery of Art, Washington, D.C.] (New Haven and London, 1994), 45–52.

68. See Füßli, *Annalen*, 23, 24; Kaufmann, *Central European Drawings*, 10–24; Lubomír Slavíček, "Dessin: 'La Prima Achatemia,'" in *La Moravie à l'âge baroque*, 247–55.

69. First published in Kaufmann, *Central European Drawings*, 23, fig. 9.

70. For Troger's drawing in Italy and the origins of his style, see Bernard Aikema, "Paul Troger: A Transalpine Journey," *On Paper* 2 (1998): 12–19.

71. For a discussion of the sources and style of Kracker's drawings at the Vienna academy, and illustrations, see Anna Jávor, "Kracker Bécsben," *Művészettörténeti Értesítő* 32 (1984): 97–211. Slavíček, "Dessin," 248, has however suggested that this style was developed in a private academy that Joseph Winterhalder the Elder may have had in Znojmo (Znaim), in southern Moravia. For Winterhalder's Trogeresque drawings, see Monika Dachs, "Joseph Winterhalder der Ältere und Paul Troger: Definitionsversuch eines Zeichenstils," *Kunstjahrbuch der Stadt Linz, 1996–1997* (1998): 124–44. In any case this style would have formed the basis for Winterhalder's nephew, Joseph the Younger, who was Maulbertsch's assistant in the 1760s and again, at Dyje, in the 1770s, and who completed projects left at Maulbertsch's death. For a recent summary of the younger Winterhalder's work, see Lubomír Slavíček, "*. . . diese herrliche Arbeit den Werken des seelg. Maulbertsch so ähnlich* . . . Der mährische Maler Joseph Winterhalder d. J. (1743–1807) im Schatten von Franz Anton Maulbertsch," in *Reiselust und Kunstgenuss*, 229–40.

72. See Monika Dachs, "Original und Kopie: Zeichnungen im Bannkreis von Paul Troger," *Pantheon* 58 (2000): 103–13.

73. See, for example, James Henry Rubin in collaboration with David Levine, *Eighteenth-Century French Life Drawing* (Princeton, 1976).

74. For the Schmutzer drawing illustrated here, see Kaufmann, *Central European Drawings*, 23, fig. 10, and further ibid., cat. no. 51, ill. 146, cat. no. 54, ill. 153, for academic studies by Matthäus Donner and Franz Xaver Messerschmidt.

75. See, for example, a drawing associated with Troger's work for Altenburg in 1742; Edmund Schilling, *Städelsches Kunstinstitut Frankfurt am Main: Katalog der deutschen Zeichnungen, Alte Meister* (Munich, 1973), 1:203, no. 2088.

76. Michael Krapf, "Paul Troger, Josef Ignaz Mildorfer, Michelangelo Unterberger: Beiträge zur Tiroler Antiklassik in Wien," *Kunsthistoriker—Mitteilungen des Österreichischen Kunsthistorikerverbandes* 2 (1985): 68–73.

77. See Elisabeth Leube Payer: ". . . daß nunmehro seine Stücke dem Maister gleich geachtet werden." "Joseph Ignaz Mildorfer und sein expressiv malerischer Stil" / ". . . that from now on his pictures are as much honoured as the master's." "Joseph Ignaz Mildorfer and his expressiv [*sic*], picturesque Style," *Belvedere* 6 (2000): 29–47 and 86–95.

78. See Monika Dachs, "Der Geschmackswandel an der Wiener Maler-Akademie um

1740: Unterberger, Troger, Mildorfer—und die Folgen," in *Strukturwandel kultureller Praxis: Beiträge zu einer kulturwissenschaftlichen Sicht des theresianischen Zeitalters*, ed. Franz M. Eybl (*Jahrbuch der Österreichischen Gesellschaft zur Erforschung des achtzehnten Jahrhunderts* 17 [2002]), 265–87; for Maulbertsch, see 273–75.

79. As suggested first by Haberditzl, *Maulbertsch*, 114–33, who believed that Maulbertsch may have assisted Mildorfer.

80. This has been an issue of some debate, because it has been suggested more than once that Maulbertsch's technical inadequacy was the initial cause for later problems with the condition of the frescoes in the Piarist church, which have been frequently restored: see, for example, Karl Möseneder, "Deckenmalerei," in *Barock*, ed. Hellmut Lorenz, vol. 4 of *Geschichte der bildenden Kunst in Österreich* (Munich, London, and New York, 1999), 369: "Die gravierenden Schäden an der Hauptkuppel entstanden durch die partiell noch unvollkommene Maltechnik Maulbertschs, die Kondenswasserbildung und Versinterungen zur Folge hatte."

However, Manfred Koller, of the Austrian Bundesdenkmalamt and a scholar who has long investigated Austrian wall painting (see n. 45 above), stresses Maulbertsch's technical mastery; he says that Maulbertsch's work is not only one of the high points of Central European baroque painting ". . . sondern zeigt auch im Technischen echte Meisterhaft" ("Zum Problem der Übermalung," 183). He also states uncategorically: "Gegen den Maler Maulbertsch kann, bei derzeitiger Kenntnis seiner Malweise, nicht der für viele andere gültige Vorwurf schlampiger Ausführung und maltechnischen Schleuderns erhoben werden" (ibid., 192).

Restoration of the Piarist church is again under discussion, but, as noted above (see n. 45), no full report is available.

81. The account offered here briefly summarizes the facts of Maulbertsch's life and work as they are presented in Garas, *Maulbertsch, 1724–1796*; Garas, *Maulbertsch: Leben und Werk*; and Haberditzl, *Maulbertsch*.

82. For an account of these paintings according to the restoration undertaken in 1967 (!), see the report of Peter Swittalek, "Die 'Wiederentdeckung' der Maulbertsch-Fresken in der Josephskapelle der Wiener Hofburg," *Österreichische Zeitschrift für Kunst und Denkmalpflege* 51 (1997): 627–36.

83. Noticeably, the only major commission that Maulbertsch had previously received was in 1764 from a cotton manufacturer to paint the frescoes (destroyed in 1944) in the parish church in Schwechat; see Garas, *Maulbertsch, 1724–1796*, 68.

84. See Geza Galavics, "Die letzten Mäzene des Barock—ungarische Kirchenfürsten," in *Künstlerischer Austausch = Artistic Exchange: Akten des XVIII. Internationalen Kongresses für Kunstgeschichte Berlin, 15.–20. Juli 1992*, ed. Thomas W. Gaehtgens (Berlin, 1993), 1:185–98.

85. These aspects of the public sphere are part of the classic definition given in Jürgen Habermas, *Strukturwandel der Öffentlichkeit: Untersuchungen zu einer Kategorie der bürgerlichen Gesellschaft* (Darmstadt and Neuwied, 1962). The theses of Habermas have been built on by many subsequent historians of the Enlightenment.

86. For an excellent recent review and critique of definitions of the Enlightenment, and also for a rejection of its restriction to France, see Carsten Zelle, "Was ist und was war Aufklärung?," in *Mehr Licht: Europa um 1770; Die bildende Kunst der Aufklärung* [exhibition catalog, Städelsches Kunstinstitut] (Frankfurt a. M., 1999), 449–59.

87. As has been argued by Franz Matsche, "Franz Anton Maulbertsch und Daniel Gran: Zur Frage des Klassizismus im österreichischen Spätbarock," in *Herbst des Barock: Studien zum Stilwandel; Die Malerfamilie Keller (1740 bis 1904)*, ed. Andreas Tacke (Munich and Berlin 1998), 203–14.

CHAPTER TWO

1. Halbturn is called Féltorony in Magyar (Hungarian), Halb Thurn in the older documents relating to payments to Maulbertsch, and often Halbthurn in more recent literature; see Julius Fleischer, *Das kunstgeschichtliche Material der Geheimen Kammerzahlamtsbücher in den staatlichen Archiven Wiens von 1705 bis 1790*, Quellenschriften zur barocken Kunst in Österreich und Ungarn (Vienna, 1932), 172–73, docs. 983 and 984, also cited in Klára Garas, *Franz Anton Maulbertsch, 1724–1796* (Graz, 1960), 247, doc. xxx, and Franz Martin Haberditzl, *Franz Anton Maulbertsch* (Vienna, 1977), 301.

2. In a list of his works that Winterhalder supplied to Jakob Schmutzer on December 12, 1796, he mentions the places where he had worked as a student with Maulbertsch (*Als Schüller Bei Selg. Maullbertsch mitgearbeith*); published in János Kapossy, *A Szombathelyi Székesegyház és Mennyezetképei* (Budapest, 1922), 112, doc. 3: the *Lusthaus* in the garden of Count Erdődy in Bratislava; a pilgrimage church in Kirchberg am Wagram; the parish church in Schwechat; Halbturn (spelled by him Halbthurn); the *sala terrena* in the Schloss in Bratislava; the Hofkapelle in Vienna; the refectory in the cloister in Louka; the church in Dyje; and the church in Hradiště u Znojma. Of these (current names of places are used here) the works in Halbturn, Dyje, Vienna, and Hradiště survive.

3. See György Kelény, *Franz Anton Hillebrandt (1719–1797)* (Budapest, 1976), 57, 108.

4. Wilhelm Mrazek, "Deckenmalerei," in *Barock in Österreich* (Vienna, 1962), 47, called the Halbturn composition along with Johann Bergl's frescoes in Melk the purest work of the rococo (*das reinste Rokokowerk*) in Austria; Karl Möseneder, "Deckenmalerei," in *Barock*, ed. Hellmut Lorenz, vol. 4 of *Geschichte der bildenden Kunst in Österreich* (Munich, London, and New York, 1999), 371, no. 126, also refers to it as rococo.

5. See the varying interpretations of Garas, *Maulbertsch, 1724–1796*; Klára Garas, *Franz Anton Maulbertsch, Leben und Werk* (Salzburg, 1974); and Haberditzl, *Maulbertsch*.

6. See in general A. Pigler, *Barockthemen: Eine Auswahl von Verzeichnissen zur Ikonographie des 17. und 18. Jahrhunderts*, 2nd ed. (Budapest, 1974), 2:26–27; for Rottmayr, see Edward A. Maser, *Drawings by Johann Michael Rottmayr* [exhibition catalog, David and Alfred Smart Gallery] (Chicago, 1980), 67–68, cat. no. 35; also Erich Hubala, *Johann Michael Rottmayr* (Vienna and Munich, 1981), 242, cat. no. z36.

7. Wilhelm Mrazek, "Studien zur Ikonologie der barocken Deckenmalerei in Österreich," in *Imagination und Imago. Festschrift für Kurt Rossacher* (Salzburg, 1983), 197, lists further paintings of the theme by Martino Altomonte (1719) in the Lower Belvedere and (1721/22) in the Upper Belvedere, Vienna; by Paul Troger (1737) in the *Marmorsaal* of the Benedictine Abbey in Altenburg; by Gran in the reception hall and in the *Großer Saal* of Schloss Hetzendorf in Vienna (1746/47), as well as in the *Festsaal* at Schloss Fridau at Obergrafendorf in Lower Austria; and by Vincenz Fischer (1753) in the "Temple of Diana" (the "*Grünes Lusthaus*") at Laxenburg.

The painting in the Lower Belvedere traditionally attributed to Chiarini has since the 1930s been assigned to Altomonte; see Hans Aurenhammer, *Martino Altomonte* (Vienna and Munich, 1965), 34, cat. no. 73; it is, however, attributed to Carlone by Amalia Barigozzi Brini and Klára Garas, *Carlo Innocenzo Carloni* (Milan, 1967), 29. For the latest information, see Wolfgang Prohaska, "*Vom Fürsten Prälaten und andere Standespersohnen hatte er öfters großmüthige Bezahlung . . . erhalten*: Der Freskant Carlo Innocenzo Carlone als Maler fürstlicher Glorie," in *Reiselust und Kunstgenuss: Barockes Böhmen, Mähren und Österreich*, ed. Friedrich Polleroß (Petersberg, 2004), 107–18, especially 107. Prohaska's notes contain references to much further bibliography on Carlone.

8. Haberditzl, *Maulbertsch*, 301.

9. See Endre Rácz, *Fertőd* (Budapest, 1972), 16–17.

10. See Mrazek, "Studien," 197–98.

11. Illustrated most recently in *Barock*, ed. Lorenz, 10; see also Thomas DaCosta Kaufmann, *Court, Cloister, and City: The Art and Culture of Central Europe, 1450–1800* (Chicago and London, 1995), 305.

12. In others, where depictions of the four seasons appear, the reference is, however, more general. See, for example, the charming vignette related to summer on the ceiling of the *Festsaal* in Altenburg: *Paul Troger und die österreichische Barockkunst* [exhibition catalog, Stift Altenburg] (Altenburg, 1963), ill. 26.

13. Karl Möseneder, *Franz Anton Maulbertsch: Aufklärung in der barocken Deckenmalerei* (Vienna, Cologne, and Weimar, 1993), 11–12.

14. Maser, *Drawings*, 41.

15. Mrazek, *Barock in Österreich*, 47; Wilhelm Mrazek, "Das Deckenfresko 'Triumph des Lichtes' im Festsaal des Schlosses Halbturn," in *Franz Anton Maulbertsch: Ausstellung anläßlich seines 250. Geburtstages; Wien Halbturn Heiligenkreuz-Gutenbrunn* (Vienna and Munich, 1974), 128–29.

16. Günter Brucher, "Deckenfresken," in *Die Kunst des Barock in Österreich* (Salzburg and Vienna, 1994), 295 n. 205.

17. Möseneder, "Deckenmalerei," 371, s. v. no. 126.

18. Bruno Bushart, "Barock und frühe Aufklärung in der österreichischen Malerei," in *Rationalität und Sentiment: Das Zeitalter Johann Sebastian Bachs und Georg Friedrich Händels*, ed. Vincenz Fischer (St. Ottilien, 1987), 275.

19. See Rolf Reichardt, "Light against Darkness: The Visual Representations of a Central Enlightenment Concept," *Representations* 61 (1998): 95–148; for German examples, see Carsten Zelle, "Was ist und was war Aufklärung?," in *Mehr Licht: Europa um 1770; Die bildende Kunst und die Aufklärung* [exhibition catalog, Städelsches Kunstinstitut] (Frankfurt a. M., 1999), 454–58.

20. "Aufklärung . . . hat bis jetzt noch kein allgemeiner, verständliches, allegorisches Zeichen . . . als die aufgehende Sonne"; quoted in Rudolf Vierhaus, *Was war Aufklärung?* (Wolfenbüttel and Göttingen, 1995), 20. For recent scholarship, see Reichardt, "Light against Darkness," and Zelle, "Was ist und was war Aufklärung?"

21. See Garas, *Maulbertsch, 1724–1796*, 119.

22. Pavel Preiss, "Alegorie výchovy mládeže v díle F. A. Maulbertsche," *Umění* 26 (1978): 348–69.

23. Bushart, "Barock und Frühe Aufklärung," 275–76; "Maulbertsch der Aufklärer," in *Franz Anton Maulbertsch und der Wiener Akademiestil* (Sigmaringen, 1994), 111–34. See further Bushart, "Die Offenbarung der göttlichen Weisheit: Zum Augsburger Bildskizze des Franz Anton Maulbertsch," *Alte und moderne Kunst* 16, no. 15 (1971): 19–31.

24. Möseneder, *Aufklärung.*

25. Bushart, "Die Offenbarung der göttlichen Weisheit"; Pavel Preiss, "Freska F. A. Maulbertsche ve filosofickém salé Strahovské knihovny," *Strahovská knihovna* 2 (1967): 217–34.

26. Karl Möseneder, "Die 'Weisheit' der Aufklärung: Maulbertschs Bibliotheksfresko in Klosterbruck und Korbers 'Historische Erklärung,'" in *Bild und Text im Dialog*, ed. K. Discherl (Passau, 1993), 169–88.

27. Jiří Kroupa, *Alchymie štěstí: Pozdní osvícentství a moravská společnost* (Brno, 1986), 162; Kroupa, "Osvícenství a jeho protipól—poznámky k námětů skic Josefa Winterhaldera ml.," *Sborník prací filosofické fakulty brněnské university*, F 34–36 (1990–92): 117–31; Kroupa, "Fresky," in Petr Kroupa, Jiří Kroupa, Lubomír Slavíček, *Premonstrátský klášter v Louce: Dějiny—umělecká vyzdoba—ikonologie* (Znojmo, 1997); J. Kroupa, "Baroque tardif et siècle des Lumiéres," in *La Moravie à l'âge baroque, 1670–1790: Dans le miroir des ombres* [exhibition catalog, Musée des Beaux-Arts de Rennes] (Paris, 2002), 337–47.

28. Anette Kruszynsi, "Franz Anton Maulbertschs 'Glorifikation Kaiser Josephs II.,'" *Jahrbuch der Kunstsammlungen in Baden-Württemberg* 24 (1987): 25–32; Helmut Börsch-Supan, "Franz Anton Maulbertsch und Berlin," in *Franz Anton Maulbertsch und sein schwäbischer Umkreis* (Sigmaringen, 1996), 224–33; Pavel Preiss, "Vom Tugendhelden zum Tyrannen: Die Umwertung Alexanders des Großen im Streiflicht der Aufklärung," in *Ex fumo lucem: Baroque Studies in Honour of Klára Garas; Presented on Her 80th Birthday* (Budapest, 1999), 1:285–98; Hans-Jürgen Lechtreck, "Herrscher im 'royaume agricole': Das kaiserliche Pflügen als Gegenstand reformabsolutistischer Bildsprache," *Zeitschrift für Kunstgeschichte* 64 (2001): 365–80.

29. For a convenient sampling of views expressed in response to this question by Kant, Erhard, Hamann, et al., see *Was ist Aufklärung? Thesen und Definitionen*, ed. Erhard Bahr (Stuttgart, 1974).

30. The pan-European aspects of the Enlightenment are evident in recent treatments by Barbara Stolberg-Rilinger, *Europa im Jahrhundert der Aufklärung* (Stuttgart, 2000), and Jonathan Israel, *Radical Enlightenment: Philosophy and the Making of Modern Thought* (Oxford, 2001). A more restrictive view is proposed by Robert Darnton, "George Washington's False Teeth," originally in the *New York Review of Books*, 27 March 1997, 34–38.

31. For a convenient recent summary in English, see Dorinda Outram, *The Enlightenment* (Cambridge, 1995), 1–13; see further Zelle, "Was ist und was war Aufklärung?"

32. Vierhaus, *Was war Aufklärung?*

33. For this subject, see Leslie Bodi, *Tauwetter in Wien: Zur Prosa der österreichischen Aufklärung, 1781–1795* (Frankfurt, 1977).

34. Marike Bückling, "'*cognosce et dignosce*'—'Erkenne und differenziere': Messerschmidt—ein Künstler der Aufklärung," in *Franz Xaver Messerschmidt, 1736–1783*, ed. Michael Krapf [exhibition catalog, Lower Belvedere] (Ostfildern-Ruit, 2002), 77, 85.

35. See Isaiah Berlin, "Herder and the Enlightenment," in *Vico and Herder: Two Studies in the History of Ideas* (New York, 1976), 143–216; Berlin, "The Counter-Enlightenment," in *Against the Current: Essays in the History of Ideas*, ed. Henry Hardy (New York, 1982), 1–24; Berlin, *Magus*

of the North: J. G. Hamann and the Origins of Modern Irrationalism, ed. Henry Hardy (Cambridge, 1993); Berlin, *The Roots of Romanticism* (Princeton, 1999), 21–45 ("The First Attack on the Enlightenment").

36. See the essays in *Mehr Licht*.

37. To follow the ideas of Isaiah Berlin, as suggested in the works cited above in n. 35; see further Berlin, "Introduction," in *The Age of Enlightenment: The Eighteenth Century Philosophers* (New York, 1956), 11–29.

38. Discussed most extensively by Möseneder, *Aufklärung*. The present book offers a different interpretation and approach, despite its apparently similar title.

39. For the eighteenth-century origins of an idea advanced by Schiller, see Jeffrey Morrison, *Winckelmann and the Notion of Aesthetic Education* (Oxford, 1996); and Wilhelm Amann, *"Die Stille Arbeit des Geschmacks": Die Kategorie des Geschmacks in der Ästhetik Schillers und in den Debatten der Aufklärung* (Würzburg, 1999).

40. See Panajotis Kondylis, *Die Aufklärung im Rahmen des neuzeitlichen Rationalismus* (Hamburg, 2002), 537–95. The discussion of "reform theology" in Kondylis is interesting to think about in relation to the "Reform Catholicism" discussed in this chapter.

41. See Jiří Kroupa, "Václav Antonín Kaunitz-Rietberg a vytvarná umění," *Studia Comeniana et historica* 18, no. 35 (1985), 78; Kroupa, "Société patriotique de Hessen-Hombourg à Brno," *Časopis Matice moravské* 113 (1994): 142–43.

42. Pavel Preiss, "Böhmen und die österreichische Malerei in der Zeit Maria Theresias und Josephs II.," in *Österreich im Europa der Aufklärung: Kontinuität und Zäsur in Europa zur Zeit Maria Theresias und Josephs II.; Internationales Symposion in Wien, 20.-23. Oktober, 1980* (Vienna, 1985), 2:650.

43. Peter Gay, *The Enlightenment: An Interpretation*, vol. 1, *The Rise of Modern Paganism* (New York, 1967).

44. This is basically the argument of Grete Klingenstein's magisterial *Staatsverwaltung und kirchliche Autorität im 18. Jahrhundert: Das Problem der Zensur in der theresianischen Reform*, Österreich Archiv (Vienna, 1970).

45. Consequently, it has received a good deal of attention: Bushart, "Die Offenbarung der göttlichen Weisheit"; Kroupa, *Alchymie štěstí*, 159–62; Möseneder, "Die 'Weisheit' der Aufklärung"; Möseneder, *Aufklärung*, 17–89.

46. Korber's statement suggests something of the spirit of the painting; *Historische Erklärung der Kalckmahlerey in Freßko, Welch in dem königl. Stif Bruck an der Taya der regulirten Chorherrn von Prämonstrat, auf dem Gewölbe des dasigen Büchersaals* (Znaym [Znojmo], n.d. [1778]), "Absicht" (also reprinted in Möseneder, *Aufklärung*, 198): "Das Licht der Natur—dieser alles vermögende Urstopf der Wissenschaften—machte den Menschen fähig, die Bedürfnißen seiner Gattung so wohl in nützlichen, als schon auch in denen dunkelsten Zeiten auszuspähen. Für seinen immerforschenden Geist wäre es schon Reitze genug bis an neue Quellen selbst vorzudringen, aus denen ihm so mancherley Wohl zuströhmte. Das erhabenste, was seine ordentlichen Nachdenken auffallen könnte, war eine alles erschaffende Weisheit und Güte; und die natürlichste Folge davon belehrte den Erdbewohner, daß er in der Erkänntniß, und in dem Dienste die so wichtige Bestimmung seines Daseyns festsetzen müsse.

"Das Wachsthum dieser Erkänntniß, und des damit nothwendig verbundenen Dienstes, ist der Zweck des Meisters, der hier gemahlet hat."

47. See Möseneder, "Die Weisheit der Aufklärung."

48. See Kroupa, "Baroque tardif et siècle des Lumiéres," 338.

49. For a fuller discussion of the subject, see Eric Garberson, *Eighteenth-Century Monastic Libraries in Southern Germany and Austria: Architecture and Decorations* (Baden-Baden, 1998).

50. See Dagmar Zimdars, "F. A. Maulbertschs Deckengemälde in der Bibliothek des ehemaligen Barnabitenklosters Mistelbach," *Österreichische Zeitschrift für Kunst und Denkmalpflege* 38 (1984): 194–99.

51. Ibid., 199.

52. Möseneder, *Aufklärung*, 88, points to the comparison.

53. See Friedrich Endl, "Ueber die wissenschaftliche Heranbildung der Piaristen im 17. und 18. Jahrhunderte. Mit besonderer Rücksicht auf die deutsche (sc. österr.) Ordens-Provinz," *Mitteilungen der Gesellschaft für deutsche Erziehungs- und Schulgeschichte* 8 (1898): 147–77. For the Piarists' relation to art, see in general Otto Biba, *Der Piaristenorden in Österreich: Seine Bedeutung für bildende Kunst, Musik und Theater im 17. und 18. Jahrhundert* (Eisenstadt, 1975).

54. See further Preiss, "Alegorie výchovy mládeže."

55. Ernst Wangermann, "Reform Catholicism and Political Radicalism in the Austrian Enlightenment," in Mikuláš Teich and Roy Porter, *The Enlightenment in National Context* (Cambridge, 1981), 128.

56. See James Van Horn Melton, *Absolutism and the Eighteenth-Century Origins of Compulsory Schooling in Prussia and Austria* (Cambridge, New York, New Rochelle, Melbourne, Sydney, 1988).

57. Klingenstein, *Staatsverwaltung und kirchliche Autorität.*

58. For this, see chiefly Peter Hersche, *Der Spätjansenismus in Österreich* (Vienna, 1977).

59. For Muratori's impact in Austria, see Eleonore Zlabinger, *Ludovico Antonio Muratori und Österreich*, Veröffentlichungen der Universität Innsbruck, 53; Studien zur Reichs-, Wirtschafts- und Kulturgeschichte, 6 (Innsbruck, 1970). This issue has, however, been variously interpreted: see Adam Wandruszka, "Die katholische Aufklärung Italiens und ihr Einfluß auf Österreich," in *Katholische Aufklärung und Josephinismus*, ed. Elisabeth Kovács (Vienna, 1979), 62–69, with ensuing discussion, 70–74; Eduard Winter, *Der Josefinismus: Die Geschichte des österreichischen Reformkatholizismus, 1740–1848* (Berlin, 1962); and T. C. W. Blanning, *Joseph II and Enlightened Despotism* (Burnt Mill, 1970), 61, 62; and Blanning, *Joseph II* (London and New York, 1994), 43–44.

60. For this information see Wandruszka, "Die katholische Aufklärung Italiens und ihr Einfluß auf Österreich," 64; Blanning, *Joseph II*, 44, quotes Peter Hersche's opinion on Muratori's text as a manifesto.

61. Klingenstein, *Staatsverwaltung und kirchliche Autorität*, 108 n. 69.

62. See ibid., 107, and Zlabinger, *Muratori und Österreich.*

63. Published in Klingenstein, *Staatsverwaltung und kirchliche Autorität*, 207–8.

64. For instance, there was institutional reform, inasmuch as it pertains to the system of courts, such as that undertaken by Leopold Egkh (or Eckh), bishop of Olomouc (Olmütz). Egkh commissioned Maulbertsch to paint the *Lehensaal*, the feudal room where the bishop held his (judicial) court, in the episcopal palace at Kroměříž (Kremsier) in 1759. Maulbertsch's painting at Kroměříž glorifies Egkh in the center of the ceiling, and through four historical examples, emphasizes the historic basis for the rights and glory of the bishopric

and its bishop. For the interpretation of the room in Kroměříž, see the general comments of Haberditzl, *Maulbertsch*, 192–218, and further Jaromír Šíp, "Společenská funkce Maulbertschovy fresky v lenním sále Kroměřížského zámku," *Umění a Svět* 2/3 (1959): 92–101; Ivo Krsek, "Ein Beitrag zum Problem des Kolorits in der 2. Hälfte des 18. Jahrhunderts (F. A. Maulbertschs Freskogemälde im Lehensaal des Kremsierer Schlosses)," *Sborník prací filosofické fakulty brněnské university*, ser. F 5 (1961): 349–66; Krsek, "Das Fresko von Franz Anton Maulbertsch im Lehensaal der Kremsierer Residenz—Zur Frage seines Kolorits," *Alte und moderne Kunst*, no. 87 (1966): 16–23; Antonín Jirka, "*Totus erat Caesareus*: Das Programm des Freskos von Franz Anton Maulbertsch im Lehensaal des Schlosses von Kroměříž (Kremsier)," in *Baroque Art in the 18th Century in Poland, Bohemia, and Hungary*, Niedzica Seminars, 4 (Cracow, 1990), 179–88, also in *Mitteilungen der Österreichischen Galerie* 32–33 (1988–89): 5–17; and Kroupa, "Osvícenství a jeho protipól," 118–19, with an important note on a document, 119 n. 11, referring to a previous publication by the same author.

65. For Biró, see József Pehm, *Padányi Biró Márton Veszprémi Püpök Élete és kora* (Zalegerszeg, 1934), and, more accessible, Gabor Tüskes and Éva Knapp, "Ein ungarischer Bischof zwischen Gegenreformation und Aufklärung: Márton Padányi Biró," *Das achtzehnte Jahrhundert und Österreich: Jahrbuch der Österreichischen Gesellschaft zur Erforschung des achtzehnten Jahrhunderts* 6 (1990/1991): 38–54.

66. See Friedrich Gerke, *Die Fresken des Franz Anton Maulbertsch in der Pfarrkirche zu Sümeg*, Akademie der Wissenschaften und der Literatur; *Abhandlungen der Geistes- und Sozialwissenschaftlichen Klasse*, no. 21 (Mainz, 1950), 7 (1547).

67. See R. J. W. Evans, "Calvinism in East Central Europe; Hungary and Her Neighbours, 1540–1700," in *International Calvinism, 1541–1715*, ed. by Menna Prestwich (Oxford, 1985), 167–96; see further, and for Calvinist art in Hungary, George Starr, "Art and Architecture in the Hungarian Reformed Church," in *Seeing beyond the Word: Visual Arts and the Calvinist Tradition* ed. Paul Corby Finney (Grand Rapids and Cambridge, 1999), 301–40.

68. This is the thrust of the article by Tüskes and Knapp, "Ein ungarischer Bischof."

69. See Michael Wagner, "Spätbarocker Kirchenbau und Frömmigkeit: Die Piaristenkirche Maria Treu in Wien" (Ph.D. diss., Vienna, 1999), 100–102, 175–77.

70. Ludovico Antonio Muratori, *Opere*, ed. Giorgio Falco and Fiorenzo Forti (Milan and Naples, n.d.), 346–47, 951–54.

71. See James Van Horn Melton, "Von Versinnlichung zur Verinnerlichung: Bemerkungen zur Dialektik represäntativer und plebeischer Öffentlichkeit," in *Österreich im Europa der Aufklärung*, 2:934.

72. Muratori, *Contra sublime loquentes in cathedra seu Dignitas Eloquentiae Popularis*, trans. Gregor Trautwein (Augsburg 1757): "Ceterum saeculo proxime elapso vere immoderatio sacrorum quorundem oratorum obtinuit, quam in architectura prudentes damnant cum risu, ornamentorum luxuries." Quoted in Frank Büttner, "Abschied von Pracht und Rhetorik: Überlegungen zu den geistesgeschichtlichen Voraussetzungen des Stilwandels in der Sakraldekoration des ausgehenden 18. Jahrhunderts in Süddeutschland," in *Herbst des Barock: Studien zum Stilwandel; Die Malerfamilie Keller (1740–1904)*, ed. Andreas Tacke (Munich, 1998), 168, 172 n. 28. The same text is cited by Büttner in the expanded version of his essay, "Das Ende des Rokoko in Bayern: Überlegungen zu den geistesgeschichtlichen Voraussetz-

ungen des Stilwandels," *Zeitschrift des Deutschen Vereins für Kunstwissenschaft* 51 (1997 [1999]), 143 n. 59.

73. ". . . die auf kleine Privat andachten, auf die Verehrung eines Heiligen und auf dessen Bildniß mehr Vertrauen setzen als auf die Verdienste Christi . . ." Quoted in Zlabinger, *Muratori und Österreich*, 122.

74. See Melton, *Absolutism and the Origins of Compulsory Schooling*, 81.

75. See Büttner, "Abschied von Pracht und Rhetorik," for a good account of the background to these decisions; see further Frank Büttner, "München und Neresheim: Kunst im Umfeld der katholischen Aufklärung," in *Mehr Licht*, 203–15.

76. Colloredo's letter ("Hirtenbrief des Erzbischofs von Salzburg, Hieronymus Graf Colloredo 1782") is published in *Der aufgeklärte Reformkatholizismus in Österreich*, Quellen zur neueren Geschichte, 33, ed. Peter Hersche (Bern, 1976), 45–101. The telling passage from the 1784 document is quoted in Möseneder, *Aufklärung*, 116: "Was den innern Kirchenputz anbelangt, da soll majestätischer Anstand, Simplizität, Ordnung und Reinlichkeit überall vorherrschen."

77. See *Der Josephinismus: Ausgewählte Quellen zur Geschichte der theresianisch-josephinischen Reformen*, ed. Harm Klueting (Darmstadt, 1995), 356–57, doc. 158.

78. Möseneder, *Aufklärung*, 116.

79. "Seit dieser Zeit hat die in den Erblanden und vorzüglich in Wien bewirkt wordene Simplifizierung des äusserlichen Gottesdienstes, und die darauf erfolgte Verminderung der gar zu zahlreichen Altäre, und überladenen Zierarten in den Kirchen, nebst der Sekularisierung vieler Klöster, diese Art Mahlereyen, die bis dahin die hiesigen Historienmahler fast ganz allein beschäftigten, sehr vermindert, und der seither entstandene, so genannte moderne Geschmack in der innern Verzierung der Häuser und Paläste, hat auch endlich die historischen Deckenmahlereyen, die, im Grunde betrachtet, doch nur unnatürliche Vorstellungen sind, selten gemacht." Hans Rudolf Füßli, *Annalen der bildenden Künste für die österreichischen Staaten* (Vienna, 1801), 1:63.

80. Wangermann, "Reform Catholicism and Political Radicalism," 131.

81. See Éva H. Balázs, *Hungary and the Habsburgs, 1765–1800: An Experiment in Enlightened Absolutism*, trans. Tim Wilkinson (Budapest, 1997), 78, 156, 356 n. 26.

82. For recent views of Kaunitz, as well as summaries of older interpretations, see *Staatskanzler Wenzel Anton von Kaunitz-Rietberg, 1711–1794: Neue Perspektiven zu Politik und Kultur der europäischen Aufklärung*, ed. Grete Klingenstein and Franz A. J. Szabo (Graz-Esztergom, Paris, New York, 1996).

83. For an excellent overview of the issues concerning the interpretation of Joseph II, although primarily concerned with the period until 1780, see Derek Beales, *Joseph II: In the Shadow of Maria Theresa, 1741–1780* (Cambridge, 1987), especially 439–79.

84. Winter, *Der Josefinismus*.

85. Blanning, *Joseph II*, 44.

86. Blanning, *Joseph II and Enlightened Despotism*, 62.

87. Hersche, *Spätjansenismus*, 69; Blanning, *Joseph II*, 45, overstates Hersche's argument.

88. See in general Melton, *Absolutism and the Eighteenth-Century Origins of Compulsory Schooling*; Blanning, *Joseph II*, 39–40.

89. See Jiří Kroupa, "Poznámky k Sonnenfelsové koncepci umění," in *Uměleckohistorický Sborník* (Brno, 1985), 201, and n. 23.

90. For the earlier reforms, see the balanced presentation of Beales, *Joseph II*. For Hungary, see Domokos Kosáry, *Culture and Society in Eighteenth-Century Hungary*, trans. Zsuzsa Béres, trans. rev. by Christopher Sullivan (Budapest, 1987), 85–86.

91. As noted by Hersche, *Spätjansenismus*, 70, who remarks that Migazzi's opposition can be dated as starting already in 1767; see further Zlabinger, *Muratori und Österreich*, and Klingenstein, *Staatsverwaltung und kirchliche Autorität*.

92. Kroupa, "Poznámky k Sonnenfelsové koncepci umění"; Jiří Kroupa, "Václav Antonín Kaunitz-Rietberg a vytvarná umení," *Studia Comeniana et historica* 18, 1985, no. 35, pp. 71–9. See also J. Kroupa, "Kaunitz and the Visual Arts," *Sborník prací filosofické fakulty brněnské university*, ser. F, 40 (1996): 7–58. For Kaunitz and the arts, see further Franz A. J. Szabo, *Kaunitz and Enlightened Absolutism, 1753–1780* (Cambridge, 1994), 200–204.

93. F. Pascher, "Joseph Freiherr von Sperges (1725–1791)," *Mitteilungen der Österreichischen Galerie* 11, no. 55 (1967), 58–59.

94. See further Möseneder, *Aufklärung*, 104–5, for a different interpretation.

95. Geza Galavics, "Barockkunst, höfische Repräsentation und Ungarn," in *Maria Theresia als Königin von Ungarn* (*Jahrbuch für Österreichische Kulturgeschichte* 10) (1984), 66.

96. See Eckhart Knab, *Daniel Gran* (Vienna and Munich, 1977), 50–73.

97. As noted by Elfriede Baum, *Katalog des Österreichischen Barockmuseums im Unteren Belvedere in Wien* (Vienna and Munich, 1980), 1:340.

98. Given in Garas, *Maulbertsch, 1724–1796*, 253, doc. lix, and frequently cited in the literature.

99. *Historische Erklärung der von Anton Maulbertsch k.k. Akademie Rath, und Kammermahler in Wien verfertigten drey Platfonds des grossen Saals in der k.k. Hofburg zu Innsbruck* (Innsbruck, 1782), in *Journal der Literatur und Statistik* 2 (1782); also printed in Garas, *Maulbertsch, 1724–1796*, 254–55, doc. lxi; see further Pascher, "Sperges," 43–44.

100. For this description, see E. Wangermann, "Maria Theresa, a Reforming Monarchy," in *The Courts of Europe: Politics, Patronage, and Royalty, 1400–1800*, ed. A. G. Dickens (London, 1977), 287; see also Kaufmann, *Court, Cloister, and City*, 453. For the program of the Innsbruck frescoes in relation to Tyrolean themes, see further Oswald Trapp, "Maria Theresia und Tirol," in *Maria Theresia und ihre Zeit: Eine Darstellung der Epoche von 1740–1780 aus Anlass der 200. Wiederkehr des Todestages der Kaiserin*, ed. Walther Koschatzky (Salzburg and Vienna, 1979), 131–37, especially 134; *Die Kunstdenkmäler der Stadt Innsbruck: Die Hofbauten*, Österreichische Kunsttopographie, 47, ed. Johanna Felmayer et al. (Vienna, 1986), 128–35, also reprinting the program published by Sperges in 1776.

101. For their relevance, see Blanning, *Joseph II and Enlightened Despotism*, 10–11, 53; and, in general, Beales, *Joseph II*.

102. This interpretation is presented by Lechtreck, "Herrscher im 'royaume agricole.'"

103. As suggested in the telling formulation of the still readable textbook by Crane Brinton, John B. Christopher, and Robert Lee Wolff, *A History of Civilization* (Englewood Cliffs, 1961), 2:62.

104. See Balázs, *Hungary and the Habsburgs*, 251–61.

105. See ibid., 82.

106. For this image, see James A. Friesen, "Franz Anton Maulbertsch und sein 'Bild der Duldung,'" *Mitteilungen der Österreichischen Galerie* 17, no. 61 (1973): 15–55; Möseneder, *Aufklärung*, 83–88.

107. See in general Galavics, "Die letzten Mäzene des Barock."

108. See most fully Béla K. Király, *Hungary in the Late Eighteenth Century: The Decline of Enlightened Despotism* (New York and London, 1969).

109. Kosáry, *Culture and Society in Eighteenth-Century Hungary*, 86.

110. Miklós Szmrecsányi, *Eger Művészetéről: Tanulmányok és jegyzetek a hazai barokk történetéhez*, ed. János Kapossy and Elemér Radisics (Budapest, 1937), 262, doc. 14.

111. See Galavics, "Die letzten Mäzene des Barock."

112. Cf. Garas, *Maulbertsch, 1724–1796*.

113. Bushart, "Die Offenbarung der göttlichen Weisheit"; Möseneder, *Aufklärung*.

114. See Robert Joseph Kerner, *Bohemia in the Eighteenth Century: A Study in Political, Economic, and Social History with Special Reference to the Reign of Leopold II, 1790–1792* (New York, 1932).

115. As stated by Dorothy Johnson, "From Savior to Supreme Being: David and Late Enlightenment Spirituality," *Abstracts*, College Art Association 91st Annual Conference, New York, 19–22 February 2003.

116. Bushart, "Die Offenbarung der göttlichen Weisheit," 30.

117. As quoted in Preiss, "Alegorie výchovy mládeže," 368 nn. 18, 19; the article in general discusses the debate over allegory.

118. Lechtreck, "Herrscher im 'royaume agricole,'" 378.

119. See Kaufmann, *Court, Cloister, and City*, 415–17.

120. Füßli, *Annalen*, 63.

121. Möseneder, *Aufklärung*, 120–21, 152–54.

122. As explicated already by Hans Tietze, "Programme und Entwürfe zu den grossen österreichischen Barockfresken," *Jahrbuch der Kunsthistorischen Sammlungen des allerhöchsten Kaiserhauses* 30 (1910): 1–28.

123. See Büttner, "Abschied von Pracht und Rhetorik."

124. See James Van Horn Melton, *The Rise of the Public in Enlightenment Europe* (Cambridge, 2001); the point is also made by Lechtreck, "Herrscher im 'royaume agricole.'"

125. See Frank Büttner, "Der Betrachter im Schein des Bildes: Positionen der Wirkungsästhetik im 18. Jahrhundert," in *Mehr Licht*, 341–49.

126. See Peter Burke, *The Fabrication of Louis XIV* (New Haven and London, 1992); this is pointed out by Blanning, *Joseph II*, 34, 52 n. 10.

CHAPTER THREE

1. Betka Matsche-von Wicht, "'die heilligkeit, die stille ordnung, das Kenliche in der Kleidung und die Wirckhsame bedeittung der Historie': Zur Lage der österreichischen Freskomalerei in der zweiten Hälfte des 18. Jahrhunderts," in *Herbst des Barock: Studien zum Stilwandel; Die Malerfamilie Keller (1740–1904)*, ed. Andreas Tacke (Munich 1998), 94, observes a difference between the fresco in Halbturn and Maulbertsch's painting in the old *Theologiesaal* of the University of Vienna, executed in 1766.

2. Hans Tintelnot, *Die Barocke Freskomalerei in Deutschland: Ihre Entwicklung und europäische Wir-*

kung (Munich, 1951), 217, noted that Pápa showed the first sign of stylistic change (*erste Stilwandel*) in Maulbertsch's work, although, as suggested in the previous note, earlier changes can be observed.

3. In a letter of 24 July 1782 Maulbertsch says that because the work at Pápa was so large he had help with the architectural painting: Andor Pigler, *A Pápai Plébániatemplom és Mennyezetképei* (Budapest, 1922), 74, doc. 16: "NB. Weillen die Arbeit groß ist so habe noch einen Gehilfen Zur Archidectur von Wien bekomen."

4. Monika Dachs, ". . . *Mahlergehilfen, Materialien, Kost und Reisespesen* . . . Der Maler Franz Anton Maulbertsch (1724–1796) als künstlerischer Unternehmer," in *Reiselust und Kunstgenuss: Barockes Böhmen, Mähren und Österreich*, ed. Friedrich Polleroß (Petersberg, 2004), 201–18, considers the issue of Maulbertsch's assistants, a problem treated more thoroughly in her *Habilitationsschrift*, "Franz Anton Maulbertsch und sein Kreis: Studien zur Wiener Malerei in der zweiten Hälfte des 18. Jahrhunderts," 3 vols. (University of Vienna, 2003).

For reasons discussed here, I believe that Maulbertsch, as head of the enterprise, can nevertheless be credited with the invention of the projects on which he and his helpers worked, and, in the examples adduced, also for significant parts of their execution.

5. The fullest effort to explicate the program at Sümeg is offered by Gerke, *Die Fresken des Franz Anton Maulbertsch in der Pfarrkirche zu Sümeg*; see further Lajos Végvári, *A Sümegi Maulbertsch Freskók* (Budapest, 1958).

6. Österreichische Galerie, Vienna; see Elfriede Baum, *Katalog des Österreichischen Barockmuseums im Unteren Belvedere in Wien* (Vienna and Munich, 1980), 1:358–59, no. 214.

7. See Pierre Minguet, *Esthétique du rococo* (Paris, 1966); Henry-Russell Hitchcock, *Rococo Architecture in Southern Germany* (London, 1968); Anthony Blunt, *Some Uses and Misuses of the Terms Baroque and Rococo as Applied to Architecture* (London, 1972).

8. Tintelnot, *Barocke Freskomalerei*, 218, already made this observation.

9. Pál Voit, *Der Barock in Ungarn* (Budapest, 1970), 97.

10. See Pál Voit, *Franz Anton Pilgram* (Budapest, 1982), 395–97.

11. As already observed in Klára Garas, *Franz Anton Maulbertsch, 1724–1796* (Graz, 1960), 131.

12. See, for example, Anna Petrová-Pleskotová, "Die spätbarocke Malerei in der Slowakei und ihre Stellung in der mitteleuropäischen Kunst," in *Late Baroque Art in the 18th Century*, Seminaria Niedzickie 4 (Kraków, 1990), 154; see also Petrová-Pleskotová, *Maliarstvo 18. storočia na Slovensku* (Bratislava, 1983), 45–48, dealing with paintings found in Slovakia that are also discussed in the present book.

13. For example, as stated explicitly by Ivo Krsek, "Malířství," in *Umění Baroka na Moravě a ve Slezsku* (Prague, 1996), 136.

14. Because this is a standard theme in the literature on the artist, only the more general lines of interpretation of Maulbertsch's work are considered here. Some attempts have been made to account for particular stages in this transformation, but no full study of the problem has yet been published.

15. See Krsek, in *Franz Anton Maulbertsch* [exhibition catalogue] (Vienna, 1974), 29. This passage, to which Franz Matsche, "Franz Anton Maulbertsch und Daniel Gran: Zur Frage des Klassizismus im österreichischen Spätbarock," in *Herbst des Barock*, 205, 211 n. 18, takes exception, is, however, but a revised and condensed version of Krsek's oft repeated theses.

See, for example, Krsek, "Ein Beitrag zum Problem des Kolorits in der 2. Hälfte des 18. Jahrhunderts (F. A. Maulbertschs Freskogemälde im Lehensaal des Kremsierer Schlosses)," *Sborník prací filosofické fakulty brněnské university*, ser. F 5 (1961): 349–66; "Das Fresko von Franz Anton Maulbertsch im Lehensaal der Kremsierer Residenz—Zur Frage seines Kolorits," *Alte und moderne Kunst*, no. 87 (1966): 16–23; *František Antonín Maulbertsch 1724–1796* (Prague, 1974).

16. Garas, *Maulbertsch, 1724–1796*, 130–34; Garas, *Franz Anton Maulbertsch: Leben und Werk* (Salzburg, 1974), 104.

17. Garas, "Maulbertsch als Maler," in *Franz Anton Maulbertsch* [exhibition catalog], (Vienna, 1974), 33; see also in general Garas, *Maulbertsch, 1724–1796*.

18. See Matsche, "Franz Anton Maulbertsch und Daniel Gran."

19. Matsche-von Wicht, "'die heilligkeit, die stille ordnung, das Kenliche in der Kleidung und die Wirckhsame bedeittung der Historie,'" says that the sort of painting implied by Maulbertsch's earlier works was attacked by the theorists of classicism as unnatural, nonsensical, and too complicated, and that it ran against their demands for simple and clear development of the pictorial objects, for restful movement, for clothing that did not balloon out too much, and for as little foreshortening as possible in ceiling paintings.

20. Matsche, "Franz Anton Maulbertsch und Daniel Gran," 205–6: "Die kunstgeschichtliche Analyse und Erklärung eines Stils ist wie im Fall Maulbertschs auch nicht durch Zitate philosophischer und kunsttheoretischer Postulate, bischöflicher Hirtenbriefe und kaiserlicher Reskripte zu ersetzen. Der Künstler und zumal der barocke Freskomaler ist und bleibt in erster Linie ein Praktiker und geht von gegebener Möglichkeiten und verfügbaren Vorbildern aus. Er knüpft immer an etwas an, das er verändert und in seinem Sinn gestaltet."

21. Ibid., 207.

22. Klára Garas, "Maulbertsch, Franz Anton," in *The Dictionary of Art* (London, 1996), 20:856.

23. In a letter of 1 May 1775 to Andrä Joseph Leicharding, Sperges said: "Ich nehme an dem ganzen aus gewissen Ursachen einen besonderen Antheil," and he determined the general iconography; see Garas, *Maulbertsch, 1724–1796*, 253–54, doc. lix.

24. Miklos Szmrecsányi, *Eger Művészetéről tanulmányok és jegyzetek a hazai barokk történetéhez*, ed. János Kapossy and Elemér Radisics (Budapest, 1937), 294.

25. To paraphrase Frank Büttner, "Der Betrachter im Schein des Bildes: Positionen der Wirkungsästhetik im 18. Jahrhundert," in *Mehr Licht: Europa um 1770; Die bildende Kunst und die Aufklärung* [exhibition catalog, Städelsches Kunstinstitut] (Frankfurt a. M., 1999), 341. See further Büttner, "Abschied von Pracht und Rhetorik: Überlegungen zu den geistesgeschichtlichen Voraussetzungen der Stilwandels in der Sakraldekorationen des ausgehenden 18. Jahrhunderts," in *Herbst des Barock*, 165–73, and Büttner, "Das Ende des Rokoko in Bayern: Überlegungen zu den geistesgeschichtlichen Voraussetzungen der Stilwandels," *Zeitschrift des Deutschen Vereins für Kunstwissenschaft* 51 (1997 [1999]): 125–50.

The slightly earlier critique of the rococo seen in a secular setting is discussed by Katie Scott, *The Rococo Interior* (New Haven, 1995), 241–65.

26. These citations are taken from the text of Colloredo's letter, printed in *Der aufgeklärte Reformkatholizismus in Österreich*, Quellen zur neueren Geschichte, 33, ed. Peter Hersche (Bern, 1976), 64, 98.

27. These lines are paraphrased from the summary presented in Rémy G. Saisselin, *The Enlightenment against the Baroque: Economics and Aesthetics in the Eighteenth Century* (Berkeley, Los Angeles, and Oxford, 1992), 55–57.

28. For a good introduction see Wilhelm Amann, *"Die stille Arbeit des Geschmacks": Die Kategorie des Geschmacks in der Ästhetik Schillers und in den Debatten der Aufklärung* (Würzburg, 1999).

29. Günther Heinz, "Veränderungen in der religiösen Malerei des 18. Jahrhunderts mit besonderer Berücksichtigung Österreichs," in *Katholische Aufklärung und Josephinismus*, ed. Elisabeth Kovács (Munich, 1979), 362: "Der Grundsatz steht deutlich fest: 'was den guten Geschmack beleidigt', d.h. soviel, daß auch Colloredo nicht mehr für die Reform des religiösen Bildwerkes anzugeben weiß als den gereinigten Geschmack Winckelmanns."

30. Johann Joachim Winckelmann, *Gedanken über die Nachahmung der griechischen Werke in der Malerei und Bildhauerkunst* (1755; reprint, Stuttgart, 1969), 38: "Die Gemälde an Decken und über den Türen stehen mehrenteils nur da, um ihren Ort zu füllen, und um die ledigen Plätze zu decken, welche nicht mit lauter Vergöldungen können angefüllet werden. Sie haben nicht allein kein Verhältnis mit dem Stande und mit den Umständen des Besitzers, sondern sie sind demselben sogar oftmals nachteilig. Der Abscheu vor den leeren Raum füllet also die Wände; und Gemälde von Gedanken leer, sollen das Leere ersetzen."

31. Quoted in E. Wangermann, "Maria Theresa, a Reforming Monarchy," in *The Courts of Europe: Politics, Patronage, and Royalty, 1400–1800*, ed. A. G. Dickens (London, 1977), 302–3.

32. For evidence on Sperges and Winckelmann, see Franz Pascher, "Joseph Freiherr von Sperges (1725–1791): Liebhaber, Förderer und Verwalter der Künste unter Maria Theresia und ihren Söhnen," *Mitteilungen der Österreichischen Galerie* 11, no. 55 (1967): 48.

33. Pavel Preiss, *Österreichische Zeichnung des 18. Jahrhunderts: Ausgewählte Werke aus Böhmischen und Mährischen Sammlungen* [exhibition catalog, Národní Galerie] (Prague, 1996), 86, no. 41, asserts that this painting, belonging to the museum at Slavkov, was from the Kaunitz collection, even though earlier sources indicated that it lacked a more certain provenance; see, for example, *Barock in Mähren*, ed. Vlasta Kratinová [exhibition catalog, Lower Belvedere] (Vienna, 1988) 47, no. 250.

34. See Jiří Kroupa, "Fürst Wenzel Anton Kaunitz-Rietberg: Ein Kunstmäzen und Curieux der Aufklärung," in *Staatskanzler Wenzel Anton von Kaunitz-Rietberg: Neue Perspektiven zu Politik und Kultur der europäischen Aufklärung*, ed. Grete Klingenstein and Franz A. J. Szabo (Graz, 1996), 360–82, and especially Kroupa, "Kaunitz and the Visual Arts," *Sborník prací filosofické fakulty brněnské university*, ser. F, 40 (1996): 7–58.

35. See Jiří Kroupa, "Poznámky k Sonnenfelsové koncepci umění," in *Uměleckohistorický Sborník* (Brno, 1985), especially 201.

36. See Steffi Röttgen, "'Antonius de Maron faciebat Romae': Intorno all'opera di Anton von Maron a Roma," in *Artisti austriaci a Roma dal Barocco alla Secessione* [exhibition catalog, Museo di Roma–Palazzo Braschi] (Rome, 1972), n.p. (17 pages); also Peter Betthausen, "Winckelmann, Anton von Maron und Wien," in Bettina Hagen, ed., *Antike in Wien* [exhibition catalog, Akademie der bildenden Künste, Vienna] (Mainz, 2002), 79–84, with the portrait of Winckelmann discussed on 85–86.

37. For Winterhalder the Younger's activities, see János Kapossy, *A Szombathelyi Székesgyház és Mennyezetképei* (Budapest, 1922), 112, doc. 3. The most recent summary on Winterhalder is provided by Lubomír Slaviček, ". . . *diese herrliche Arbeit den Werken des seelg. Maulbertsch*

so ähnlich . . . Der mährische Maler Joseph Winterhalder d. J. (1743–1807) im Schatten von Franz Anton Maulbertsch," in *Reiselust und Kunstgenuss*, 229–40.

38. I am grateful to Jiří Kroupa for alerting me to the connection between Maulbertsch and Schweigel; the summary is my own.

39. This is observed by Miloš Stehlík, "Sochařství," in *Umění Baroka na Moravě a ve Slezsku* (Prague, 1996), 431, cat. no. 170.

40. For Schweigel's writings, see C. Hálová-Jahodová, "Andreas Schweigel, Bildende Künste in Mähren," *Umění* 20 (1972): 168–87.

41. For this text, see most recently Pascal Griener, "La *connoisseurship* européenne au service de la création artistique allemande: les *Lettres* de Christian Ludwig von Hagedorn," in *Théorie des arts et création artistique dans l'Europe du Nord du XVe au début du XVIe siècle*, ed. Michèle-Caroline Heck et al. (Villeneuve d'Ascq, 2001), 333–54.

42. This is part of a debate carried on by Matsche, "Franz Anton Maulbertsch und Daniel Gran," 206–8, with Garas. In the light of the discussion to be presented in chapter 4, it is, however, not adequate to describe their theory as classicistic.

43. This story remains to be told in full: for some of the earlier history, see Thomas DaCosta Kaufmann, "Before Winckelmann: Towards the Origins of the History of Art," in *Knowledge, Science and Literature in Early Modern Germany*, ed. Gerhild Scholz Williams et al., University of North Carolina Studies in the Germanic Languages and Literatures, 116 (Chapel Hill, N.C., 1996), 71–89. See further Kaufmann, "Antiquarianism, the History of Objects, and the History of Art before Winckelmann," *Journal of the History of Ideas* 62 (2001): 523–41.

44. See Leslie Bodi, *Tauwetter in Wien: Zur Prosa der österreichischen Aufklärung, 1781–1795* (Frankfurt a. M., 1977), 39f.

45. See James Van Horn Melton, *The Rise of the Public in Enlightenment Europe* (Cambridge, 2001); more generally see Jürgen Habermas, *Strukturwandel der Öffentlichkeit: Untersuchungen zu einer Kategorie der bürgerlichen Gesellschaft* (Darmstadt and Neuwied, 1962); for the situation in France, see Thomas E. Crow, *Painters and Public Life in Eighteenth-Century Paris* (New Haven and London, 1985).

46. Bodi, *Tauwetter in Wien*, 45: "Es muß aber auch betont werden, daß man um 1785 schon durchaus von einer aktiven, räsonierenden, kritischen öffentlichen Meinung in Wien sprechen kann, die sich in Broschüren, Zeitschriften, Lesekabinetts, Kaffeehäusern, Salons und weitverästelten, das ganze gesellschaftliche Leben durchsetzenden Freimauerlogen ihre eigenen Organe geschaffen hat."

47. Garas, *Maulbertsch, 1724–1796*, 248, doc. xxxix.

48. *Wienerisches Diarium*, no. 21, 14 March 1770; also cited in Garas, *Maulbertsch, 1724–1796*, 248–49, doc. xl.

49. "Winkelmanns Buch von der Allegorie ist zu bekannt als dass wir es hier anzuführen nötig hatten," cited in Garas, *Maulbertsch, 1724–1796*, 249, doc. xl.

50. Ibid., 250, doc. xliii.

51. Ibid., 252, doc. lvi.

52. Ibid., 253, doc. lvi.

53. Quoted by Günther Heinz, "Bemerkungen zur Geschichte der Malerei zur Zeit Maria Theresias," in *Maria Theresia und ihre Zeit*, ed. Walter Koschatzky (Salzburg, 1979), 277.

54. This connection is made in Günther Heinz, "Veränderungen in der religiösen Malerei des 18. Jahrhunderts mit besonderer Berücksichtigung Österreichs," in *Katholische Aufklärung und Josephinismus*, ed. Elisabeth Kovács (Munich, 1989), 350–51, and Heinz, "Die bildende Kunst der Epoche Maria Theresias und Josephs II.," in *Österreich im Zeitalter des aufgeklärten Absolutismus*, ed. Erich Zöllner (Vienna, 1983), 192. For the notion of painterly pyrotechnics, see above and Thomas DaCosta Kaufmann, *Court, Cloister, and City* (Chicago, 1995), 426–31.

55. See Hildebrand Dussler, "Ein Kunstgeschichtler reist im Herbst 1776 durch Nieder- und Oberbayren [*sic*]," in *Zwischen Donau und Alpen: Festschrift für Norbert Lieb zum 65. Geburtstag* (Munich 1972), 333–34.

56. Garas, *Maulbertsch, 1724–1796*, 269, doc. cxiv.

57. Ibid., 265, doc. cv.

58. See the discussion in Helmut Börsch-Supan, "Franz Anton Maulbertsch und Berlin," in *Franz Anton Maulbertsch und sein schwäbischer Umkreis* (Sigmaringen, 1996), 224–33, especially 225.

59. Garas, *Maulbertsch, 1724–1796*, 269, doc. cix.

60. Hans Rudolf Füßli, *Annalen der bildenden Künste für die österreichischen Staaten* (Vienna, 1801), 60.

61. Gerda Mraz, "Contract des H. Mahlers Maulpärtsch," in *Ex fumo lucem: Baroque Studies in Honour of Klára Garas; Presented on Her Eightieth Birthday* (Budapest, 1994), 1:138.

62. Garas, *Maulbertsch, 1724–1796*, 253, doc. lviii.

63. Szmrecsányi, *Eger Művészetéről*, 299, doc. 7: "Anbey folget ein Entwurf und Zeichnung der Architectur Verziehrungen, der blawon umfange, Gurten und Holgurten mit ihren Antic-Verzierung . . ."

64. Szmrecsányi, *Eger Művészetéről*, 262, doc. 14.

65. For a discussion of Szily and the works done in Szombathely, see further Géza Galavics, "Das Bistum von Szombathely als Kunstwerk," in *Gedenkausstellung des architekten Melchior Hefele (1716–1794)* [exhibition catalog, Szombathelyi Képtár] (Szombathely, 1994), 111–13.

66. See Kapossy, *A Szombathelyi Székesgeyház és Mennyezetképei*, 102–3, doc. 7.

67. Pigler, *A Pápai Plébániatemplom*, 52, 51.

68. Ibid., 52.

69. G. J. Dlabacz, *Allgemeines historisches Künstlerlexikon für Böhmen und zum Theil auch für Mähren und Schlesien* (Prague, 1815), vol. 2, col. 283–84.

Robert Waisenberger, "Franz Anton Maulbertsch und seine Beziehung zu Wien," in *Wien zur Zeit von Franz Anton Maulbertsch* [exhibition catalog, Historisches Museum der Stadt Wien] (Vienna, 1974), 7, reads this story in such a way as to imply that Maulbertsch could still learn from the technical side of the problem of painting the frescoes in the Piarist church that he had not mastered in his youth: "Die Fresken erschienen freilich in vieler Beziehung, vor allem, was die technische Seite des Problems betrifft, noch unbewältigt. Maulbertsch äußerte im Alter, daß er in diesem frühen Werk gemacht habe, immer noch lernen könne."

Regardless of the issue of technical difficulties and problems that may have been present in the execution of the frescoes in the Piarist church, given that Maulbertsch had long since mastered such problems of painting walls and ceilings, it seems reasonable to assume that other issues were involved in his continuing study of this work. See the discussion in chapter 1 and further comments on Maulbertsch's technique in chapter 4.

70. Similar prints are to be seen on walls, on cabinets, and in hallways in the Szombathely bishop's palace.

71. Pigler, *A Pápai Plébániatemplom*, 73, doc. 15, and 79, doc. 29.

72. For these painters and the related institution, see Hagen, *Antike in Wien*.

73. Garas, *Maulbertsch, 1724–1796*, 130–31.

74. For this point, see Saisselin, *The Enlightenment against the Baroque*. See also the comments by Heinz, "Die bildende Kunst der Epoche Maria Theresias und Josephs II.," 192.

75. Winckelmann, *Geschichte der Kunst des Altertums*, bk. 4, translated as *A History of Ancient Art*, trans. G. Henry Lodge (1849–72; reprint, New York, 1968), reprinted in *Art in Theory, 1648–1815: An Anthology of Changing Ideas*, ed. Charles Harrison, Paul Wood, and Jason Gaiger (Oxford, 2000), 469–70.

CHAPTER FOUR

1. Ivo Krsek, "Ein Beitrag zum Problem des Kolorits in der 2. Hälfte des 18. Jahrhunderts (F. A. Maulbertschs Freskogemälde im Lehensaal des Kremsierer Schlosses)," *Sborník prací filosofické fakulty brněnské university*, ser. F 5 (1961): 349–66; Krsek, "Das Fresko von Franz Anton Maulbertsch im Lehensaal der Kremsierer Residenz—Zur Frage seines Kolorits," *Alte und moderne Kunst*, no. 87 (1966): 16–23; and Krsek, *František Antonín Maulbertsch* (Prague, 1974).

2. Krsek, "Ein Beitrag zum Problem des Kolorits," has, for example, compared the color relationships and contrasts in Maulbertsch's painting to the art of Delacroix, *plein air* painting, and expressionism.

3. Svetlana Alpers and Michael Baxandall, *Tiepolo and the Pictorial Intelligence* (New Haven and London, 1994), 69.

4. Gerda Mraz, "Contract des H. Mahlers Maulpärtsch," in *Ex fumo lucem: Baroque Studies in Honour of Klára Garas; Presented on Her Eightieth Birthday* (Budapest, 1994), 138. The last term reads in the original: "Die Wände in der ganzen Kirchen zwischen der Architectur mit einem lieblichen und hellen Fäberl anzulegen, und zu distinguiren."

5. There is a lengthy literature on this topic. For a summary of some of the meanings of the term, see the somewhat polemical account by Claudia Swan, "Ad vivum, naer het leven, from the life: Defining a Mode of Representation," *Word and Image* 11 (1995): 355–72, which, however, does not deal with the theoretical aspect of the discussion broached here.

6. Klára Garas, *Franz Anton Maulbertsch, 1724–1796* (Graz, 1960), 242, doc. viii, 28 July 1752: "Absoluta fuit a pictore Maulberes Cuppula Presbyterii, cuius artificium ab omnibus quidem probatum fuit, et alterius pictoris qui adornavit Architecturam reiectum."

7. ". . . und zur Auszierung erforderlichen Gold-Bliken nach möglicher Kunst und seiner besten Wissenschaft ausmahlen . . . ," first published in Antonín Breitenbacher, *Dějiny arcibiskupské obrazárny v Kroměříži: Archivní studie* (Kroměříž, 1927), 2:181.

8. Garas, *Maulbertsch, 1724–1796*, 253, doc. lviii.

9. For the most recent information on the altarpieces, see *Umělecké Památky Moravy a Slezska*, ed. Bohumil Samek (Prague, 1999), 2:496.

10. János Kapossy, *A Szombathelyi Székesgeyház és Mennyezetképei* (Budapest, 1922), 112, doc. 3.

11. See Sibylle Puhl, "Das Primatialpalais in Preßburg," in *Gedenkausstellung des Architekten Melchior Hefele* [exhibition catalog, Szombathelyi Képtár] (Szombathely, 1994), 71–78.

12. See Ferenc Dávid, "Ein Entwurf von Maulbertsch Architekturmaler von Győr und die Ikonographie der Erneuerung des Doms," in *Ex fumo lucem*, 2:141–56.

13. Miklos Szmrecsányi, *Eger Művészetéről tanulmányok és jegyzetek a hazai barokk történetéhez*, ed. János Kapossy and Elemér Radisics (Budapest, 1937), 294, no. 1.

14. Ibid., 299, no. 7.

15. Ibid., 262, no. 14: "Diese vorgemelte Khunst stücke, mit gröster Liebhafftigkeit, und alles lieblichs Colirt Khunst Mässig zu Mahllen, und hertzustellen verspreche, und mich obligire."

16. Szmrecsányi, *Eger Művészetéről*, 294, no. 1.

17. See Paul Taylor, "The Concept of Houding in Dutch Art Theory," *Journal of the Warburg and Courtauld Institutes* 55 (1992): 210–32.

18. Szmrecsányi, *Eger Művészetéről*, 299, no. 7.

19. Kapossy, *A Szombathely Székesegyház és Mennyezetképei*, 108, no. 18.

20. "Die Lichter und Schatten sind ohne schreyenden Contrast, in einer verständigen Vereinigung, die das Auge entzückt, aber ihm zugleich den angenehmen Wechsel, und die nöthigen Rueplätze anweist, die das Zauberwerk des Helldunkeln ausmachen. Die Figuren . . . sind edel und charakterisirt; das ganze Bild mit drey Farben, aber mit der nämlichen Freyheit des Pinsels ausgeführt." *Wienerisches Diarium*, no. 21, 14 March 1770; also cited in Garas, *Maulbertsch, 1724–1796*, 248–49, doc. xl.

21. "Er weiß Licht und Schatten wohl zu vertheilen und ihnen ein reizendes Colorit zu geben, das ob es schon bunt ist, doch selbst auf Kalch angenehm bleibt, die Kenner überrascht, und die Unwissenden bezaubert." Garas, *Maulbertsch, 1724–1796*, 253, doc. lvi.

22. Ibid., 247, doc. xxxii.

23. It also describes them as having "Pracht und Geschmack in Kleidungen, nicht minder das steigende und weichende in einem vollkommenen Grad" (magnificence and taste in the clothing, attaining a perfect degree of modeling). Garas, *Maulbertsch, 1724–1796*, 254, doc. lx.

24. Börsch-Supan, "Franz Anton Maulbertsch und Berlin," 225.

25. Cited according to C. Hálová-Jahodová, "Andreas Schweigel, bildende Künste in Mähren," *Umění* 20 (1972): 175.

26. ". . . mit allen Gratien, guter Ordnung, einen schönen angenehmen geschmolzenen Collerit." Ibid., 184.

27. Ibid.

28. See Bernard Teyssèdre, *Roger de Piles et les débats sur le coloris au siècle de Louis XIV* (Paris, 1957).

29. Roger de Piles, *Cours de peinture par principes*, with a preface by Jacques Thuillier (1708; Paris, 1989, 148, 217; de Piles, *Dialogue sur le coloris* (Paris, 1673), 4, 29.

30. De Piles, *Cours de peinture par principes*, 65.

31. De Piles, *Dialogue sur le coloris*, 12–13: "La beauté du coloris ne consiste pas dans une bigarure de couleurs differents: mais dans leur juste distribution, en sorte que les objets qui sont peints ayent le même couleur que les veritables, que la pierre peinte, par example, resemble à la pierre naturelle, et que les carnations paroissent de veritable chaires. Et enfin

non seulement chaque objet particulier represente parfaitement la couleur de ceux qu'il imite, mais que tous ensemble fassent une agréable union dans tout le Tableau.

32. *Einleitung in die Malerei aus Grundsätzen* (Leipzig, 1760); de Piles's *Abrégé de la vie des peintres* (Paris, 1699) had been translated as *Historie und Leben der berumtesten europaeischen Mahler* (Hamburg, 1710); his *Abrégé d'anatomie* (Paris, 1666) as *Kurze Verfassung der Anatomie* (Berlin, 1706).

33. Christian Ludwig von Hagedorn, *Betrachtungen über die Mahlerey* (Leipzig, 1762), 647n, 64n.

34. Ibid., 647.

35. Ibid., 278, 301, 647, 637, 640, 679.

36. Ibid., 47.

37. *Des Herrn Pernety Handlexikon der bildenden Künste* (Berlin, 1764), 45.

38. Ibid., 46: "Unterm Colorit sind zwey Stücke begriffen, die Lokalfarbe und das Helldunkle. Die Lokalfarbe ist diejenige, welche einem jeden Gegenstande eigen ist, und welche der Maler durch die Vergleichung muß geltend machen; diese Kunst erfordert Überdieß die Kenntniß der Natur der Farben, nämlich ihrer Antipathie und Sympathie. Das Helldunkle erhebet die Lokalfarben und die ganze Zusammensetzung des Gemäldes; es bestimmt, durch die Austheilung der Lichter und der Schatten."

39. Ibid., 47–48.

40. Ibid., 49: "Noch weniger bestehet die Schönheit des Colorits des Ganzen eines Gemäldes in dem Bunten der verschiedenen Farben, sondern in einer richtigen Austheilung derselben, geleitet von der Kenntniß der Freundschaft, welche sie unter einander haben, damit sie sich einander unterstürtzen und erheben . . . so hängt seine Schönheit [i.e., des Colorits] von der Brechung und Mischung der Farben auf der Palette ab . . . und daß endlich nicht allein ein jeder Gegenstand vollkommen die Farben derjenigen, welche der Maler zu copiren sich vorgesetzt hat, vorstelle, sondern auch, daß sie alle zusammen eine angenehme Einheit, und eine verführerische Harmonie ausmachen."

41. With regard to this treatise, see John Gage, *Color and Meaning: Art, Science, and Symbolism* (Berkeley and Los Angeles, 1999), 23–24, 173–74, 243.

42. This was noticed by Jacqueline Lichtenstein, *The Eloquence of Color: Rhetoric and Painting in the French Classical Age*, trans. Emily McVarish (Berkeley, 1993), 220.

43. For views of the sublime, Burke's place in them, and the implications for the arts, see in general Samuel Monk, *The Sublime: A Study of Critical Theories in XVIII-Century England* (New York, 1935).

44. This point is made by Frank Büttner, "Der Betrachter im Schein des Bildes: Positionen der Wirkungsästhetik im 18. Jahrhundert," in *Mehr Licht: Europa um 1770; Die bildende Kunst und die Aufklärung* [exhibition catalog, Städelsches Kunstinstitut] (Frankfurt a. M., 1999), 344.

45. See Karl Viëtor, "Die Idee des Erhabenen in der deutschen Literatur," in *Geist und Form: Aufsätze zur deutschen Literaturgeschichte* (Bern, 1952), 234–66; Immanuel Jacob Pyra, *Über das Erhabene: Mit einer Einleitung und einem Anhang mit Briefen Bodmers, Langes und Pyras*, ed. Carsten Zelle (Frankfurt a. M., Bern, New York, Paris, 1991).

46. Hagedorn, *Betrachtungen*, 642.

47. Ibid., 688.

48. See in general, Monk, *The Sublime*, 164–202.

49. This phrase, *la mente del Pittore deve sempre tendere al Sublime, all'Eroico, alla Perfezione*, is part of a larger quotation attributed to Tiepolo in the *Nuova Veneta Gazetta* of 20 March 1762, cited in Francis Haskell, *Patrons and Painters: Art and Society in Baroque Italy* (New York, 1963), 253 n. 2.

50. A. [Anselm] Elwert, *Kleines Künstlerlexikon oder raisonnirendes Verzeichnis der vornehmsten Maler und Kupferstecher* (Giessen and Marburg, 1785), 115–16: "Maulbertsch (Anton, lebte in Wien um 1775). Er malte in einem grosen, erhabnen Stil Historien, meist auf nassen Kalk, in denen man Figuren voller Geist und Feuer, ein schönes Kolorit und grose Kompositionen findet, hingegen tadelt man seine unrichtige Zeichnung und seine zu grosgefaltete Gewänder."

51. See Monk, *The Sublime*, 191.

52. Most recently by Franz Matsche, "Franz Anton Maulbertsch und Daniel Gran: Zur Frage des Klassizismus im österreichischen Spätbarock," in *Herbst des Barock: Studien zum Stilwandel; Die Malerfamilie Keller (1740 bis 1904)*, ed. Andreas Tacke (Munich and Berlin, 1998), 214.

53. See Garas, *Maulbertsch*, 1724–1796, 284, doc. clxvi.

54. For the reorganization and new display of the collections, see Debora J. Meijers, *Kunst als natuur: de Habsburgse schilderijengalerij in Wenen omstreeks 1780* (Amsterdam, 1991; also in German as *Kunst als Natur: Die Habsburger Gemäldegalerie in Wien um 1780* [Vienna, 1995]).

55. I am grateful to Frances Huemer for pointing out that Maulbertsch's coloring does really not resemble that of Rubens at all.

56. Otto Benesch, "Maulbertsch: Zu den Quellen seiner malerischen Stiles," *Städel-Jahrbuch* 3 (1924): 107–76.

57. Alpers and Baxandall, *Tiepolo and the Pictorial Intelligence*, 66.

58. See Manfred Koller, "Zur maltechnischen Lehre an der Wiener Kunstakademie im 18. Jahrhundert," *Barockberichte* 11/12 (1995): 421.

59. For the fresco technique used by Maulbertsch and other contemporary painters in Austria, see Manfred Koller, "Arbeitsmethoden barocker Freskomaler in Österreich," *Barockberichte* 2 (1990): 41–72; see further Koller, "Zum Werkprozeß spätbarocker Freskanten: Martin Knoller, Josef Schöpf und ihr Nachlaß im Stift Stams in Tyrol," in *Herbst des Barock*, 97–108; Koller, "Die Wandmalereitechniken der Neuzeit," in *Reclams Handbuch der künstlerischen Techniken*, 2:213–398; Koller, "Barocke Wand- und Deckenmalerei in Österreich—Technologie und Restaurierung," *Barockberichte* 34/35 (2003): 325–31.

60. See Alpers and Baxandall, *Tiepolo and the Pictorial Intelligence*, 74–78.

61. Garas, *Maulbertsch*, 1724–1796, 250, doc. xliii.

62. Ibid., 255, doc. lxiii.

63. Cited in Hálová-Jahodová, "Andreas Schweigel, Bildende Künste in Mähren," 175.

64. ". . . da dessen Talent nicht benützet, was zur Ausführung in diesen Zeiten Grose Eigenschaft der Befärbung, so wohl, als Pensels Ausführung eines Maulpersch bedarf . . . ," cited in Kapossy, *A Szombathely Székesegyház és Mennyezetképei*, 112, no. 2.

65. Hans Rudolf Füßli, *Annalen der bildenden Künste für die österreichischen Staaten* (Vienna, 1801), 1:59: ". . . die nähmlich einen schnellen, lebhafte, und das Auge reitzenden Eindruck zu machen pflegen: grandiöse, reich, aus stark bewegten Bildern bestehende Compositionen, Kenntniß der Optik und Perspektive, allgemeine akademische Wissenschaft

der Verhältnisse des menschlichen Körpers, eine harmonische Farbenmischung, in großen Massen idealisirte Drapperien, wilkürlich [*sic*] Anwendung des Lichtes und Schattens, nebst einem markigen und kühnen Auftrag des Pinsels, charakterisiren so wohl ihre als die Werke fast aller andern gleichzeitigen Geschichtmahler."

66. Alpers and Baxandall, *Tiepolo and the Pictorial Intelligence*, 76.

67. Winckelmann, *Essay on the Beautiful in Art (1763)*, in Winckelmann, *Writings on Art*, ed. David Irwin (London, 1972), 100.

68. Benesch, "Maulbertsch."

69. See Monika Dachs, "Neue Überlegungen zum sogenannten Selbstporträt des Franz Anton Maulbertsch," *Barockberichte* 16/17 (1998): 50; Dachs, "*. . . Mahlergehilfen, Materialien, Kost und Reisespesen* . . . Der Maler Franz Anton Maulbertsch (1724–1796) als künstlerischer Unternehmer," in *Reiselust und Kunstgenuss: Barockes Böhmen, Mähren und Österreich*, ed. Friedrich Polleroß (Petersberg, 2004), 201–18. Dachs considers the issue of Maulbertsch's assistants in her *Habilitationsschrift*, "Franz Anton Maulbertsch und sein Kreis: Studien zur Wiener Malerei in der zweiten Hälfte des 18. Jahrhunderts," 3 vols. (University of Vienna, 2003). See also Dachs, "Franz Anton Maulbertsch in Langenargen," *Barockberichte* 16/17 (1998): 7 n. 15.

70. Brno, Moravský Zemský Archiv, G11 FM 60, 17v. This document is published as part of the papers of the Moravian scholar J. P. Cerroni, without recognition that the notes are in fact autobiographical, in Marie Lomičova, "Rukopis o umění J. P. Cerroniho," *Umění* 26 (1977): 64–78.

Winterhalder's work is surveyed in Lubomír Slaviček, "*. . . diese herrliche Arbeit den Werken des seelg. Maulbertsch so ähnlich* . . . Der mährische Maler Joseph Winterhalder d. J. (1743–1807) im Schatten von Franz Anton Maulbertsch," in *Reiselust und Kunstgenuss*, 229–40.

71. Garas, *Maulbertsch, 1724–1796*, 284, docs. clxv and clxvi.

72. See Franz Martin Haberditzl, *Franz Anton Maulbertsch* (Vienna, 1977), 370–71.

73. Andrea Pozzo, *Der Mahler und Baumeister Perspectiv* (Augsburg, 1749); sections on fresco painting from this German edition of the treatise are printed in *Maurer, Kalk und Sand oder der Maler Franz Anton Maulbertsch: Materialien zu Leben und Werk, 1724–1796*, ed. Nora and Gerhard Fischer (Vienna, 1998), 87–99.

74. The most recent, and accessible, overview of the work of Kracker is provided by Anna Jávor, "*. . . der Stift Bruk verschaffte ihm viele Arbeiten besonder im hungarischen Stift Jazo* . . . Der Maler Johann Lucas Kracker (1719–1779) im Dienste der Prämonstratenser," in *Reiselust und Kunstgenuss*, 187–200.

75. See Richard Shiff, *Cézanne and the End of Impressionism* (Chicago and London, 1984).

76. Concerning this point, see in general Thomas Puttfarken, *Roger de Piles's Theory of Art* (New Haven and London, 1985).

77. See Lichtenstein, *The Eloquence of Color*, 165, 159.

78. See Thomas Crow, "The Critique of Enlightenment in Eighteenth-Century Art," *Art Criticism* 3 (1987): 27.

79. See Thomas DaCosta Kaufmann, *Cloister, Court, and City: The Art and Culture of Central Europe, 1450–1800* (Chicago, 1995), 456.

80. Crow, "The Critique of Enlightenment," 27.

81. Clement Greenberg, "Towards a Newer Laocoon," first published in *Partisan Review* 7 (1940): 296–310.

82. See, for instance, *Journal de Eugène Delacroix* (Paris, n.d. [1932]), 3 vols.; Stendhal, *Salons*, ed. Stéphane Guégan and Martine Reid (Paris, 2002), 141; Charles Baudelaire, *Art in Paris, 1845–1862*, trans. and ed. Jonathan Mayne (London and New York, 1965), 48–52, 64–65.

83. As emphasized by Lichtenstein, *The Eloquence of Color*, 163.

84. For the continuing relevance of debates of the *cinquecento* and eighteenth century for the nineteenth century, see especially Gage, *Color and Culture*.

85. Wassily Kandinsky, *Über das Geistige in der Kunst* (Munich, 1912), 37–42, translated in part in Herschel B. Chipp, *Theories of Modern Art* (Berkeley, Los Angeles, and London, 1968), 152–55.

86. E.g., Krsek, *František Antonín Maulbertsch*; Robert Rosenblum, *Modern Painting and the Northern Romantic Tradition: Friedrich to Rothko* (New York, Evanston, San Francisco, and London, 1972).

87. See Anna C. Chave, *Mark Rothko: Subject in Abstraction* (New York and London, 1989), 180–83.

88. Rosenblum, *Modern Painting and the Northern Romantic Tradition*, 216, 218.

89. Crow, "The Critique of Enlightenment."

Index